Dilemmas of Sustainable Urban Development

Dilemmas of Sustainable Urban Development offers valuable insights into a difficult line of work whose practice inevitably requires a confrontation with fundamental conflicts between divergent goals, and therefore also demands difficult choices and compromises. With contributions from leading academics and expert practitioners, this book provides readers with diverse international case studies which highlight and examine the concrete challenges of practicing sustainable urban development.

The examples in this book touch upon all aspects of sustainable urban development work, from City Hall to the local park. All of the cases unfold in their own specific contexts under particular circumstances—but from each one of them there are general lessons that can be used to inform practice. This book is essential reading for anyone who is active as a student, researcher, or practitioner in the field of urban development.

Jonathan Metzger is Professor in Urban and Regional Studies at the KTH Royal Institute of Technology in Stockholm, Sweden. Most of his research deals with decision making concerning complex environmental issues—often (but not exclusively) with a focus on urban and regional policy and politics. In his work he relates to, and finds inspiration in, research debates within the subject areas of planning studies, human geography, science and technology studies, and organization studies.

Jenny Lindblad is a PhD candidate in Urban and Regional Studies at the KTH Royal Institute of Technology, Stockholm, Sweden. Her dissertation explores bureaucratic practices in French urban planning, and particularly the implications of contexts as a setting for, and a product of, planning. Broadly, her research inquires how material infrastructures shape urban geographies. Jenny is trained in social anthropology, and is an associated member of the research center Profession, Architecture, Ville et Environnement (PAVE) of the École Nationale Supérieure d'Architecture et de Paysage de Bordeaux.

Dilemmas of Sustainable Urban Development

A View from Practice

Edited by
Jonathan Metzger and Jenny Lindblad

NEW YORK AND LONDON

First published 2021
by Routledge
52 Vanderbilt Avenue, New York, NY 10017

and by Routledge
2 Park Square, Milton Park, Abingdon, Oxon OX14 4RN

Routledge is an imprint of the Taylor & Francis Group, an informa business

© 2021 Taylor & Francis

The right of Jonathan Metzger and Jenny Lindblad to be identified as the authors of the editorial material, and of the authors for their individual chapters, has been asserted in accordance with sections 77 and 78 of the Copyright, Designs and Patents Act 1988.

All rights reserved. No part of this book may be reprinted or reproduced or utilised in any form or by any electronic, mechanical, or other means, now known or hereafter invented, including photocopying and recording, or in any information storage or retrieval system, without permission in writing from the publishers.

Trademark notice: Product or corporate names may be trademarks or registered trademarks, and are used only for identification and explanation without intent to infringe.

Library of Congress Cataloging-in-Publication Data
Names: Metzger, Jonathan, 1978- editor. | Lindblad, Jenny, editor.
Title: Dilemmas of sustainable urban development : a view from practice / edited by Jonathan Metzger and Jenny Lindblad.
Identifiers: LCCN 2020007326 (print) | LCCN 2020007327 (ebook) |
ISBN 9780367266592 (hardback) | ISBN 9780367266608 (paperback) |
ISBN 9780429294457 (ebook)
Subjects: LCSH: Sustainable urban development. |
City planning--Environmental aspects.
Classification: LCC HT241 .D55 2020 (print) | LCC HT241 (ebook) |
DDC 307.1/416--dc23
LC record available at https://lccn.loc.gov/2020007326
LC ebook record available at https://lccn.loc.gov/2020007327

ISBN: 978-0-367-26659-2 (hbk)
ISBN: 978-0-367-26660-8 (pbk)
ISBN: 978-0-429-29445-7 (ebk)

Typeset in Sabon
by Taylor & Francis Books

Contents

List of Illustrations vii
List of Contributors viii
Acknowledgements xiii

Introduction: A Practice-Centered Approach to Dilemmas of
Sustainable Urban Development 1
JONATHAN METZGER AND JENNY LINDBLAD

1 Law. Sustainable Development in English Planning Law: Golden
   Thread or Black Swan 21
   SUE CHADWICK

2 Politics. Who Stands Up for Ecology? The Politics of Sustainable
   Land Use in Stockholm 39
   SABINA EDELMAN

3 Concretization. Sustainability in City Management and Urban
   Planning in Gothenburg: From Vague Vision to Social Inclusion
   Activities 50
   PETRA ADOLFSSON AND SARA BRORSTRÖM

4 Strategy. What Is More Important than Getting Things Done?
   Learning from Sustainable Sydney 2030 67
   MARTIN KORNBERGER

5 Best Practices. Contradictions of the 'Green City' in Germany 75
   SAMUEL MÖSSNER AND ROB KRUEGER

6 Mobility. Promises of Intermodality for Sustainable Mobility in
   Bordeaux 86
   PATRICE GODIER AND GUY TAPIE

7 Complexities. Construction Sites of Sustainable Low Carbon Transition in Paris: Snapshots of Internal Organization, Energy Plans and Technical Infrastructure 101
JONATHAN RUTHERFORD AND SYLVÈRE ANGOT

8 Values. Valuing Sustainability in Bordeaux: Should the Grass Be Cut? 115
JENNY LINDBLAD

9 Programming. Programming Urban Transitions in Practice 129
JONAS BYLUND

10 Evidence. Evidence-Based Urban Development: Beyond the Urban Anecdotes? 147
MAGNUS JOHANSSON AND JOAKIM FORSEMALM

11 Smart. Climate-Smart Cities?: A Corporate Takeover of Urban Environmental Governance in Malmö 160
DARCY PARKS

12 Ownership. Delivering Sustainable Development: Landownership and Accountability in Cambridge 175
SOPHIA PEACOCK AND PHIL ALLMENDINGER

13 Tools. Realizing the Vision of a Socially Inclusive RiverCity 194
JACOB LINDKVIST, KRISTIAN KÄLL AND ANDERS SVENSSON

14 Commons. Producing Collaborative Sustainable Urban Development: Experiences of Water Management in Bangalore, India 201
HITA UNNIKRISHNAN, VANESA CASTÁN BROTO AND HARINI NAGENDRA

15 Expectations. Hope and Despair: Professionals' Struggle to Navigate Multiple Planning Ideas in a Public–Private Collaboration in Gothenburg 217
MARI KÅGSTRÖM

16 Concluding Commentary. Will Sustainability Be Replaced by Resilience, and If So, Why? 231
BARBARA CZARNIAWSKA

Index 235

Illustrations

Figures

2.1	Ecologically valuable forest in the Stockholm area	42
3.1	Gothenburg: View from the Lipstick	51
6.1	The Pont de Pierre in Bordeaux after it was closed to car traffic	87
8.1	View from the construction site overlooking the recently paved road and the wetland area	116
8.2	A section of the park area in between the recent constructions	123
9.1	Photo (left) taken at the JPI Urban Europe Policy Conference 2019, in the plenary room of the Committee of the Regions, EU. Photo (right) shows a typical meeting room with the EC Interservice Group on Urban Development. Both settings are located in Brussels	133
10.1	Four types of problem structures (Forsemalm et al. 2019, after Hoppe 2010)	151
10.2	UN-Habitat's five principles as a city block	155
10.3	Evidence-based development model (Forsemalm et al. 2019)	157
11.1	Map of Malmö with the Western Harbour (solid rectangle), Hyllie (dotted line), Hyllie station (unfilled triangle) and the proposed location of Eon's wind turbine (solid triangle). The west side of the map shows the Öresund Bridge towards Copenhagen	164

Tables

3.1	Translation of sustainability: part of various contextual outcomes in urban planning	63
12.1	Interviewees	191

Contributors

Petra Adolfsson (PhD, University of Gothenburg) is an Associate Professor in the Department of Business Administration at the University of Gothenburg, Sweden. Her research focuses on public management, sustainability, professions, and change. She has extensive experience of conducting qualitative research, for example using photographs as part of her field work. Her research has been published in *Financial Accountability & Management* and the *British Journal of Management*.

Phil Allmendinger is Professor of Land Economy and Head of the School of the Humanities and Social Sciences at the University of Cambridge. Recent books include *Neoliberal Spatial Governance* (Routledge, 2016), *Planning Theory* (Palgrave Macmillan, 2011, new edition 2017), *Soft Spaces of Governance in Europe: A Comparative Perspective* (with Graham Haughton, Jörg Knieling, and Frank Othengrafen, Routledge, 2015), *Displacing the Political: Democratic Deficits in Contemporary European Territorial Governance* (with Jonathan Metzger and Stijn Oosterlynck, Routledge, 2014).

Sylvère Angot (PhD, Paris Est University) is an Associate researcher at LISIS (Laboratoire Interdisciplinaire Sciences Innovations Sociétés). His research focuses on reforms and mergers within the French State territorial administration (2009–2015), especially in the field of energy renovation of housing. He has published in particular *The unthoughts of new public organizations* (Millénaire 3 - Grand Lyon, 2018).

Sara Brorström (PhD, University of Gothenburg) is an Associate Professor in the Department of Business Administration at the University of Gothenburg, Sweden. Her research focuses on city development processes, sustainability practices, public sector collaborations, and public sector strategic management. Her research has been published in *Financial Accountability & Management*, the *Scandinavian Journal of Management*, *Cities*, and the *International Journal of Public Sector Management*.

Vanesa Castán Broto is a Professorial Fellow in the Urban Institute at the University of Sheffield, UK, where she researches ecological futures, climate change governance, and urban sustainability transitions. Her latest books are *Urban Energy Landscapes* (Cambridge: Cambridge University Press) and *Urban Sustainability and Justice* (London: ZED Books). In 2016, she was awarded the Philip Leverhulme Prize for contributions to Geography.

Jonas Bylund is a Program Manager at the Swedish Centre for Innovation and Quality in the Built Environment (IQS) and a member of the JPI Urban Europe Management Board since 2013. His main responsibility is science-policy communication and to develop urban research and innovation funding calls with affiliated funding agencies as well as other initiatives. He is trained in human geography (PhD) and social anthropology, with a specific research focus on the knowledge practices in planning and environmental sciences.

Sue Chadwick is a planning solicitor and independent academic. She is a Strategic Planning Advisor working for Pinsent Masons LLP. Sue has combined practical experience with teaching and has been Director of Studies at Magdalene College, University of Cambridge, and a part-time lecturer for the Department of Land Economy. She completed a PhD in planning law in 2017 and has written books on neighbourhood planning and planning decisions.

Barbara Czarniawska is a Senior Professor in Management Studies at GRI, School of Business, Economics and Law at the University of Gothenburg, Sweden, and *Doctor honoris causa* at the Stockholm School of Economics, the Copenhagen Business School, the Helsinki School of Economics, and Aalborg University. She takes a feminist and processual perspective on organizing, recently exploring connections between popular culture and practice of management and robotization of work. She is interested in the techniques of fieldwork and in the application of narratology to organization studies.

Sabina Edelman worked as a political advisor and expert in urban planning and development for the Swedish Green Party in Stockholm during 2015–2019. She holds a Master's degree in civil engineering of urban management and architecture. Sabina's work has focused on questions about the implementation of urban sustainability in local administrations.

Joakim Forsemalm is Associate Professor in Ethnology at Radar arkitektur & planering in Gothenburg, Sweden, where he is both a researcher and practitioner. He is associated with the Gothenburg Research Institute and has been publishing on urban learning processes and knowledge management for the past decade. In 2019, he published a handbook (in Swedish) for planners, architects, and other urban professionals on evidence-based urban development, together with Magnus Johansson.

Patrice Godier is a senior researcher in Sociology at the École Nationale Supérieure d'Architecture et de Paysage de Bordeaux, a member of the research center Profession, Architecture, Ville et Environnement (PAVE) and of the Centre Émile

Durkheim (CNRS, University of Bordeaux). His work focuses on metropolitan facts, urban design, space fabrication, and energy transition with the objective of analyzing the way in which urbanization constitutes a key to the 'work of societies' in general.

Magnus Johansson has a PhD in Pedagogy. He divides his time between Malmö University, Department of Urban Studies, and RISE (Research Institute of Sweden) were he works as a senior researcher in the unit for Sustainable Cities and Communities. In 2019, he published a handbook (in Swedish) for planners, architects, and other urban professionals on evidence-based urban development, together with Joakim Forsemalm.

Martin Kornberger received his PhD in Philosophy from the University of Vienna in 2002. Prior to joining the University of Edinburgh as Chair in Strategy he worked at the University of Technology Sydney as associate professor in design and management, and as research director of the Australian Creative Industry Innovation Centre; at Copenhagen Business School as professor for strategy and organization; and at EM Lyon, France. Since 2011 he is also a research fellow at the Vienna University of Economics and Business. With a background in the Humanities and an eclectic bookshelf behind him, his research focuses on strategies for and organization of new forms of distributed collective action.

Robert Krueger is a human geographer whose scholarship and teaching focus on creating sustainable, socially just improvements to development projects in the global north and south. He has worked in countries in North America, Europe, Asia, and Africa, on issues of economic development and institutional change. His scholarship and teaching challenge conventional notions of economic development, economy-environment relationships, and social change.

Mari Kågström is a researcher at the Swedish University for Agricultural Sciences (SLU). Her research focuses on practitioners' possibilities to make a difference in the fields of environmental assessment and environmental policy integration. As a researcher and practitioner with over 15 years of experience as a consultant, Mari's work bridges the gap between academia and practice. In parallel with her research she currently acts as senior advisor at the Swedish consulting firm Tyréns AB.

Kristian Käll has 15 years' experience in the fields of social sustainability, human rights, and inclusive urban development. He is currently part of Älvstranden utveckling AB, a municipal developing company developing the RiverCity Gothenburg project. In his work, Kristian aims to find innovative ways to combat segregation, and focuses on testing schemes for inclusive housing in partnership with private sector developing companies. Kristian has a Master's in Social Science.

List of Contributors   xi

Jenny Lindblad is a PhD candidate in Urban and Regional Studies at KTH Royal Institute of Technology, Stockholm. Her dissertation explores bureaucratic practices in French urban planning, and particularly the implications of contexts as a setting for, and product of, planning. Broadly, her research inquires how material infrastructures shape urban geographies. Jenny is trained in social anthropology, and an associated member of the research center Profession, Architecture, Ville et Environnement (PAVE) of the École Nationale Supérieure d'Architecture et de Paysage de Bordeaux.

Jacob Lindkvist is a professional working within the field of sustainable urban development. In recent years he has been involved in environmental and social sustainability issues both in Sweden and internationally. His work revolves around the challenges of tomorrow's cities, setting sustainability targets in order to respond to the environmental conditions and societal needs. Jacob has a Master's degree in environmental science and economics from the University of Gothenburg, Sweden.

Jonathan Metzger is Professor in Urban and Regional Studies at the KTH Royal Institute of Technology in Stockholm, Sweden. Most of his research deals with decision making concerning complex environmental issues—often (but not exclusively) with a focus on urban and regional policy and politics. In his work he relates to, and finds inspiration in, research debates within the subject areas of planning studies, human geography, science and technology studies, and organization studies.

Samuel Mössner holds a professorship for spatial planning and sustainability in the Institute of Geography at University of Münster, Germany. Earning his PhD in 2004 in human geography from the University of Kiel, he has worked at LMU Munich and the University of Freiburg. He is the author of several articles and books on urban social policy and governance, social movements and protests, as well as sustainable urban development. Most recently, he co-authored "Adventures in Sustainable Urbanism" (SUNY, 2019).

Harini Nagendra is Professor of Sustainability at Azim Premji University, India. Her research focuses on social-ecological transformations in South Asia. Nagendra has over 150 research publications. Her book *Nature in the City: Bengaluru in the Past, Present, and Future* (Oxford University Press, 2016) examines the implications of environmental change for cities of the global South. She received an Elinor Ostrom Senior Scholar award in 2013, and the Clarivate-Web of Science India Research Excellence award for interdisciplinary research in 2017.

Darcy Parks is a postdoctoral researcher at the Department of Thematic Studies—Technology and Social Change at Linköping University, Sweden. His research interests include sustainability transitions, planning, smart cities and the use of information and communications technology in infrastructure.

His dissertation investigated the influence of smart city ideas on urban environmental governance in Malmö. He has received degrees in engineering (University of Waterloo, Canada) and sustainability studies (Linköping University), and has worked as an energy consultant in Toronto, Canada.

Sophia Peacock holds a PhD from the University of Cambridge. Her dissertation examined the politics and discourses of spatial governance policy reform in England, with a focus on localism, devolution and decentralization. Sophia currently works as a policy advisor in the Ministry of Housing, Communities and Local Government.

Jonathan Rutherford is a senior researcher at LATTS (Laboratoire Techniques, Territoires et Sociétés), at Paris Est University and the École des Ponts engineering school (France). His research focuses on the processes and politics of urban socio-technical change through a focus on the shifting relations between infrastructure and cities. He has co-edited special issues of *Urban Studies and Energy Policy*, the Routledge volume *Beyond the Networked City* (2016) and the book *Redeploying Urban Infrastructure: The Politics of Urban Socio-Technical Futures*.

Anders Svensson is an architect and project leader in the Planning department in Gothenburg, Sweden, with a focus on strategical issues. Anders has over 35 years of experience in architectural practice and planning. Since 2010, he has worked as a project manager and coordinator on the RiverCity development project. Anders is currently the project manager for the revision of the comprehensive plan for the city center of Gothenburg.

Guy Tapie is Professor of Sociology at the École Nationale Supérieure d'Architecture et de Paysage de Bordeaux, a member of the research center Profession, Architecture, Ville et Environnement (PAVE), and the Centre Émile Durkheim (CNRS, Université de Bordeaux). He is thesis director at the Doctoral School of Health and Public Policies of the University of Bordeaux, France. His work focuses on the production of housing, the manufacture of the city, and architectural issues in contemporary society.

Hita Unnikrishnan is a Newton International Fellow at the Urban Institute, University of Sheffield, UK, and a visiting faculty at the Azim Premji University, Bengaluru, India. Her research explores the historical and contemporary vulnerabilities of the social ecological system represented by the urban commons of Bangalore, particularly within the contexts of inclusivity and sustainable urban development. She was a recipient of the Prof. Elinor Ostrom Fellowship on Practice and Policy on the Commons in 2013.

Acknowledgements

The contributions in this book have grown out of the papers and discussions at the workshop 'Difficult Doings: Investigating the Challenging Practice of Sustainable Urban Development,' which was organized at Clare College, University of Cambridge, from 17–19 April 2018. The transdisciplinary international workshop was conducted as part of the Organizing Sustainable Cities project funded by the Swedish Research Council (Vetenskapsrådet, grant #2014–01414). We wish to thank the project participants (in alphabetical order): Petra Adolfsson, Phil Allmendinger, Barbara Czarniawska, Martin Kornberger, and Sophia Peacock.

The idea behind the workshop was to generate a space for mutual exchange between academic researchers who have an explicit interest in the situated practices of sustainable urban development with reflective practitioners who deal with these type of issues in their everyday work. The discussions covered everything from 'the street level' to the 'strategy room', and from the suburban lawns of Bordeaux to sailing schools in Gothenburg and urban macaque management in New Delhi, but—importantly—all focused on the concrete practices, and practical challenges, of attempting to somehow concretize sustainable urban development in these different settings.

We wish to thank Phil Allmendinger for hosting the conference at Clare College. We also acknowledge the support of the Vinnova-funded Decode project, for which we are grateful to the project manager, Björn Hellström.

Introduction

A Practice-Centered Approach to Dilemmas of Sustainable Urban Development

Jonathan Metzger and Jenny Lindblad

Sustainable Urban Development: Ambiguous Concept and Multiple Object

A decade ago, Gunder and Hillier (2009: 20) proclaimed that "sustainable development is the now dominant spatial planning narrative." A recent survey among over 500 European planning practitioners from a large sample of countries and different professional specializations, conducted within the Organizing Sustainable Cities research project, also evinced that this claim to a large extent still seems to hold true. When asked "How central is the specific concept of 'sustainable development' to your professional practice at present?", and provided with a five-grade scale from 'Not important at all' (1) to 'Very important' (5), no less than 84% of the respondents scored a 4 or 5, with 61% choosing the highest possible rating. Additionally, the great majority of the respondents also stated that the centrality of the concept to their professional practice had indeed increased in recent years.

But even if the concept of sustainable development still appears to constitute a central point of reference for urban development and planning practice in many places, this insight tells us very little about the substantial meaning given to the concept in relation to the concrete work being performed by the responding urban professionals. In a review of the urban professional practices that were associated with the concept in the European Union (EU) at that time, Cooper and Symes (2009) highlight the inherently contestable nature of the meaning ascribed to sustainable development. They cite Pearce et al. (1989) as being able to account for no less than 60 detailed, but partially or fully incongruent, definitions of the term. Needless to say, since then the flora of such definitions has proliferated even further (see also e.g., Hajer, 1995).

Relating the above inherent ambiguity of the concept of sustainability to the question of concrete urban development practice, it is obvious that with such a range of diverse meanings in circulation, any idea of some form of easy and direct 'implementation approach' towards the practical realization of sustainable urban development will be misguided. There are even those who contend that given the fundamentally ambiguous meaning of the concept of sustainability, we would do better to discard it completely, given the risk that it may otherwise in practice simply come to function as an empty shell that can be filled with whatever concrete policy practice one wishes, e.g., unthoughtful pro-growth agendas (Swyngedouw, 2007). This is certainly a legitimate concern. Nonetheless, there is a risk that sweeping philosophical dismissals come to stand in the way of a better understanding of the myriad urban development practices that are already going on all around the world in the name of sustainable development. Every day, thousands of urban professionals go to work with a job description that in one way or another contains the concept of sustainable development. Krueger and Gibbs (2007: 1) cite a report by the council of Local Governments for Sustainability (formerly known as the International Council for Local Environmental Initiatives), which concluded that over 6,000 local governments in 113 countries have adopted sustainability initiatives since the early 1990s, and this was already in 2002. A decade and a half later, the sustainability ideology has grown ever more dominant and the number of policy interventions made in the name of sustainability has multiplied exponentially. In an extensive review of existing research on urban sustainability policy, Bulkeley (2010: 231) concluded that "fundamental questions" concerning e.g., "the sociotechnical networks through which policies are mediated, have to date been neglected." While there are some studies that do grapple with these questions (see e.g., Rutland and Aylett, 2008; Olsson, 2009; Gustafsson & Mignon, 2019), there is still a dearth of research that engages with the discrepancies and frictions within and across city administrations, which far too often tend to be treated as coherent 'black boxes' in existing research on the practical doings of sustainability policy. In contrast, the sensibility that underpins this book is that even if we are critical, or even condemning, of some of the policy that is being promoted under the label of sustainable urban development, the only way to be so in an informed manner is to first strive to learn to understand better the details of the work that is currently being performed in the name of sustainability: what are the prerequisites and outcomes of those actions, and which are the challenges that those who perform this work wrestle with daily?

With regard to these already existing practices of sustainable urban development, the diversity of work tasks and professional domains within any given city administration reveals that even if all the employees of such an organization were to have a shared, precise understanding of the meaning and essence of the term 'sustainable development,' which in itself is highly improbable if not impossible, the ways in which they might practically approach the manifestation of this meaning in the form of concrete decisions, priorities, and activities within their professional domain would nonetheless, by necessity, differ wildly. Thus, no matter the degree of clarity or not on the conceptual level (e.g., through a consensus that its essence is embodied in the currently popular United Nations Sustainable Development Goals), the practical 'doing' of urban sustainable development within complex organizations inevitably will come to present itself as the manifestation of a 'multiple object.' This is a concept introduced by Annemarie Mol (2002) in a very different context, the study of atherosclerosis diagnosis and treatment in a hospital, to highlight how many of the practices she observed that a body underwent in such a process actually enacted the nature and symptoms of the illness in very different ways, some of which seemed not even to go together at all. Focusing her analysis on the divergent practices of the hospital and the different ways in which they enacted the illness in different moments and spaces of the diagnostic and treatment process, Mol (2002) notes that

> If practices are foregrounded there is no longer a single passive object in the middle, waiting to be seen from the point of view of seemingly endless series of perspectives. Instead, objects come into being—and disappear— with the practices in which they are manipulated.
>
> (p. 5)

Staying in the discipline of anthropology, another interesting way to approach the inherent vagueness of the concept of sustainable development is to approach this as to some extent constituting a new, contemporary universal value. Studying how universal values are practically enacted in the world, Anna Lowenhaupt Tsing (2005) has suggested that these processes always generate *friction*:

> Through friction universals become practically effective. Yet they can never fulfill their promises of universality. Even in transcending localities, they don't take over the world. They are limited by the practical necessity of mobilizing adherents. Engaged universals must convince us to pay attention to them. All universals are engaged when considered as practical projects accomplished in a heterogeneous world ... To study engagement requires turning away from formal abstractions to see how universals are used.
>
> (pp. 8–9)

Tsing further argues that "Actually existing universalisms" are hybrid, transient, and "involved in constant reformulation." Therefore, it is crucial to always study the articulation of such universals in a situated manner—that is— in the concrete times and spaces in which they are deployed and invoked, given that "engaged universals are never fully successful in being everywhere the same because of this same friction" (Tsing, 2005: 9–10).

What would it imply, then, to translate Mol's conceptualization of the multiple object and Tsing's understanding of friction-ridden universals-in-practice into the domain of sustainable urban development? First, it means that in the corridors of a city administrative building, the way that sustainable development is being practically done in a room at one end of the hall may indeed radically differ from the way it is being enacted 10 doors down, on the other side of the corridor. Second, bar some grand leaps of imagination or the exercise of quite crude interpretive violence, these divergent versions of sustainable urban development probably cannot be added up into a single coherent whole. For sure, there will probably be manifest and potential overlaps between some of the versions of how urban sustainability is being done at any given time, but there will most probably also be other aspects in which some versions directly conflict. According to such an approach, how—or rather, if—the various ways in which sustainable urban development is practically enacted in the different departments of a city administration are somehow coordinated in some aspect or another, and how this coordination is achieved (and at what cost), remains an empirical question. What we can be certain about when it comes to sustainable urban development, is that the multiplicity of practices coupled with the existing substantive ambiguity of the concept itself will quite expectedly lead to those engaged in practices related to sustainable urban development commonly facing frictions in the form of *dilemmas* in their everyday work situations. Indeed, they face dilemmas particularly if their work bridges traditionally separated spheres of expertise in the way that much urban sustainability work does today.

Conceptualizing Dilemmas

The concept of 'dilemma' certainly has a pedigree in studies of practical professional decision-making. Nonetheless, classic works such as Horst Rittel and Mel Webber's *Dilemmas in a General Theory of Planning* (1973) or Michael Lipsky's *Street Level Bureaucracy: Dilemmas of the Individual in Public Services* (1980) do discuss concrete dilemmas in detail, but scarcely elaborate on the meaning of the term itself. In a paper that aims at providing a more thorough discussion of the concept of dilemma and its applicability within the social sciences, Höijer et al. (2006) suggest that a basic working description of a dilemma would be that of a "situation of difficult choice, either because of the circumstance that all available alternatives have undesirable consequences, or because of incompatible demands that have to be fulfilled." As we will find amply illustrated in the chapters that follow, such situations of difficult choice are far from unfamiliar for those working to realize sustainable urban development, and perhaps are also to be expected, given the wide remit of goals and ambitions that this term can be interpreted to encompass. As has also been discussed previously by many, including e.g., Metzger and Rader Olsson (2013) in relation to sustainable urban development experiences in Stockholm, this produces a need to reflect over difficult and sometimes directly tragic trade-offs between equally desirable goals.

However, dilemmas need not stem only from direct and explicit goal conflicts. Chiming with many of the narratives contained in this book, Höijer et al. (2006) suggest that even if traditionally associated with a difficult choice between equally valuable goals or opportunities, or between two things we equally wish to avoid, the notion of dilemma can also be applicable in situations where a clear-cut goal is established, but where the difficult choice nonetheless "concerns which way to best achieve what one desires."

Noting that dilemmas need not be monumental earth-shaking events, Höijer et al. (2006) propose that dilemmas may be more mundane "relatively common aspects of socio-cultural life—whether as basic contradictions within intellectual ideologies, or between ideas and practices in mundane life, or between practices in different situations," thus opening up the possibility to study such dilemmas in relation to everyday practices and experiences.

Following from the above, in this book we use the notion of dilemma in a broad sense to denote any type of troubling impasse that generates a sense of dissonance in situations of everyday decision-making. Taking into consideration the broad range of backgrounds, research approaches, and writing styles of the contributions in the present volume (more on this below), it is not surprising that the dilemmas of sustainable urban development presented in these pages display a broad range not only of types and topics of dilemmas, but also a wide variety among the persons actually posing or describing the dilemma in question. In some cases it is urban practitioners themselves, either in the role of interviewee or directly as an author. In other cases, it is an academic researcher who depicts what they sense to be a dilemma of practice, no matter whether the practitioners themselves describe it in these terms or not. We believe that this multitude of perspectives is helpful in that it clearly highlights that some dilemmas are more visible from the position of those directly situated in the doings themselves, whereas others may only become visible when viewing a practice unfolding from somewhat more afar, and the opportunity such a research approach allows for 'zooming out' and tracing broader patterns of development.

A pertinent question to raise at this point is: why focus so exclusively on that which is difficult at a time when many professionals are desperately searching for practices that can be promoted as 'solutions,' as in practices that can be argued to actually provide a productive way forward towards more sustainable urban futures? On a general note, Höijer et al. (2006) suggest that focusing on dilemmas helps to highlight the challenges that arise when any proposed 'solution' hits the ground in a specific place and time; in other words it provides a better understanding of "the sense-making and decision-making of institutions and people in their societal contexts." More recently, and speaking directly to urban professional practitioners, Wrangsten and Bylund (2018, quoted in Chapter 9 in this volume) suggest that sustainable urban development work generally relates to many different targets and goals at the same time, which often result in a set of strategies or actions pursued in parallel to or disconnected from each other. While some targets and goals support each other, many often turn out to be in direct or oblique conflict or friction. Consequently, practitioners and strategists tend to encounter dilemmas rather than simple problems with an easy fix readily available.

The question of dilemmas thus goes fundamentally to the heart of how we pose the whole problem of sustainable urban development. Perhaps it does not suffice that we understand this as a 'problem' begging for 'solutions.' Rather, no matter how seemingly self-evidently good in itself, any form of supposed 'solution' will—when it is deployed in a complex urban environment that is delicately entangled in cultural, political, and social processes—inevitably generate dilemmatic situations (see also Rittel & Webber, 1973). However, if we take this as a given, it also means that the emergence of such dilemmas does not imply that the proposed intervention in itself is wrong-headed, but simply that we must expect that any such ambition—whether it later turns out to be for better or worse—can be expected to come up against serious challenges that will need to be properly articulated and thought-through. This in turn poses a demand for a habit of continuous collective reflection-in-practice (Schön, 1983) regarding how to perform thoughtful and responsible "situated ethical judgement" (Campbell, 2006).

Relating to the above, it is our hope that at least some of the copies of this book will end up in the hands of not only academic researchers and teachers, but also people who either have, or are studying towards, a career as urban professionals. For those already working in urban development the book can be used as an inspiration and a point of departure for discussions with colleagues regarding similar dilemmas in their own professional practice. For those who are heading towards a future as professionals in the field, the book can hopefully function as a showcase of some of the types of dilemmas that they themselves may come to face, so as to better prepare them for the types of challenges that they can reasonably expect to be confronted with in their future work life. In this regard, we would even dare to claim that even if the label under which the concrete work is performed is shifted from 'urban sustainability' to some currently more in-vogue term such as 'zero emission,' 'decarbonization,' 'urban transition,' etc., the dilemmas that are outlined in this book can nonetheless be expected to remain broadly similar.

A View from Practice

In their discussion of dilemmas Höijer et al. (2006) stress the importance of recognizing that in reality these are seldom confronted in abstract terms, but rather as concrete situations, and that consequently it is crucial that dilemmas are understood "in relation to socially and culturally specific contexts." Along similar lines, Vanesa Castán Broto (2019) has recently called for a research approach that takes into consideration the radical "messiness" of any already existing, situated urban sustainability work, far beyond the neatness of clear-cut and carefully ordered abstract frameworks. This brings us to the subtitle of this book, 'A View from Practice.' This does not imply that our analysis takes its departure from some form of formalized 'practice theory' (cf. e.g., Schatzki, 1996; Reckwitz, 2002). Instead, we simply asked the contributors to not ground their chapters in some overwhelmingly theoretical conundrum, but rather to take as their point of departure all the practices of urban sustainable development that go on 'on the ground' every day. And proceeding from there we asked them to attempt to stake out some of the most pressing challenges that can be identified in relation to those situated experiences of urban sustainability work.

Thus, rather than presenting the contributors with a strict, predefined theoretical framework, we asked them to consider urban sustainability from the perspective of practice according to their own understanding of what this would imply. From that basic instruction and discussions among all the contributors during a two-day workshop held early in the process of developing the present book, they have applied their own preferred approach to flesh out and reflect on the dilemmas that they themselves have identified. In some cases, these approaches are presented in the form of an explicit theoretical and methodological positioning, but even so, we have aspired to keep the academic ruminations to a minimum, so as to retain a focus on the concrete, situated challenges in the different relevant contexts that they discuss. These contexts range from boardrooms to park grounds; from the semi-secluded programming of EU policy to the conflicted management of polluted Indian lakes; and from questions of strategy on the grandest urban scale in Sydney to controversies over the cutting of grass in a local housing area in Bordeaux. Each of them calls attention to some critical challenge in the practical 'doing' of sustainable urban development, highlighting the frictions that are generated when the vague and multiple policy object of 'sustainable development' is to be translated into some form of action in relation to a particular urban issue within a pre-existing local context.

The chapters are by no means well-polished examples of 'good practice,' rather they focus on that which is difficult—the situations and choices that beg any simple answer with regard to how to prioritize or proceed. As a collective, the contributors to this volume share the conviction that an attentiveness to these concrete challenges on the ground can provide some significant insights about the broader questions regarding the possibilities and limitations of contemporary practical approaches to urban sustainable development and all the goal conflicts, value clashes and fractured polities that these must constantly handle. The chapters in this book all approach this task differently. The book contains contributions from professional academic researchers as well as active urban practitioners. Consequently, the chapters evince a broad variety of styles of reflecting and writing, based on the divergent experiences and modalities of discourse that are established in these different communities of practice. When approaching the individual contributions, we therefore urge the reader to keep in mind that all the contributors have their specific professional prerequisites and conventions to relate to in their thinking and writing. For instance, our practitioner contributors have to some extent perhaps been challenged to move out of their comfort zones by not necessarily portraying their home organizations in a spotlessly positive guise, while professional academics have been implored to minimize the amount of abstract theoretical reasoning so as to instead place the concrete practices in question at the center of their contributions, with a view to making the book accessible not only to professional academics but hopefully also to students or other interested practitioners.

Content of the Book

The contributors to this volume have all approached the task of furthering knowledge about the situated practice dilemmas of sustainable urban development in somewhat different ways. The book is structured so that each contribution circles around a key theme, or keyword, that features in the title. Furthermore, they all directly relate to some specific place or situation, which can range from a local neighborhood to a national, or even transnational, setting. Each chapter examines a central dilemma, or—as is often the case—a delicately entangled assortment of them. The chapters thus present a variety of foci, styles, and geographical and professional settings. Nonetheless, there are also evident and manifest overlaps between the different chapters in the form of partial connections with regard to the types of dilemmas they discuss and highlight. The remainder of this Introduction will therefore consider the following chapters individually, and will also attempt to highlight some of the thematic parallels and overlaps between them.

Dilemmas of Definition and Realization

One of the central dilemmas that emerges from the 'view from practice' presented in the chapters of this book concerns the multifariousness and inherent ambiguity of the concepts of sustainability and sustainable development. This leaves the field open to variegated and sometimes conflicting interpretations of the essential meaning of these terms, not only in a general sense but also in relation to their implications for urban development practice. In her chapter on the intense contestation surrounding the proper legal interpretation of the term 'sustainable development' in the United Kingdom's National Planning Policy Framework (NPPF), presented under the keyword of 'law,' Sue Chadwick unpicks the confusion that has emerged in UK legal practice, also at the highest levels of the system, when policy definitions of sustainable development come to diverge radically from more well-established holistic understandings of the concept. Chadwick shows that even though the whole 2012 NPPF framework rests upon an apparent presumption in favor of sustainable development, in effect it produced a circular argument, whereby the substantial meaning of 'sustainable development' was simply that embodied by the various policies presented in the framework, the effects of which came across to many people—including leading judges—as providing anything but a road towards a sustainable future. Thus, argues Chadwick, even if sustainable development was sold as a 'golden thread' of the NPPF, in effect it constituted a 'black swan' in legal terms.

What Chadwick's chapter aptly illustrates is the dramatic difference that the way we understand a term can make, particularly in the detail-sensitive but decisive practice arena of law where all meaning must be carefully spelt out and scrutinized. In other contexts, for instance the world of formal politics, such meanings are often only more implicitly communicated, and the surreptitious sliding between different shades of meaning of a concept can instead present both challenges and frustrations for practitioners. On this topic, Sabina Edelman's chapter recounts and discusses a conflict over the establishment of a nature reserve in the centrally located Årsta forest in the City of Stockholm. As Edelman shows in Chapter 2, from her position as an insider in the process it was quite clear that the different parties in the ruling political coalition had different political priorities with regard to the development of the area. What was particularly frustrating and confusing was that they all invoked the concept of sustainable development to argue for their conflicting positions. Edelman suggests that this confusion is fueled by the now well-established 'three-dimensional' understanding of sustainability as composed of ecological, social, and economic aspects. However, rather than conceptualizing this as a triple baseline, where all the dimensions must be considered, in practice this has led to the different aspects being pitted against each other in political debate. Edelman suggests that in Stockholm the social dimension has recently taken precedence over ecological concerns on the political agenda. Thus, Edelman pointedly argues, "in the rhetorical competition with municipal incomes, housing for youth and more employment—ancient deciduous forestland simply did not stand a chance."

Both Chadwick and Edelman's chapters thus evince that far from merely constituting a philosophical question the contestation over the definition of the term sustainable development in political decision-making and legal practice makes a concrete difference to outcomes on the ground. Thus, the mere invocation of the concept of sustainability clearly offers no shortcuts around the always contentious situated balancing between conflicting goals and goods. Considering the inherent vagueness of the concepts of sustainability and sustainable development, how can they ever be concretized into interventions in a built environment? And yet they are. But how, then, is the line traced from vague ideas and ambitions to concrete project outcomes, and what are the challenges for practice in such processes? Writing under the heading of 'concretization,' in Chapter 3 Petra Adolfsson and Sara Brorström utilize the concept of 'translation' to explore how notions of sustainable development were translated into urban strategy in the city of Gothenburg, and later into very concrete activities in an urban environment—the new Jubilee Park. Adolfsson and Brorström suggest that in this case, sustainability remained uncontroversial so long as it was merely part of a vaguely expressed vision. However, when it was to be transformed into concrete ways of working, and into actual local planning projects, things came to a head and differences between interests and actors had to be addressed. Nevertheless, the authors argue that the overarching strategic plans and goals did have an impact upon the unfolding of more concrete interventions in the urban environment, sometimes in unexpected ways. Consequently, they suggest that the idea of sustainable urban development can be seen to have inspired various city actors who have taken part in the process of finding a shared vision of the future city, and has prompted new ways of taking an inclusive approach towards in urban planning.

Also focusing on the question of results or outcomes, and relating even more directly to the keyword of 'strategy,' in Chapter 4 Martin Kornberger asks whether the lack of concretization is always a sign of failure and eventually concludes that this may not be the case. Having followed the process of formulation and adaptation of the Sustainable Sydney 2030 urban strategy for almost a decade, Kornberger admits that purely from an implementation perspective, the strategy can be understood as a failure, considering that only one out of 10 identified key projects was realized after almost 10 years, and even in that case it remained doubtful to what extent it actually contributed towards the realization of the overall goals of the strategy. Yet, puzzlingly, many key actors insisted that the strategy was a resounding success. Kornberger asks why this might be the case, and proposes that the strategy was considered successful not just because it delivered what it set out to do, but because it succeeded in engaging a wide range of key actors as well as the public in a process that changed their mentality and equipped them with a new language to talk about urban challenges, thus instigating a collective learning journey. So even if the strategy did not deliver some concrete form of sustainability in the short term, nonetheless it generated the necessary preconditions for potentially doing so in the longer term.

Together, the contributions of Adolfsson, Brorström, and Kornberger show that relative to the realization of broad ambitions, our understanding of the concrete effects and outcomes will be dependent on both the geographical and temporal scale of scrutiny—and this is in itself a particular type of dilemma.

Dilemmas of Space and Time

Dilemmas of space and time, or rather, of spacing (scaling) and timing of urban sustainability work, is a recurrent topic in the contributions to this volume, and is often interwoven with other types of challenges and issues. Questions of space and scaling are given particular attention in Chapter 5 by Samuel Mössner and Rob Krueger. The authors problematize the notion of 'best practice' in sustainable urban development by way of a thorough analysis of the broadly lauded urban sustainability policies of the German cities Freiburg and Münster. In their examination of these policies they show that they are problematically myopic in their unswerving geographical focus on what goes on within the boundaries of a particular city, while to some extent ignoring the city's interdependence with a broader urban hinterland. Mössner and Krueger argue that the circulation of superficial best practice examples, and the lack of a relational understanding of urban sustainability that they build on, ignore the particularities, specific local circumstances, and contradictions that are immanent to all planning and practice. The strong city focus of best practice narratives, and its underpinning understanding of cities as discrete objects, directly counteracts a relational understanding of urban sustainability. Furthermore, best practice examples problematically tend to underplay the political and contested nature of sustainability, and obfuscates the existing deep conflicts—both at the local level and more broadly—regarding what constitutes a pathway towards a truly sustainable future.

Chapter 6 by Patrice Godier and Guy Tapie, which focuses on 'mobility,' to a large extent circles around the question of geographical scaling and boundaries. The chapter presents and analyzes the ambition to develop Bordeaux's overarching transport system under the aegis of 'intermodality,' and raises the question of how to get all the residents of the broader Bordeaux region figuratively and literally 'on board' on this journey towards a more climate-friendly, and supposedly sustainable, overall urban transport solution. Similarly to Mössner and Kreuger, the chapter raises questions about the viability of ambitions to transplant best practice recipes across contexts, testifying to the doubts among local traffic planners in Bordeaux that what works in Paris may not be easily applicable in Bordeaux, and, furthermore, that the solutions that work well in the more densely populated central parts of the city may not be easily applicable to the more sprawled outskirts of the functional urban area. The authors also raise the troubling question of inequalities in the offer of attractive, climate-friendly transport options to different populations within the urban region. They point towards the reality of 'mobility precariousness' for large parts of the population, thus clearly demonstrating the entanglement of questions of sustainability with socio-economic and spatial issues—issues that were catapulted into the limelight with the eruption of the French *gilets jaunes* (yellow vests) movement in 2018.

Staying in France, in their chapter on 'complexities,' Jonathan Rutherford and Sylvère Angot introduce the reader to the multiple and fractured spatialities of sustainability practice in the city of Paris. Focusing on how meaningful responses to big issues are constructed on a daily basis in different sites of urban sustainability work, the chapter speaks directly to the notion of urban sustainability as a multiple object. Rutherford and Angot explore three heterogeneous sites, each of which relates to the internal organization of public authority action, the production of energy plans, and the very apparent reconfiguration of technical infrastructure. They argue that these sites of action are emblematic of the kinds of issues facing local actors on the ground as they attempt to develop a sustainable Paris. Continuing its very close examination of urban development practice, the chapter situates the complexity of the changes that are required in the many small and tangible practices that are engaged by people across the city in different settings. The readers are left to judge for themselves whether these dispersed actions add up to something that deserves to be labeled as a proper transition towards a sustainable urban future. Were they posed this questions, the contributors to this book would individually probably have returned with very different views on this matter, which again points towards the essential contestability of the underlying ideas.

Furthermore, Rutherford and Angot's chapter does not only problematize the spatialities, but also the temporalities—or timescales—of urban sustainability work. The latter question is also largely the focus of Jenny Lindblad's chapter on 'values.' Drawing on the interdisciplinary research area of valuation studies, Chapter 8 investigates the interplay between the formation of values and practices of evaluation in sustainable urban development projects in Bordeaux. Central to the chapter is the question of responsibility over time, and what happens when the ownership of a project shifts across the various stages of its realization and completion. By way of a discussion regarding controversies over the management of vegetation, circling around the issue 'should the grass be cut or not?,' Lindblad demonstrates that 'being sustainable' is not a stable end-state for urban areas, but instead requires continuous work towards aligning efforts, attention, and resources, since an achievement at one point in time may be overthrown and rendered considerably unsustainable at a later stage. Similarly to Rutherford and Angot, she argues that work towards sustainable urban development is a matter of micro decisions that are happening throughout the course of realizing construction projects, as well as in the sets of relations emerging after the completion of the construction phase. Furthermore, these are precarious potential achievements that in practice can be expected to demand a constant, ongoing struggle to avoid becoming reversed or perverted further on.

In addition to the above, the contributions by Lindkvist et al. in Chapter 13 and Edelman in Chapter 2 in this volume all point towards the importance of attending to the flow of events and the chronologically extended, and sometimes dispersed, character of urban sustainability practice. These are processes that tend to aim to produce effects in the long term, which turns the timing of scrutiny into an incessant topic of debate, namely when is it the right time to assess the outcomes of a specific action or intervention? Whatever the particular situated answer that is provided to this question, there is no doubt that the views from practice presented in this book above all point towards the acute demand for a spatially and temporally relational understanding of urban sustainability work across well-established scales and boundaries and without any form of fixed time horizon. The challenge of achieving urban sustainability thus admits no possibility of a final solution. There can only ever be repeated attempts at *resolution*, as Rittel and Webber (1973) famously remarked in their characterization of complex planning problems, long before the concept of sustainability burst onto the scene.

Dilemmas of Knowledge

Another key problem that Rittel and Webber raise regarding such 'wicked' problems is the question of how one can even achieve a proper knowledge of the characteristics of such entangled problematics. They suggest that the definition of what constitutes relevant and valid knowledge in relation to complex planning problems is itself a key arena of contestation and disagreement. This insight puts the spotlight on the question of the practices through which we produce and validate knowledge, and highlights the dilemma of the substance and modalities of knowledge that are relevant for sustainable urban development. A number of the chapters already introduced in various ways relate to such dilemmas, which are distinctly present for instance in the chapters by Mössner and Krueger, Rutherford and Angot, and Lindblad. In his chapter on 'programming,' Jonas Bylund specifically focuses on the agenda-setting for knowledge production relating to sustainable urban development.

Bylund's chapter takes the reader to the different types of rooms in which this agenda is negotiated in different ways. Specifically, he walks the reader through the development process of the Strategic Research and Innovation Agenda for the European transnational research program, JPI Urban Europe, explaining the 'dilemma-driven' approach that underpins this initiative. Bylund takes us through four different rooms that are of relevance to the production of knowledge regarding sustainable urban development, and utilizes them to discuss similarities and differences in the discussions that go on in these different sessions. At the centre of the argument is the challenge of producing the conditions for truly transdisciplinary knowledge production for sustainable urban transitions, which demands the development of knowledge formats and processes that both make sense and come across as interesting and relevant to urban practitioners and academics alike. The chapter also takes a meta-perspective and turns a critical eye onto the workshop that was the catalyst for this book. While lauding its transdisciplinary ambition, it also problematizes some of the academic conventions that still stand in the way of a deeper engagement across such interfaces, particularly with regard to the way in which academics relate to and produce texts.

Another take on knowledge practice for sustainable urban development is presented in Magnus Johansson and Joakim Forsemalm's chapter on 'evidence' for sustainable urban development. Relating their thinking to the 'evidence-based turn' in policy-making in the early 2000s, Johansson and Forsemalm suggest that professional urban planners seldom use research in a systematic way. Similarly to Bylund in Chapter 9, they suggest that, when asked, planners generally state that they find research literature too abstract, too theoretical, and too narrow, and that it has little relevance to professional practice. Far from arguing for a return to modernistic and reductionist ways of urban planning and development, the authors nonetheless suggest that there is a need for a more systematic approach to the utilization of a broad range of knowledge in urban planning. In the chapter, the authors present and debate a method that they have developed with the purpose of producing, identifying, and systematizing various types of evidence, including the experience of professionals; the deep knowledge of the everyday life among stakeholders in districts; the vast and complex data and knowledge that emerges from organizations; and knowledge that can be gleaned from scientific literature. Based on live tests of the method in collaborative work with a public housing agency in a so-called particularly vulnerable area in Gothenburg, and drawing on Rittel and Webber's typology of 'wicked' and 'tame' problems, they argue that different kinds of evidence should be used actively for accomplishing the opening-up and closing-down of issues, ideas, projects, and processes in sustainable urban planning practice. This, they suggest, paves the way to more innovative and creative learning among professionals.

In their chapter, Johansson and Forsemalm highlight the dilemma of producing openings and closures by way of knowledge practices. While thoughtful and reflexively produced simplifications are always necessary foundations for any form of action in relation to wickedly complex problems, the closure generated by focusing on a specific knowledge base is always risky and to some extent arbitrary. But, as they argue, "At the end of the day, professional planners need to close down and frame complex issues in order to fulfil an assignment such as the production of a plan or the development of an urban district" (see Chapter 10 in this volume). This insight brings into stark relief the inherent power dynamics relating to such knowledge practices—an insight which also resonates very closely with the chapters by Rutherford and Angot as well as Lindblad. Together they aptly illustrate that knowledge is by no means the neutral ground of settling controversies over sustainable urban development, but, on the contrary, is often that which is crucially at stake in such conflicts. Rutherford and Angot, Johansson and Forsemalm, as well as Bylund all raise the question of whether or not it is possible to aim for a unified paradigm of knowledge production in relation to sustainable urban development, or indeed if this pursuit is in vain. The authors appear to be taking somewhat different positions on this issue, which further highlights the contested nature not only of the substance of relevant knowledge for sustainable urban development, but also the potentially productive modalities and media of knowledge, whereby Johansson and Forsemalm as well as Bylund and Lindblad all problematize the question of knowledge translation and valorization at the interfaces between different professions and communities.

Dilemmas of Collaboration and Conflict

A focal point in Kornberger's chapter is the 'governance gaps' that tend to mire contemporary urban areas, and the dependence of public authorities upon a plethora of public and private organizations for the potential realization of urban sustainability ambitions, for example. Such challenges, demanding a response through broadened and deepened collaboration between diverse sets of actors for the realization of urban sustainability agendas, can also be found in many of the other previously discussed chapters. Whatever the specific details of unique national and local governance arrangements, in this volume collaborative ambitions reveal themselves as a *sine qua non* for any form of sustainable urban development practice within contemporary fractured urban governance landscapes. However, the processes and arrangements through which such collaborations come about appear to be far from unproblematic. On the contrary, the view from practice demonstrates that they generate a great deal of friction and some distinct dilemmas for those who are tasked with putting together and carrying through various cooperative constellations.

In his chapter under the heading of 'smart,' Darcy Parks follows a collaboration project between a municipal planning authority and a private utility company in Malmö's Hyllie neighborhood. The purpose of the collaboration was to make good on the promise to the public as well as to providers of central government funding of delivering a 'climate-smart' city district. The challenge that arose was not only to enable a shift from sustainable to climate-smart city, but also to do so in collaboration with a for-profit energy utility. The chapter does not only investigate the mutation of broad sustainability ambitions into a more technology-focused climate-smart agenda. By staying close to the practitioners on the ground and their daily struggles, it carefully scrutinizes whether the city government, in its partnership with the multinational utility company, fell victim to some form of 'corporate takeover' of its politics, as some of the existing literature on the smart city ambitions of urban administrations would lead a casual observer to expect. However, Parks shows that even though the project ended up fulfilling the energy company's goals to a larger extent than those of the municipality, the reason for this was not the fault of the private company. Rather, there were other factors at play, in particular opposition from other parts of the municipal organization. In the chapter, Parks lucidly describes and analyzes the logic whereby city governments are pushed to make big promises with regard to the potential sustainability achievements of public-private partnerships in urban development projects, as a common prerequisite for securing national funding support. Nonetheless, when sometimes unrealistic expectations go unfulfilled due to projects becoming mired in technical, administrative, and political complexities, practitioners are left with the unsavory task of explaining how this apparent failure is in fact a constructive learning experience.

Another chapter which focuses on collaboration dynamics and public-sector dependency on private actors for goal-delivery is Sophia Peacock and Phil Allmendinger's contribution on the topic of 'ownership.' Their contribution puts the spotlight on the capacity of local governments in the UK to realize their ambitions to achieve sustainable urban development by being willing to examine the process of the realization of a housing area with high sustainability ambitions, namely the University-owned Eddington development in Cambridge. The chapter illustrates that while achieving sustainable development is necessarily a public concern, due to the setup of the British planning system (see Chadwick in Chapter 1 in this volume), responsibility for implementing sustainable urban development has in recent years increasingly fallen on private actors, primarily developers and landowners, who are, for the most part, driven by profit motives. As a consequence, ambitious local councils—such as that in

Cambridge—are forced to put a great deal of effort into developing a good relationship with those developers that are committed to sustainability as part of their business model and values. Nonetheless, the authors show that often, even for the most long-term investors and landowners, economic considerations may come to stand in the way of sustainability concerns. They point to the need to shift the balance of scales somewhat further in the direction of public ownership of the tools for not only promoting, but also demanding a broader and deeper consideration of sustainability concerns in planning processes.

Peacock and Allmendinger's contribution highlights the crucial importance of attending to and scrutinizing the concrete conditions under which collaborations for urban sustainable development take place. Crucially, the chapter also stresses the considerable power of landowners in deregulated planning systems. This is also a central concern in the contribution from Jacob Lindkvist, Kristian Käll, and Anders Svensson on the topic of 'tools.' Their chapter discusses the development of RiverCity Gothenburg, currently the most extensive urban development project in Northern Europe. They focus on the social dimension of sustainability and highlight the need for a fundamentally collaborative approach to fulfilling the vision of an area that, through its mix of activities and residents, contributes to ameliorating the deep socio-economic disparities in the city. Similarly to Peacock and Allmendinger, they assert that the current planning system in Sweden does not provide municipalities with adequate tools for highlighting the importance of socio-economic integration in new urban areas. A central dilemma in the ambition to utilize the RiverCity project to counteract the widening social rifts in the city is thus the challenge of working to achieve a socially sustainable urban future within the context of a national system that does not provide strong policy tools for making this possible. Consequently, any such development becomes dependent upon the solid commitment of local politicians, the facilitation and advocacy skills of local public servants and committed urban professionals, as well as the ability of property developers to commit to a holistic and long-term perspective on urban value-creation.

Much of the collaborative work in the area of sustainable urban development is framed under the aegis of 'coproduction.' In their chapter, under the heading of 'commons,' Hita Unnikrishnan, Vanesa Castán Broto, and Harini Nagendra warn that the set of practices that are related to this concept is by no means innocent or unproblematic, but rather can be expected to become deeply enfolded in the complexities of the power dynamics of any given setting in which they are deployed. The authors examine the governance of urban artificial lakes, previously constructed to function as freshwater tanks or reservoirs, in Bangalore, India. Having suffered decades of neglect, pollution, and environmental degradation, many of the lakes are currently undergoing radical transformations due to a transfer of power to new arrangements of responsibility that are framed as community-based solutions. Writing from an explicit perspective of admiration for all the activists and civil society actors who have engaged in cleaning up the lakes and enabling them to flourish, the authors nonetheless caution that these processes also represent a layered political struggle that involves boundary-making activities in which the dynamics of power tend to exclude some already socially marginalized and vulnerable groups who are dependent on the lakes for their livelihoods. Relating this to the concept of coproduction, the authors caution that one should be careful to assume that any application of this concept will have unconditionally emancipatory effects, while nonetheless suggesting that situated reflection on complexities associated with coproduction could potentially be used as a tool to engage with notions of urban sustainability and social justice.

Unnikrishnan, Castán Broto, and Nagendra's contribution, together with the chapters by Godier and Tapie and Mössner and Kreuger, serve to illuminate the very real conflicts that can be expected to surface or emerge through the frictions that any attempt at realizing ambitions towards sustainable urban development inevitably will produce. Sometimes these conflicts will relate to overtly distributional issues, such as the intolerable personal cost of a supposedly sustainable lifestyle or home, or the exclusion of many people from their means of earning a living. However, as evinced by these chapters, such overt issues of social justice and equality often also become deeply entangled in questions of a more delicate political, ethical, or cultural nature, and, again, trouble our understanding of what the concepts of sustainability and sustainable urban development can fundamentally be taken to mean (see also Bylund's reference to Jacques Rancière in Chapter 9 in this volume).

Dilemmas of Engagement and Frustration

Given all the challenges and dilemmas recounted above, how do professionals tasked with effecting sustainable urban development in their everyday work even manage to cope? In her contribution to this book on the topic of 'expectations,' Mari Kågström closely follows a group of sustainability process managers working on the RiverCity project in Gothenburg, and focuses on the emotional dimension of their struggle to promote multidimensional sustainability in this groundbreaking development for the city.

These ambitious but also necessary collaborative arrangements (see also Chapter 13 by Lindkvist et al.) turn out to be mired in the various parallel ideas about what collaboration should comprise and how it should be managed that are held by different actors involved in the processes. These ideas tend to emphasize different, sometimes conflicting, values and point in different directions with regard to what should be prioritized and how power and responsibilities should be distributed between different categories of involved parties. Kågström follows the process managers through moments of buoyant confidence and hope, as well as frustration and even despair, in their struggle to ensure that the private-public collaboration they are involved in will eventually leads to something that they can honestly claim is moving in the direction of a more sustainable urban development. As Kågström writes, this is a story in which the professionals are torn between pride, happiness, fatigue, and doubt as the fortunes of their high ambitions ebb and flow with the twists and turns of the clashing agendas, expectations, and logics of action of different involved actors.

What we find in Kågström's chapter, as in so many others in this book, are hard-working, doggedly committed and often visionary urban professionals, who struggle to fulfil monumental ambitions in fractured urban governance landscapes, in situations where they are nonetheless reliant on the goodwill and long-term engagement of other actors on the inside and outside of city administrations if they are to have any chance in succeeding to any degree whatsoever. In his chapter, Parks suggests that this organizational complexity and accompanying vagueness, paralleled by ambitious goals, sets practitioners up for failure. However, as evinced in the chapter by Rutherford and Angot, for example, even in less high-profile and seemingly more mundane situations, important issues can get lost in the mess of daily working life—the 'mangle of practice' (cf. Pickering, 1995).

These conditions all come together to put a great deal of pressure on the individuals who are tasked with realizing these ambitions and who step in to fill nebulous governance voids through negotiating ambiguous policies and vague mandates. The chapters of this book also give ample evidence of the passionate engagement, deep sense of mission and obligation, and almost heroic degree of perseverance that can be found all around the world among practicing urban professionals. Nonetheless, zooming out, the deck may sometimes seem to be stacked against them. In many parts of the world, public administrations are blatantly under-resourced. As Bylund points out in Chapter 9, even though staff are generally skilled in their areas of expertise they simply do not have sufficient time or attention to actually be able to do all that is asked of them. Taking these preconditions into consideration, the question arises as to what can reasonably be expected and asked of the individual urban professional when it comes to assuming responsibility for producing results under these circumstances. At least Kågström is unequivocal in her judgement that these conditions put excessive pressure on individual professionals. The price paid at an individual level can even be that of tragedy, as Bylund candidly points out: "What we see are burnouts by those that try to engage beyond the typical checkboxes forms in public organizations" (see Chapter 9 in this volume).

One of the questions we are thus left struggling with is this: taking all this into consideration, how forgiving should we be regarding apparent failures to realize the currently highly ambitious goals for sustainable urban development around the world? And if what we are seeing can indeed be qualified as failures, where should we place the blame for this? In none of the chapters in this volume do professionals come across as devious, unengaged, or incompetent— quite on the contrary. Nonetheless, they are forced to constantly navigate and struggle with almost insurmountable institutional and political obstacles. The closer we get to practice and the conditions under which it unfolds in these chapters, the less it seems that practitioners are able to shape the fundamental design of the processes and end results that they moving towards. In her concluding commentary, which discusses the ongoing discursive shift towards the prioritization of 'resilience' in urban development practice, Barbara Czarniawska also alludes to how urban sustainability work has become increasingly squeezed by various forms of austerity politics.

Thus, one of the lessons that appears to emerge from the focus on the specificities of concrete sustainable urban development practice is that investigations of the conditions under which this work is currently being performed must not only strive to keep sight of the concrete ground on which unique episodes of practice unfold, but also strive to lift the gaze towards a more collective level to detect patterns across the unique cases. In doing so, it becomes reasonable to start asking whether ambitions, mandates, and resources are reasonably matched. Do the existing arrangements give those who are tasked with making progress on the ground a fair chance of achieving ambitious goals, or are they—as Parks suggests—working under conditions that set them up for failure and disappointment? If so, what must change for circumstances to become more favorable, or at least manageable? Here, researchers acting within the academic context can hopefully fulfil a function in acting as 'critical friends,' by listening to, validating, and contextualizing the situated experiences of practice—thus helping to make sense of them and contributing to an enhanced capacity for reflection and sympathetically critical analysis. Realizing this potential requires active engagement and effort from academics and practitioners alike. Our hope as editors is that the present volume, and the work that has gone into it, will constitute one small step on the road towards initiating such a process of collective reflection.

References

Bulkeley, H. (2010). Cities and the governing of climate change. *Annual Review of Environment and Resources*, 35.

Campbell, H. (2006). Just planning: The art of situated ethical judgment. *Journal of Planning Education and Research*, 26(1), 92–106.

Castán Broto, V. (2019). Climate change politics and the urban contexts of messy governmentalities. *Territory, Politics, Governance*, 1–18.

Cooper, I, & Symes, M. (2009). *Sustainable Urban Development*. Vol. 4: *Changing Professional Practice*. Abingdon: Routledge.

Gunder, M., & Hillier, J. (2009). *Planning in Ten Words or Less: A Lacanian Entanglement with Spatial Planning*. Farnham: Ashgate.

Gustafsson, S., & Mignon, I. (2019). Municipalities as intermediaries for the design and local implementation of climate visions. *European Planning Studies*, 1–22. DOI: doi:10.1080/09654313.2019.1612327.

Hajer, M.A. (1995). *The Politics of Environmental Discourse: Ecological Modernization and the Policy Process*. Oxford: Clarendon Press.

Höijer, B., Lidskog, R., & Uggla, Y. (2006). Facing dilemmas: Sense-making and decision-making in late modernity. *Futures*, 38(3), 350–366.

Krueger, R., & Gibbs, D. (2007). Introduction: Problematizing the politics of sustainability. In R. Krueger & D. Gibbs (Eds.), *The Sustainable Development Paradox: Urban Political Economy in the United States and Europe*. New York: Guilford Press, pp. 1–11.

Lipsky, M. (1980). *Street-Level Bureaucracy: Dilemmas of the Individual in Public Services*. New York: Russell Sage Foundation.

Metzger, J., & Rader Olsson, A. (Eds.) (2013). *Sustainable Stockholm: Exploring Urban Sustainability in Europe's Greenest City*. New York: Routledge.

Mol, A. (2002). *The Body Multiple: Ontology in Medical Practice*. Durham, NC: Duke University Press.

Olsson, J. (2009). Sustainable development from below: Institutionalising a global idea-complex. *Local Environment*, 14(2), 127–138.

Pearce, D.W., Markandya, A., Barbier, E.B. (1989). *Blueprint for a Green Economy*. London: Earthscan.

Pickering, A. (1995). *The Mangle of Practice: Time, Agency, and Science*. Chicago: University of Chicago Press.

Reckwitz, A. (2002). Toward a theory of social practices: A development in culturalist theorizing. *European Journal of Social Theory*, 5(2), 243–263.

Rittel, H.W., & Webber, M.M. (1973). Dilemmas in a general theory of planning. *Policy Sciences*, 4(2), 155–169.

Rutland, T., & Aylett, A. (2008). The work of policy: actor networks, governmentality, and local action on climate change in Portland, Oregon. *Environment and Planning D: Society and Space*, 26(4), 627–646.

Schatzki, T.R. (1996). *Social Practices: A Wittgensteinian Approach to Human Activity and the Social*. Cambridge: Cambridge University Press.

Schön, D.A. (1983). *The Reflective Practitioner: How Professionals Think in Action*. New York: Basic Books.

Swyngedouw, E. (2007). Impossible sustainability and the postpolitical condition. In R. Krueger & D. Gibbs (Eds.), *The Sustainable Development Paradox: Urban Political Economy in the United States and Europe*. New York: Guilford Press, pp. 13–40.

Tsing, A.L. (2005). *Friction: An Ethnography of Global Connection*. Princeton, NJ: Princeton University Press.

Wrangsten, C., & Bylund, J. (2018). *A Dilemma-Driven Approach to Urban Innovation*. Retrieved March 23, 2020, from https://jpi-urbaneurope.eu/news/a-dilemma-driven-approach-to-urban-innovation/.

Chapter 1

Law

Sustainable Development in English Planning Law: Golden Thread or Black Swan

Sue Chadwick

Swan Lake is a ballet associated primarily with exquisite music, inspired choreography and the talents of dancers such as Margot Fonteyn and Anna Pavlova. But while the ballet may be associated with beauty and grace, the core narrative is one of deceit. The young Prince Siegfried falls in love with Odette, the white swan queen and at their next meeting he binds himself to her—or at least to the woman he believes her to be. Too late, he realizes that this woman is the sorcerer's daughter in disguise and tragedy ensues.

Sustainable development is a concept with a multiplicity of meanings but no formal or legal definition. It is most frequently defined through an overt or implicit reference to the 'Brundtland' definition used in the report 'Our Common Future' in 1987: "Humanity has the ability to make development sustainable to ensure that it meets the needs of the present without compromising the ability of future generations to meet their own needs" (World Commission on Environment and Development, 1987). In terms of planning policy, it is the ultimate white swan, a way to meet the planning needs of now and hereafter without compromising either.

The National Planning Policy Framework (the 'Framework'), adopted as the central national planning policy for England in March 2012, claimed that sustainable development would be a 'golden thread' around which planning decisions would be woven. Placing sustainable development as a primary consideration when planning for or approving new developments apparently secured a beneficial policy objective as a central consideration in all planning decisions.

This chapter is an unblinkered exploration of the use of the term sustainable development in the Framework and the updated 2019 version of the same document. It asks whether planning and development practitioners have been enchanted by these traditionally benevolent associations of sustainable development into accepting the term at its face value, while leaving its empirical functionality unquestioned. The chapter asserts that the term as defined in and constrained by the Framework is instead used to help to promote a pro-growth agenda in the teeth of local policies designed to prevent precisely those developments. In this context, the language of the Framework has been just as deceptive—and arguably just as destructive—as the magic spells woven in *Swan Lake*.

This chapter begins with an explanation of the interaction between law and policy in English planning law and the origins of the concept of sustainable development in international and national policy. It briefly summarizes the political context of the Framework and the way in which that document defines and constrains the use of the term sustainable development with a new 'tilted balance' in its favor in the context of planning decisions. It considers how the Framework-specific concept of sustainable development has been considered in case law, and focuses on one case in particular: the 'Hopkins Homes' decision considered by the Supreme Court in 2017, and what it did—and did not— achieve in terms of how sustainable development should be interpreted. The chapter ends by reviewing the updated Framework that was adopted in 2019 and modified the following year and considers, based on recent case law, whether the new Framework promises any hope for a more genuine application of the concept of sustainable development in the future.

The English Legal System

The United Kingdom does not have a codified constitution but is ruled through the intersecting scope of authority of three institutions: Parliament (comprising the Queen, the House of Commons, and the House of Lords); an executive government; and an independent judiciary. The Queen is the head of state of the UK but, by constitutional convention, she does not become publicly involved in the party politics of government, so her powers are exercised through that government. Parliament's functions include making laws and scrutinizing executive actions of ministers through a variety of mechanisms including select committees, parliamentary questions, oral and written statements, and debates. Executive government powers are exercised by ministers and are derived from legislation passed by Parliament. Ministers are subject to an overarching duty to act in accordance with the law and to account to Parliament for their actions. They are supported by impartial civil servants and often depend on those civil servants for decision making, although ministers ultimately take responsibility. The judiciary is independent of both the executive and Parliament. Judges interpret and apply the law and can rule on whether ministerial action is carried out lawfully, through a process known as judicial review. Statutory powers are interpreted and refined through the case law created when the use of those powers is challenged through judicial review, and this body of case law is generally referred to as common law.

Parliament, government ministers, and the courts all play a part in planning law. Parliament makes the legislation that regulates the planning system, (with the most relevant for the purpose of this chapter being the Town and Country Planning Act 1990). In terms of executive government, the relevant department is the Ministry of Housing Communities and Local Government currently headed by Secretary of State Robert Jenrick ('the minister'). The principal function of this ministry is to maintain and update central government planning policy through the Framework, National Planning Policy Guidance and Written Ministerial Statements. The minister also has the power to determine individual planning applications, although these planning decisions are generally administered and determined by the Planning Inspectorate, a branch of the civil service in which inspectors will use their independent judgment to consider applications, but always in the name of the minister.

The minister thus has two roles: formulating and adopting policy government policy which represents national rather than local concerns, and acting as the arbiter of how it is applied, which may also be politically motivated. As the 2001 'Alconbury' case recognized: "No one expects the inspector to be independent or impartial in applying the Secretary of State's policy."[1] Two cases have questioned the validity of the power of the minister both to set policy and to determine how it is applied:

- The Alconbury ruling of 2001 concerned the legitimacy of the planning appeals system as an independent and impartial tribunal for the purpose of Article 6 of the European Convention. The House of Lords ruled that there was no violation of the principle because of the independent system of judicial review and so a government minister could be both a policy maker and a decision taker.
- These principles were confirmed in the 2016 'West Berkshire' decision challenging the legitimacy of a Written Ministerial Statement on affordable housing.[2] This decision confirmed that the minister was entitled to express his policy in unqualified terms, and as both policy maker and decision taker was entitled to prefer his policy to that of a local authority.

The local planning authority may make the initial judgment, but so long as the minister does not frustrate or prevent the operation of the statutory principles underpinning that decision he or she is free to apply an entirely different emphasis.

Planning Decisions

The decision-making process associated with considering and determining applications for planning permission is regulated through the use of two intersecting legal requirements, referred to in this chapter as the 'legal text':

- Section 70(2) of the Town and Country Planning Act 1990 requires the decision maker to "have regard to the provisions of the development plan, so far as material."
- Section 38(6) of the Planning and Compulsory Purchase Act 2004 requires decisions to be made "in accordance with the plan unless material considerations indicate otherwise."

Decisions to approve or refuse development are one of the most visible—and contested—regulatory functions with both positive and negative outcomes for all parties involved. For developers and landowners, they are the means by which development potential can be exploited but can also constitute a significant barrier between land ownership and land value. For local communities, they can represent unwanted diminution of amenity as well as job creation, economic regeneration, and the provision of affordable housing. Individual local authorities decide most planning applications, either through a planning committee made up from a selection of the council's members or by individual planning officers. However, when planning applications are refused, the applicant can appeal and the appeal is determined by an independent inspector. In addition, some planning applications are themselves determined by the minister.

Because of their value and significance, planning decisions are regularly contested by way of judicial review by anyone with sufficient 'interest' in the application. That review is available to the applicant, the local authority, or individuals or groups who are particularly affected by the decision. A claim for judicial review involving planning matters begins in the Planning Court, which is part of the Administrative Court within the Queen's Bench Division of the High Court. An appeal from a High Court decision is heard by the civil division of the Court of Appeal, while the Supreme Court is the final court of appeal for all civil cases in the UK.

The Planning Balance

Planning applications are required to be determined by the legal test set out above but this incorporates two non-legal considerations: the development plan and material considerations. This creates a wide discretionary space within which both must be taken into account and weighed against each other. The determination of planning decisions is essentially an exercise of judgment, not law, carried out by members of the public, planning officers, or government officials rather than lawyers, and requires due weight to be given to local planning policies and a wide range of other considerations. This process of weighing plan policies against other considerations is generally referred to as the 'planning balance.'

The development plan is the document or documents prepared by a local planning authority individually or in cooperation with one or more local planning authorities. Development plans relate to the development and use of land in the area; they allocate sites for particular uses and set out a range of policy objectives formulated and adopted at the local level and reflecting local sociopolitical concerns. Documents such as strategic or development management policies will generally be within the definition of a development plan, and in London the London Plan will always be part of the development plan. Neighborhood plans are also, as a matter of law, part of the development plan. The legal test situates the development plan as the primary consideration, and the requirement to 'have regard' to the development plan operates as a presumption in favor of its policies. This was recognized by the landmark 1997 'City of Edinburgh' case, in which it is stated that "the development plan is no longer simply one of the material considerations ... there is now a presumption that the development plan is to govern the decision on an application for planning permission."[3]

The other factor to be taken into account is material considerations. There is no statutory definition of this, but the 'Stringer' case established the common law principle that "any consideration which relates to the use and development of land is capable of being a planning consideration."[4] This means that the scope of material considerations is not only wide, but will fluctuate depending on the particular proposal considered. Some considerations are material as a matter of law, such as emerging neighborhood plans, or require specific tests to be applied; for instance, European Directives relating to the environment require specific information to be supplied and that the effects on the environment must be taken into account at the earliest possible stage. When a development involves or affects a listed building or conservation area then the local authority must have special regard to that status.

The Framework is itself a material planning consideration and in addition it lists a number of policy designations that must be given particular weight when they are relevant to part or all of the development in question. They are listed in the footnote to paragraph 11 and include Sites of Special Scientific Interest; land designated as Green Belt, Local Green Space, an Area of Outstanding Natural Beauty, a National Park (or within the Broads Authority) or defined as Heritage Coast; irreplaceable habitats; designated heritage assets; and areas at risk of flooding or coastal change. There is also a range of matters that are accepted, through practice and case law, to be material to most if not all planning decisions. National policy is one of them—the Framework, the online national planning policy guidance, and Written Ministerial Statements. Emerging local and neighborhood plans, previous planning appeal decisions, representations from the local community, public benefits offered as part of a particular application, health and safety concerns—particularly those related to diet and obesity—the planning history of the site, and policies contained in documents other than the development plan fall within this group.

While all of these matters are capable of being material to a planning application, the weight accorded to them will depend on a number of factors including relevance to the development as a whole, how widely the policy was consulted, how recently the policy was adopted, and the extent to which it is consistent with the superior policy context.

The relatively simple words of the legal test frame a very complex balancing process. The decision-making context mutates with each application but, fundamentally, it requires the decision maker to know what the relevant development plan policies are, the merits of a particular proposal against those policies, and then to take into account all other material considerations, including relevant local and national policies. The combination of the range of circumstances that need to be taken into account, and the significance of the interests vested in the process, has made the determination of planning applications a particularly contentious area of planning law. And where the local development plan contains local policies that conflict with national policy, it will become a battleground between those competing and/or conflicting policy objectives. Once adopted, the Framework introduced not only a national policy document into this contested space, but also a new policy consideration altogether—the concept of sustainable development.

Sustainable Development

As mentioned above, sustainable development is traditionally associated with a responsible approach to growth, sensitive to the needs of the wider society so that what is done now does not harm existing communities, use up existing resources or otherwise impact too heavily on the needs of future generations. However, no definition that either embodies or requires these principles to be relied on or complied with has ever been adopted. Instead, it has remained a policy aspiration with a meaning left available to be diffused by the addition of further criteria and principles. This is evident in the way that the term has been defined since the original Brundtland definition. The 2001 European Strategy for Sustainable Development explicitly relied on Brundtland for its understanding of sustainable development, while the 2002 United Nations (UN) Summit on Sustainable Development introduced three 'pillars'—social, economic, and environmental—that are commonplace today. The updated version of the UN definition from 2009 added a fourth pillar of governance alongside five new principles of economic prosperity, social equity, environment protection, and international responsibilities.

Sustainable development was no more clearly defined in English policy. In 1993, the Under Secretary of State for the Environment proposed that it should incorporate two dimensions—domestic and international—while the Foreword to the 1994 Sustainable Development Strategy identified four relevant principles: (1) that decisions should be based on the best possible scientific information and analysis of risks; (2) that where there is uncertainty and potentially serious risks exist, precautionary action may be necessary; (3) that ecological impacts must be considered, particularly where resources are non-renewable or effects irreversible; and (4) that cost implications should be brought home directly to the people responsible. An updated version of the Strategy in 2005 introduced a new set of indicators, four new priorities and five new principles (Department of Environment, Food and Rural Affairs, 2005). However, the term was never formally defined, as Allmendinger has noted: "[t]he government set out four aims for sustainable development in its 1999 strategy ... it was unclear what such entreaties actually meant" (Department of Environment, Food and Rural Affairs, 2005, p. 142). In terms of the English planning system, the concept of sustainable development was just one policy consideration among many others.

When the 2011 UK coalition government was elected, it inherited a very broad concept of sustainable development. Within a year, the new government began to develop and promote a particular understanding of the term. The report *Mainstreaming Sustainable Development* that was issued by the Department of Environment, Food and Rural Affairs explained that it means "making the necessary decisions now to realise our vision of stimulating economic growth and tackling the deficit" (2011). In addition, the coalition government announced its intention to import this version of sustainable development into the planning system. The government announced in the 2011 budget its intention to create a national planning policy document that would include a presumption in favor of sustainable development "so that the default answer to development is 'yes'" (Government of the United Kingdom, 2011, p. 29).

The coalition's concept of sustainable development was therefore quite different to that promoted in Brundtland and subsequent policy documents. It shifted the concept from one associated with restrained growth mindful of the needs of future generation to one manifested primarily through the promotion of growth. In addition, it proposed for the first time to embed this version of sustainable development into core national planning policy. This proposal became a reality within a year of the coalition's election.

The 2012 Planning Framework and the Tilted Balance

Following two consultations, the Framework was published on 27 March 2012. It included a "presumption in favour of sustainable development that is the basis for every plan, and every decision" (Ministry of Housing, Communities & Local Government, 2012, p. i). Sustainable development became, for the first time in its history, a central consideration of English planning policy. Some of the traditional concepts of sustainable development were retained. For instance, the Brundtland definition of sustainable development emphasizing the consolidating of needs today without comprising those of future generations was retained on one page, while on another sustainability was referred to as having three dimensions: economic, social, and environmental. However, in terms of planning decisions, its meaning was highly constrained with the key sentences in paragraphs 6 and 14.

Paragraph 6 stated that "[t]he policies in paragraphs 18 to 219, taken as a whole, constitute the Government's view of what sustainable development in England means in practice for the planning system" (Ministry of Housing, Communities & Local Government, 2012, p. 2). This paragraph introduced a framework-specific definition that was ring-fenced by the content of the Framework itself. Planning decision makers assessing whether or not a proposal was sustainable were not free to decide what sustainable development meant in terms of their own or any other policies, but only whether the proposal could demonstrate compliance with the Framework. Paragraph 14 introduced a presumption in favor of sustainable development as defined in paragraph 6.

Paragraph 14 stated that, when applied to planning applications, sustainable development meant "approving development proposals that accord with the development plan without delay" (Ministry of Housing, Communities & Local Government 2012, p. 4). In addition, "where the development plan is absent, silent or relevant policies were out-of-date," sustainable development meant "granting permission unless any adverse impacts of doing so would significantly and demonstrably outweigh the benefits, when assessed against the policies in this Framework taken as a whole; or specific policies in this Framework indicate development should be restricted" (Ministry of Housing, Communities & Local Government, 2012).

The foreword to the Framework described the paragraph 14 presumption as a "golden thread running through both plan-making and decision-taking" (Ministry of Housing, Communities & Local Government, 2012, p. i). However, this was not a presumption in favor of a general concept of sustainable development, but the customized definition in paragraph 6 requiring conformity with the Framework itself. In addition, sustainable development was not an adjective describing development, but a function. Where a development plan was absent, silent or out of date, paragraphs 6 and 14 operated as a joint trigger mechanism, requiring decision makers to apply the Framework policies in preference to those in the local plan for the area. This became known as the 'tilted balance.'

The consequences of the intersection of paragraphs 6 and 14 were profound for decisions made under the legal test. In spite of the established presumption in favor of the development plan, which is enshrined in law, there was now a new policy presumption that all decision makers were required to apply in specific circumstances. Where it applied, councils' development plan policies would lose their usual status in favor of the paragraph 6 concept of sustainable development, so that the proposal would be assessed primarily on its compliance with the Framework rather than local policies.

Sustainable Development and the Courts

The new presumption was profoundly disruptive. It introduced a policy imperative that in many cases would require national policy considerations to be applied in favor of local ones. The courts had always recognized that it is for decision makers (local authorities, planning inspectors, and the Secretary of State) to exercise judgment in how policies should be applied. However, it was also established that the proper interpretation of planning policy was for the courts to decide and that failing to interpret a policy properly would be considered a legal defect.[5]

Although the courts could not interfere with the application of the concept of sustainable development in the Framework, they could advise on its interpretation and it was not long before they were drawn into arguments about it. Some judges struggled to define sustainable development at all. In 'Brown,'[6]

Justice Collins complained that "[t]he word sustainable in the NPPF [the Framework] is not defined; the reader has to work through some 200 paragraphs which indicate what particular matters can be taken into account," while in 'Earl Shilton,'[7] Justice Hickinbottom noted that there was in fact no definition of sustainable development in the Framework. A more problematic issue for several judges was whether a concept of sustainable development beyond that set out in paragraphs 6 and 14 should be applied, and this resulted in divergent approaches.

'William Davis'[8] in 2013 was the first case to consider the paragraph 14 presumption. The application in question was for a residential development that conflicted with a local development plan policy to protect green wedges of countryside between villages. The local authority refused permission on the basis that the proposal was unsustainable because of the conflict with the local policy, and this decision was upheld on appeal and by the court in the subsequent challenge to the planning inspector's decision. The judge also commented that "it would be contrary to the fundamental principles of NPFF if the presumption in favor of development in paragraph 14 applied equally to sustainable and non-sustainable development." This appeared to reflect recognition of a concept of sustainable development outside the narrow definition in paragraph 6 based on the wider economic, social, and environmental dimensions rather than compliance with the Framework alone.

The recognition in 'William Davis' of a stand-alone consideration based on these broader considerations was followed in a number of subsequent cases:

- In 'Trafford'[9] in 2014, Justice Stewart included an appendix headed "Whether the Proposal Would Be Sustainable Development?" and involved a full assessment of the environmental impact of the development before concluding that it was sustainable.
- In 'Gallagher Estates'[10] in 2014, Justice Hickinbottom stated that sustainable development was to be defined in terms of development which meets the needs of the present without compromising the ability of future generations to meet their own needs.
- Justice Hickinbottom repeated this approach in 'Malvern Hills'[11] in 2015, stating that sustainable development "is to be defined in terms of development which meets the needs of the present without compromising the ability of future generations to meet their own needs."
- In 'Wychavon'[12], Justice Coulson stated that "it is quite wrong to say that a presumption in favour of sustainable development does not exist in the NPPF outside paragraph 14."

In contrast, a separate thread of case law was emerging which took a much narrower approach, assessing sustainable development only in terms of the paragraph 6 definition and the paragraph 14 presumption. For example, the 'Scrivens'[13] case of November 2013 concerned a development of 'autarkic' homes with an environmentally neutral footprint and the judge was invited to agree that they were sustainable because they complied with a 'Pentalogy' of environmental policies. He declined to do so and showed a marked preference for compliance with the Framework rather than those environmental policies: "The NPPF refers to the need to protect the environment and to recognise the intrinsic character and beauty of the countryside ... sustainability is not limited to the Pentalogy."

- 'Bloor Homes'[14] in 2014 involved a residential development refused by the local authority because the proposal conflicted with development plan policies protecting green wedges of countryside. Lord Justice Lindblom gave no consideration to the objective meaning of sustainable development beyond the Framework, referring only to paragraph 6 and focused instead on a detailed interpretation of paragraph 14 and the meaning of "absent," "silent," and "out of date."
- In the 'Dartford'[15] decision in 2014, the local authority refused permission for a residential development because the development was in breach of policies protecting open spaces. The council, referring explicitly to 'William Davis,' claimed that the inspector should have considered whether the proposal was in keeping with 'sustainable development' before applying paragraph 14 of the Framework. Justice Patterson disagreed and applied a restricted, framework-specific interpretation of sustainable development.
- 'Barwood Strategic Land'[16] reviewed a planning inspector's decision that had taken social, economic, and environmental dimensions into account. The High Court ruled that this was the wrong approach. If a plan was up to date with a five-year housing land supply then development was automatically sustainable.

Even this relatively small sample of the cases shows that the courts were regularly ruling on the 'meaning' of sustainable development in the Framework without reaching a consistent conclusion. Nevertheless, for either party disgruntled with the other's view of whether or not paragraph 14 applied, the only option (other than the very limited one of a planning appeal) was a court challenge. This effectively drew the courts into assessing the meaning of individual Framework policies to rule on whether the paragraph 14 presumption was correctly applied. The process of reluctant interpretation reached its climax with the 'Suffolk Coastal' decision of the Supreme Court in April 2017.[17]

Game of Homes: A Planning Saga

By the time the Supreme Court was drawn into ruling on the meaning of six words, two further paragraphs of the Framework had joined paragraphs 6 and 14 as an issue regularly considered by the courts. One, paragraph 47, set out what was required to demonstrate that the local authority had a five-year supply of deliverable land for the development of housing. The second, paragraph 49, required that "relevant policies for the supply of housing" should not be considered "up to date" (Ministry of Housing, Communities & Local Government, 2012, p. 13), unless the authority could demonstrate that it had designated sufficient land in its plan to provide the required the five-year supply of deliverable land.

The significance of these two paragraphs and their interrelationship with paragraph 14 was critical for local authorities seeking to preserve the status of their local development plans in the decision-making process. If the local authority had the required five-year land supply, their development plan policies would retain their dominance in the planning decision process and the traditional planning balance would apply. However, should a local authority not have the required supply of deliverable houses, paragraph 47 automatically rendered all of their "policies for the supply of housing" automatically out of date, no matter how recently the plan had been adopted. Instead, the application of the paragraph 14 presumption—in effect a presumption in favor of the Framework—would be applied because of the way paragraph 6 defined the concept.

The attention of applicants and decision makers therefore turned to the meaning of the phrase 'policies for the supply of housing' in circumstances in which the local authority could not show that it had the necessary planned supply of housing land. Applicants promoting developments that were non-compliant with development plans wanted the phrase to be interpreted broadly and apply to as many policies as possible. Local authorities understandably argued for a narrow definition, thus limiting the potential damage to their development plan policies, and their weight in the planning process. By the time the Supreme Court resolved the position with its ruling in the 'Suffolk Coastal' decision in May 2017, the interrelationship between paragraphs 6, 14, 47, and 49 had been the subject of a number of judgments: Justice Lang in 'William Davis'[18] and 'Wenman'[19]; Justice Lewis in 'Cotswold'[20] and 'South Northamptonshire'[21]; and Justice Lindblom in 'Crane'[22] and 'Phides.'[23]

Matters came to a head with a case that began with an application for 26 homes in January 2013 made by Hopkins Homes to Suffolk Coastal District Council. The site was designated as historic parkland, not housing, and the application was also in conflict with development plan policy SP29 which allowed new development only if it "of necessity requires to be located there." The Council refused permission, partly in reliance on SP29, and Hopkins Homes appealed the decision. If, as Hopkins Homes argued, policy SP29 was a 'policy for the supply of housing,' then the absence of a five-year supply of housing land meant that it must be considered "out of date" and the tilted balance would apply. If, as the Council argued, it was not, then it would retain its status as an up-to-date development plan policy and could legitimately rely on its prominence in the traditional planning balance.

The planning inspector supported the Council's position, and Hopkins Homes challenged that decision. Justice Supperstone issued his judgment in January 2015,[24] and adopted a relaxed approach to the understanding of what a housing policy was, ruling that policy SP29 was a policy for the supply of housing, that it did come within the scope of paragraph 49, and that the inspector's misinterpretion was a legal defect. The original decision to refuse permission was quashed.

Within four weeks, another judge had ruled in relation to a proposal for a residential development in Willaston Cheshire.[25] The development was in conflict with development plan policies, including policy NE4 protecting 'green gaps' between villages, and the Council refused permission in partial reliance on that conflict. However, and as with the other application, the Council did not have a five-year supply of housing land. On appeal, the developer argued that policy NE4 was a policy for the supply of housing and had to be considered out of date. This was a very similar situation to the Hopkins Homes application. If, as the applicant argued, policy NE4 was a 'policy for the supply of housing' then it was also out of date and could be overridden by the paragraph 14 presumption in favor of sustainable development as defined by the Framework. If it was not, then it would retain the weight traditionally accorded to development plan policies.

On appeal, the inspector agreed with the applicant's position and granted permission for the development. The council challenged that decision and again the High Court was asked to rule. Justice Lang took the opposite approach to Supperstone and applied a much stricter interpretative approach and ruling that "[t]he immediate context of paragraph 49 suggests that the minister intended to refer to policies for the *supply of housing* rather than to any policy which may have the indirect effect of restricting housing development." She agreed with the council that NE4 was not a housing policy, did not come within the scope of paragraph 49 of the Framework, and that it was an "error of law" to say that it did. The original decision to refuse permission was reinstated.

When both parties appealed against the Supperstone/Lang judgments, the cases were conjoined and considered in a judgment issued on 17 March 2016[26] with Lord Justice Lindblom providing the main opinion. This identified the central question: should decision makers apply a 'narrow' or 'broad' interpretation of paragraph 49? A narrow interpretation would limit the application of paragraph 49 to "policies dealing only with the numbers and distribution of new housing"; a wide one would include policies "whose effect is to restrain the supply by restricting housing development in certain parts of the authority's area."

He ruled that a broader interpretative approach should be adopted with the Framework interpreted in the context of its primary goal of delivering more housing, and stated that "[i]nterpreting the policy in this way does not strain the natural and ordinary meaning of the words its draftsman has used. It does no violence at all to the language." He agreed with Justice Supperstone that the inspector had adopted too narrow a definition and overruled Justice Lang's judgment commenting that "her interpretation of the policy was not correct."

The judgment was highly significant. For local authorities without a five-year supply of housing land as required by paragraph 47, it meant that *any* policy that could—directly or indirectly—restrict housing developments would come within the scope of paragraph 49 and automatically trigger a presumption in favor of 'sustainable development,' as defined by the NPPF. For developers, there was a much greater scope to argue that a wider range of policies were out of date, opening up much greater opportunities for the tilted balance to be applied, effectively assessing applications with reference to the Framework rather than local development plan policies.

The case was again subject to an appeal in the Supreme Court which issued its judgment in May 2017.[27] Lord Carnwath began by noting the slight absurdity of the situation: "[u]naided by the legal arguments, I would have regarded the meaning of paragraph 49 itself, taken in context, as reasonably clear, and not susceptible to much legal analysis." He followed Lang's original 'narrow' approach and ruled that it was wrong to "adopt a reading of paragraph 49 which not only changes its language, but in doing so creates a form of non-statutory fiction." He also stressed that the weight given to policies should be a "pure planning judgment, not dependent on issues of legal interpretation" and that there should be no "legalistic exercise" to decide whether policies were within paragraph 49. Lord Gill also disagreed with the interpretative principles set out by Lord Justice Lindblom and echoed Lord Carnwath's opening remarks when he noted that "[t]o some extent the issue in these cases has been obscured by the doctrinal controversy." For practitioners and decision makers the Supreme Court decision brought welcomed clarity to the question of how the key Framework policy should be interpreted by decision makers.

Sustainable Development: Residual Issues

The case resolved the meaning of the six words it was asked to consider, but it did not limit the role of lawyers as interpreters of policy. The judgment did not address the wider question of how a policy document that was designed to place sustainable development at the heart of the planning system had instead become a battleground for lawyers arguing over the meaning of individual words. In fact, it could not because the Framework as drafted was destined to become a war of competing interpretations. Paragraph 14 is not a definition of sustainable development, but a trigger requiring a presumption in favor of sustainable development to be applied when any local plan policy is absent, silent, or out of date. Policy makers, decision takers, planning inspectors, barristers, and judges use the words 'sustainable development' as a clearly defined term when they are in effect referring to a process. The primary consideration for decision makers in this process is not the sustainability of the development but whether development plan policies are absent, silent, or out of date and are thus displaced by paragraph 14. If they have, and the paragraph 14 presumption is applied, the question to be considered is not whether the development is sustainable by any traditional understanding of the term but if it is sustainable as 'defined' in paragraph 6—in other words, if it is in conformity with the Framework. These are questions of linguistic interpretation rather than an assessment of sustainability and so tend to be argued by lawyers not planners.

Unsurprisingly, the meaning and interpretation of sustainable development, as defined and applied by paragraphs 6 and 14 of the Framework, has remained contentious:

- In the 'St Modwen'[28] judgment issued in 2017 an inspector's decision to refuse permission was challenged primarily on the basis that the paragraph 14 presumption was misapplied because the words "supply" and "delivery" in paragraph 47 were not properly interpreted.
- The 'Jelson'[29] decision in 2018 again challenged an inspector's decision based on misinterpretation of paragraph 47—this time the words "full, objectively assessed needs."
- The 'Braintree'[30] judgment in 2018 involved the interpretation by a planning inspector of paragraph 55 of the Framework that states: "to promote sustainable development in rural areas … [l]ocal planning authorities should avoid new isolated homes in the countryside." The central issue was once again one of linguistic interpretation so that Lord Justice Lindblom was compelled to consider the meaning of the word in isolation and did so in great detail: "Derived originally from the Latin word 'insula,' meaning an 'island,' it carries the ordinary sense of something that is … [placed] or standing apart or alone; detached or separate from other things or persons; unconnected with anything else; solitary."

Although he is a master of linguistic interpretation, Lord Justice Lindblom has been equally articulate in expressing concern at the extent to which it has become a matter of legal argument. In 'St Modwen,' Lindblom commented that "this court has cautioned against the dangers of excessive legalism infecting the planning system … There is no place in challenges to planning decisions for the kind of hypercritical scrutiny." In 'Jelson,' he commented that the submissions on misinterpretation "collide with the most basic principle in the court's jurisdiction to review planning decisions, which is that matters of planning judgment are not for the court."

The 2019 Framework

So long as the Framework imposed a presumption in favor of sustainable development and restricted that definition to development that was in conformity with the Framework, arguments for and against sustainable development were destined to begin and end with discussions on the meaning and application of Framework policies. In April 2014, The Communities and Local Government Select Committee launched an inquiry into the operation of the

National Planning Policy Framework and published its report in December.[31] The Committee's first recommendation was that paragraph 6—the statement that the policies in paragraphs 18 to 219, taken as a whole, constitute the Government's view of what sustainable development means in practice—should be removed, and that the page 2 definition—clearly referencing Brundtland—should "stand on its own." The Government began a consultation on a replacement document that ran from December 2015 to February 2016, with a further consultation following on from publication of the Housing White Paper ran from March to May 2018. The final document ('the 2018 Framework') was introduced to Parliament by the Secretary of State for Housing, Communities and Local Government on 24 July 2018.[32]

The new Framework document accepted the Committee's recommendation by removing paragraph 6 and incorporating a new paragraph 7 which states that "[at] a very high level, the objective of sustainable development can be summarised as meeting the needs of the present without compromising the ability of future generations to meet their own needs." The new Framework does not, however, address the fundamental issue with the 2012 document. The presumption in favor of sustainable development is retained in Paragraph 11. For decisions on individual applications the presumption means

> approving development proposals that accord with an up-to-date development plan without delay … where there are no relevant development plan policies, or the policies which are most important for determining the application are out-of-date, granting permission unless: the application of policies in this Framework that protect areas or assets of particular importance provides a clear reason for refusing the development proposed; or any adverse impacts of doing so would significantly and demonstrably outweigh the benefits, when assessed against the policies in this Framework taken as a whole.
> (Ministry of Housing, Communities & Local Government, 2019, p. 6)

In the specific context of planning decisions, sustainable development still cannot be defined on its own terms or with reference to its policy context, but instead continues to rely on a 'meaning' that is indissolubly yoked to the Framework policies themselves. The white swan/black swan issue remains: decision makers are continuously required to assess sustainable development in terms of the Framework with their discretionary scope significantly limited to whether or not its policies provide a reason for refusal, or the impacts outweigh the benefits, as assessed against the Framework. Indeed, in the 'Paul Newman New Homes' case decided in September 2018 the judge began his ruling with the comment that "This is yet another case in which the interpretation of the National Planning Policy Framework, the Framework, is at issue, and in particular the circumstances in which what planning jargon calls the 'tilted balance' comes into play."[33]

Conclusion

The English planning system is distinguished by the prominence of planning policy in the legal test applied to all decisions made on development proposals and the statutory provisions are in effect no more than a procedural scaffold within which a weighing process known as the 'planning balance' is carried out. The Government's planning Framework is a relevant, material consideration in the determination of each and every application for planning permission. As soon as a development policy is out of date, the presumption in favor of sustainable development as constrained by the content of the Framework overrides the usual weight attributed to development plan policies and becomes the primary consideration for whether or not planning permission should be granted.

In the 'Braintree'[34] case, Lord Justice Lindblom said that "over-interpretation of a policy can distort its true meaning." In the case of sustainable development this is exactly what has happened. Development proposals continue to be assessed in the context of a presumption in favor of sustainable development, but the assessment is not based on the environmental, social, and economic credentials of that development so much as its conformity with the Framework. That process continues to be overseen by a small number of planning judges who regularly state that interpretation is for the courts yet rarely question the meaning of the term itself. The presumption in favor of sustainable development remains one that can be used to restrict or permit planning permission for a wide range of developments, with little or no regard to its meaning in the context of planning policy or traditional conceptions of the term.

The 2012 Framework was claimed to be a document that secured the 'white swan' of sustainable development at its heart, but proved impossible for the concept to avoid drowning in the murky waters of linguistic interpretation. In the new Framework, sustainable development is still a 'black swan': the words are no more than a linguistic façade that undermines, rather than preserves the Brundtland principles from which sustainable development evolved.

Notes

1 *Alconbury* [2001] UKHL 23; [2001] NPC 90, [2001] 20 EGCS 228, [2002] Env LR 12, [2003] 2 AC 295, (2001) 3 LGLR 38, [2001] UKHRR 728, [2001] 2 All ER 929, (2001) 82 P & CR 40, [2001] 2 WLR 1389, [2001] HRLR 45, [2001] JPL 920, [2001] 2 PLR 76, [2001] [117].
2 *Secretary of State for Communities and Local Government v. West Berkshire District Council & Anor* [2016] [2016] WLR 3923, [2016] 2 P &CR 8, [2016] 1 WLR 3923, [2016] PTSR 982, [2016] WLR(D) 260, [2016] EWCA Civ 441, [2016] JPL 1034.
3 *City of Edinburgh Council v. Secretary of State for Scotland and Others* [1997] WLR 1447, [1997] 3 PLR 71, [1997] UKHL 38, [1998] 1 All ER 174, [1997] 1 WLR 1447, 1998 SC (HL) 33.
4 *Stringer v. Minister of Housing and Local Government* [1970] 1 W.L.R.1280 [1294G].

5 *City of Edinburgh Council v. Secretary of State for Scotland and Others* [1997] WLR 1447, [1997] 3 PLR 71, [1997] UKHL 38, [1998] 1 All ER 174, [1997] 1 WLR 1447, 1998 SC (HL) 33.
6 *Brown v. Carlisle City Council* [2014] EWHC 707.
7 *Earl Shilton Action Group, R (on the application of) v. Hinckley and Bosworth Borough Council & Ors* [2014] EWHC 1764.
8 *William Davis Ltd & Anor v. Secretary of State for Communities and Local Governments & Anor* [2013] EWHC 3058 (Admin).
9 *Trafford Borough Council v. Secretary of State for Communities & Local Government & Anor* [2014] EWHC 424 (Admin).
10 *Gallagher Estates Ltd & Anor v. Solihull Metropolitan Borough Council* [2014] EWHC 1283 (Admin).
11 *Malvern Hills District Council v. Secretary of State for Communities and Local Government & Anor* [2015] EWHC 2244 (Admin).
12 *Wychavon District Council v. Secretary of State for Communities and Local Government & Anor* [2016] EWHC 592 (Admin), [2016] WLR(D) 158, [2016] PTSR 675.
13 *Scrivens v. Secretary of State for Communities & Local Government* [2013] EWHC 3549 (Admin).
14 *Bloor Homes East Midlands Ltd v. Secretary of State for Communities and Local Government & Anor* [2017] PTSR 1283, [2014] EWHC 754 (Admin).
15 *Dartford BC v. Secretary of State for Communities and Local Government* [2014] EWHC 2636 (Admin).
16 *Barwood Strategic Land II LLP v. East Staffordshire Borough Council & Anor* [2017] WLR(D) 445, [2018] PTSR 88, [2017] EWCA Civ 893.
17 *Suffolk Coastal District Council v. Hopkins Homes Ltd & Anor* [2017] PTSR 623, [2017] JPL 1084, [2017] 4 All ER 938, [2017] 1 WLR 1865, [2017] WLR(D) 319, [2017] WLR 1865, [2017] UKSC 37.
18 *William Davis Ltd & Anor v. Secretary of State for Communities and Local Governments & Anor* [2013] EWHC 3058 (Admin).
19 *Wenman v. Secretary of State for Communities and Local Government* [2015] EWHC 925 (Admin).
20 *Cotswold District Council v. Secretary of State for Communities and Local Government and others* [2013] EWHC 3719 (Admin).
21 *South Northamptonshire Council v. Secretary of State for Communities and Local Government and Robert Plummer* [2013] EWHC 4377 (Admin).
22 *Crane v. Secretary of State for Communities and Local Government* [2015] EWHC 425 (Admin).
23 *Phides Estates (Overseas) Ltd v. Secretary of State for Communities and Local Government* [2015] EWHC 827 (Admin).
24 *Hopkins Homes Ltd v. Secretary of State for Communities and Local Government & Anor* [2015] CN 177, [2015] EWHC 132 (Admin).
25 *Cheshire East Borough Council v. Secretary of State for Communities and Local Government & Anor* [2015] EWHC 410 (Admin).
26 *Suffolk Coastal District Council v. Hopkins Homes Ltd & Anor* [2016] WLR(D) 151, [2016] EWCA Civ 168, [2016] PTSR 1315.
27 *Suffolk Coastal District Council v. Hopkins Homes Ltd & Anor* [2017] PTSR 623, [2017] JPL 1084, [2017] 4 All ER 938, [2017] 1 WLR 1865, [2017] WLR(D) 319, [2017] WLR 1865, [2017] UKSC 37.
28 *St Modwen Developments Ltd v. Secretary of State for Communities and Local Government & Ors* [2018] PTSR 746, [2017] EWCA Civ 1643.
29 *Jelson Ltd v. Secretary of State for Communities and Local Government & Anor* [2018] EWCA Civ 24.

30 *Braintree District Council v. Secretary of State for Communities and Local Government & Ors* [2018] EWCA Civ 610.
31 House of Commons Community and Local Government Committee *Operation of the National Planning Policy Framework Government* Fourth Report HC 190.
32 Hansard 24 July 2018 HCWS925.
33 *Paul Newman New Homes Ltd v. Secretary of State for Housing Communities and Local Government & Anor* [2019] EWHC 2367 (Admin).
34 *Braintree District Council v. Secretary of State for Communities and Local Government & Ors* [2018] EWCA Civ 610.

References

Allmendinger, P. (2016). *Neoliberal Spatial Governance*. New York: Routledge.

Department of Environment Food and Rural Affairs (2005). *Securing the Future UK Government Sustainable Development Strategy*. CM 6467. London: DEFRA.

Department for Environment, Food and Rural Affairs (2011). *Mainstreaming Sustainable Development: The Government's Vision and What this Means in Practice*. London: DEFRA.

Government of the United Kingdom (2011). *Budget*. London: HM Treasury.

Ministry of Housing Communities & Local Government (2012). *The National Planning Policy Framework*. Retrieved March 23, 2020, from https://webarchive.nationalarchives.gov.uk/20180608095821/https://www.gov.uk/government/publications/national-planning-policy-framework–2.

Ministry of Housing Communities & Local Government (2019). *The National Planning Policy Framework*. Retrieved March 23, 2020, from www.gov.uk/government/publications/national-planning-policy-framework–2.

World Commission on Environment and Development (1987). *Our Common Future*. London: Oxford University Press.

Chapter 2

Politics

Who Stands Up for Ecology? The Politics of Sustainable Land Use in Stockholm

Sabina Edelman

It is chilly in the corridors and there is a draft from the large windows of the impressive but slightly outmoded City Hall building. Our quick internal preparatory chat is cut short by the typical 'ding-dong' of the doorbell to our party's office. The councilors from the other parties in the ruling municipal coalition enter in a nonchalant manner, clearly feeling at home on the premises from many previous meetings. Their acquaintance with our office corridors have of course also been conditioned on the preceding 20 years of meetings and discussions during which we have debated the proposed new nature reserve which also constitutes the focal point of this particular get-together.

"Coffee?" The door is closed.

"We need to increase the size of the Årsta nature reserve by another hectare so that our proposal is bigger than that of the previous majority government, and includes more ecological features," says the representative of one of the coalition parties in an authoritative tone.

"What magnitude of reduction in housing would that require?" asks another representative. It is a rhetorical question, given that everyone in the group knows full well what the answer is. Someone else replies that any change must not demand more expensive groundwork, seeing that the end result of the whole project should be affordable new homes.

Goal Conflicts in Stockholm Land Politics

The dialogue above is a fairly typical example of the type of discussion that took place between key elected representatives from the Red-Green-Pink coalition government during the period 2014–2018 on the topic of potential new nature reserves within the City of Stockholm. It might even be a symbolic example of any discussion concerning ecological values and city planning. In the case of the new nature reserves, goals for securing the protection of undeveloped greenfield land for the benefit of future generations were pitted against goals for producing an adequate supply of housing, also with reference to the well-being of the aforementioned future residents. The issue had been actualized through the political agreement to produce plans for 130,000 new dwellings and seven new nature reserves within the ruling coalition's term of office. Moreover, previous political majorities had tried to agree on a boundary for the Årsta reserve, but without any success.

In this chapter, I will highlight the dilemma of sustainable land use, and in particular I will delve more deeply into what I find to be fundamental goal conflicts that lurk within current usage of the concept of sustainability in this area. As I have worked for a number of years as a political advisor to the Green Party in the City of Stockholm regarding issues of urban development and planning, this chapter will take a 'view from politics' on these issues. In what follows I will draw heavily on my experience of the internal debates regarding the formation of new nature reserves in the city during the period 2014–2018, when the city was governed by a coalition of the Social Democrats, the Left Party, the Green Party, and the Feminist Initiative (I should add that I have witnessed similar discussions on goal conflicts as an official in the urban planning office of another Swedish municipality). To illustrate these goal conflicts within the use of the concept of sustainability in relation to land use, I will utilize the planning of the Årsta nature reserve as an example. The reserve was finally instituted by decision of the city council in January 2018. The scene described at the opening of the chapter is an example of how the ruling coalition's political negotiations took place.

The development of land to facilitate urban growth is an increasingly pressing question, both at the global level and locally in Stockholm. In the planning of current and future land use, conflicting interests must be weighed against each other—for instance, an increased production of dwellings to tackle housing shortages as against the preservation of natural lands to secure ecological and recreational functions. When the balance is considered on a broader geographical scale, it is often not too controversial to point out different land use areas. The challenge arises when space is more limited, for instance in local land use plans, and where the conflict between uses becomes very clear and distinct. In such debates, 'sustainability' tends to become an oft-repeated motive for many different positions. I want to exemplify this idea through the political controversy within the ruling majority about the Årsta nature reserve and how it could be boiled down to a conflict concerning what is considered to be the true essence of 'sustainability,' and the goal conflicts that these divergent ideas generated. The housing question was important to all the coalition parties during their term in office, but the difference between them lay in what was understood to be a *sustainable* path towards new housing development. In brief, I understood that for the Social Democrats and the Left Party a sustainable housing policy meant focusing on combating segregation by means of new housing construction, whereas the Green Party took the position that sustainable development must pay critical attention to the protection of valuable green space.

To take a further step back, perhaps the central question that lies behind this chapter is this: why is it so difficult to achieve sustainable urban development? As a professional working in the area of urban development I know that it is not wholly unheard of to place the burden of the blame on the politicians, who are deemed to be inefficient, ignorant, or unresponsive. Political will and a good evidence base are of course crucial, but even when these conditions are met, this ambition can be hard to realize. During the 2014–2018 political term, in addition to the agreement on seven new nature reserves, there existed an agreement among the governing parties to construct 40,000 new dwellings in Stockholm by 2020 in order to tackle an increased rate of urbanization and expected population growth. The political majority had picked up on public concern that the current housing stock did not meet existing needs, and that the increased demand for housing was also putting pressure on the remaining green space, particularly that adjacent to high-density developed areas. Consequently, it was decided that additional housing would be built sustainably, and in phases, so as not to "risk the quality of life for present and future residents," as stated in the city budget. The idea was to both preserve nature and build new homes.

The Green Party, which profiles itself as a modern ecological party with a nuanced politics and a focus on long-term sustainability, held 16 seats in the city council (equivalent to approximately 16% of the popular vote). It may appear self-evident that buildings that are constructed under the aegis of such leadership will be focused on sustainability, but criticisms were nonetheless voiced. These concerns were often expressed by interest groups or local residents, but sometimes also by academics and other more impartial commentators. So, what was it that was going wrong in their eyes? Of course, there is not a single answer to this question, but one challenge that was recurrent during my tenure as political advisor concerns situations in which goal conflicts within the realm of sustainability turn commitments that may come across as self-evident into bones of contention. No one would claim that they do not want to protect urban nature, but nonetheless the example that I will be discussing shows that when opinion-makers pit the protection of nature against the need for housing, it becomes difficult for individual parties and politicians to stand up for nature. The malleability of the concept of sustainability enables actors to stress the need for social sustainability as being more pressing and superseding a more holistic understanding of the concept, or one that more strongly emphasizes the ecological dimension. In the Red-Green-Pink majority of 2014–2018, a social understanding of sustainability appeared to have a stronger political backing than the ecological perspective, which from my perspective led to a situation in which ecological concerns repeatedly risked becoming deprioritized. Below, I will illustrate this concern through a discussion of the process of delineating and instituting the Årsta nature reserve.

42 Sabina Edelman

Figure 2.1 Ecologically valuable forest in the Stockholm area.
Source: Sabina Edelman.

The Political Process of the Årsta Nature Reserve

The area under consideration for the Årsta reserve occupies approximately 70 hectares of natural space right outside the innermost core of Stockholm, and for a long time has been used for recreational purposes by local residents, and to some extent also by inhabitants of other parts of the city. It is located along a sloping ridge which makes accessibility to some parts of the site somewhat challenging, but it is well-served by public transport and provides easy access to many other public services. The site is located in a very popular residential neighborhood with a mixed typology, and many property developers have expressed an interest to develop the land in and around the area. Due to the development pressure, actors including the regional County Administrative Board have been pushing for the protection of green spaces, which are known to be home to many animal species and to contain a great number of old trees. During the run-up to the 2014 elections plans for developing a nature reserve in parts of the area were already under consideration by the city administration. Discussions among the coalition parties took as their starting point the preceding preparatory work. Another important precondition for the negotiations was the established city praxis of demanding that individual development projects took responsibility for their own expenses. Some of the planned interventions in the area that were aiming at facilitating better accessibility to the green spaces incurred costs that needed to be covered by funds garnered from giving up land for development. However, I will not go into this issue in detail here since the pros and cons of this way of financing public authority urban development costs is a somewhat different discussion.

The City of Stockholm's comprehensive plan has an overarching goal to ensure 'efficient land use' within the city and regulates land use on a very rough spatial level in a legally non-binding fashion. Planning for future green spaces is based on knowledge concerning national and regional green corridors and networks. 'Sustainable land use' is a political formulation that has been employed in Sweden in recent years to attempt to encompass all three sustainability dimensions (i.e., ecological, economical, and socially sustainable development). In principle, everyone agreed to the need for such a sustainable land use politics, but since land politics in practice is discussed in relation to every (legally binding) local development plan or individual development project, the drawing of concrete boundaries between different land uses becomes a recurrent political issue in the politics of the City. The dominant ideal pattern of urban density, and the related ambition that urban development should not be spread out, but rather should become more concentrated, does, however, generate challenges for green spaces, which cannot be piled up on each other in the same way as apartments or offices. Instead, what tends to happen is that the planning guidelines for green spaces are shifted, so that rather than placing demands on the extent of green space they focus on functional and qualitative norms. However, professional urban ecologists tend to question how much the manifest spatial extent of green space can actually be shrunk without losing key functions. Nonetheless, there were no minimal standards set for natural spaces in urban development plans in Stockholm during the 2014–2018 political term, even though functional quality assurance instruments such as 'Green Space Factor' calculations were in regular use. With regards to 'social sustainability', a Commission for a Socially Sustainable Stockholm was appointed during the 2014–2018 term, with the purpose of strengthening the social dimension of sustainability work in the city. One of the key areas of the commissions' work focused on housing. In the area of land use, social sustainability can for instance be about facilitating the planning of affordable dwellings, housing for marginalized residents, and ensuring that schools are within walking distance of housing areas – but it can also be about making sure that residents have access to green spaces. No other similar commission was set up to develop the other dimensions of the sustainability concept. These preconditions might be understood as risking policy decisions to become somewhat lopsided and one-dimensional.

The case of Årsta concerned the critical land use question with regard to the drawing of the border between housing development and a new nature reserve, but elsewhere it might for instance concern the separation of industrial and residential space. This can in some cases lead to a political discussion in which different societal goals are pitted against each other, even though they are all put forward in the name of sustainability. Since there are few established standards regarding the extent of green space in new local development plans, there is always a political worry from the Green side that this is a quality that will be overlooked or deprioritized in land use decisions, particularly so when considering that new dwellings, as well as schools and green spaces can all be rhetorically dressed as contributing to 'sustainable urban development.' For instance, goals of social sustainability can be pitted against ecological sustainability in a competition for space between housing development and nature preservation. Suddenly, seemingly absurd questions arise and answers need to be given, such as: 'is a biotope for frogs more important than 100 new apartments?' Posed on the scale of a single development plan, such questions will always give the wrong answer, no matter which side wins.

In my role as political advisor I had the opportunity to be part of the discussions among the coalition government regarding the Årsta nature reserve. From the outset, many politicians had their doubts about the administration-initiated proposal, not least because of the lack of political sponsorship, but also due to deficiencies with regards to accessibility. Depending on exactly how the boundaries of the nature reserve were drawn, this intervention could potentially serve to achieve a number of different political goals. Under the leadership of the Red-Green-Pink alliance, the City of Stockholm prioritized accessibility and affordable housing development, and therefore the politicians saw this as an opportunity to develop a new proposal that would better mirror their idea of urban development 'for the benefit of all.' Urban nature would be made accessible to all, and not only to the privileged residents of the local neighborhood. It was suggested that certain types of buildings and related services could function as portals to the area for visitors from other parts of the city. Another parameter that was introduced into the discussion was the social value that a nature reserve could provide. Areas of the reserve with the greatest ecological value were of course to be preserved, but the creation of more spaces for recreation and play were also considered to strengthen social sustainability and were introduced into the discussions regarding the drawing of boundaries for the reserve. It was likely that many of these divergent goals and interests could be resolved through negotiation, but the real stumbling block was the introduction into the puzzle of the wish to also contribute to tackling the housing shortage. Nonetheless, or perhaps precisely for that reason, the housing issue became the centerpiece of the discussions. As the discussions progressed, the politicians came to promise a solution that would facilitate both the construction of X number of apartments, while at the same time protecting urban nature and producing a high-quality urban environment. But anyone who attempted to probe the agreement on exactly which ecological values had been taken into consideration during the drawing-up of the boundaries of the nature reserve would draw a blank.

Based on the interest expressed by the property developers the city planners consequently suggested that 1,000 new apartments could be developed on the edge of the Årsta forest as a solution to both finance the investments for the reserve and to provide a contribution to the housing development goals set by the city—as well as all the other goals the politicians had set for the reserve. Since the new boundary allowing for this development was a revision of a pervious proposal it did not need to be put through a new public consultation. Instead, the relevant administrative departments developed a set of questions and answers regarding all the qualities and functions that the reserve and the development thereof should provide, and how. It is worth mentioning that although the entire reserve compromised approximately 70 hectares of land, it was the pockets of land located around the border, measuring approximately 10 hectares, that became controversial. Local residents and concerned ecologists formed interest groups protesting against the proposed reserve boundary. The politicians were suspected of having colluded with commercial developers, and to be serving their interests. The activists began requesting copies of the politicians' e-mail correspondence in accordance with the Swedish right-of-access principle. In the end, the reserve was instituted in January 2018. The majority of the parties voted for the proposal, but not all. Some thought that the decision to proceed should have been preceded by a more thorough inventory of the ecological values, others that the natural area should have been preserved in its entirety and no developments at all allowed. It was a contentious decision, and a number of parties had changed their position during the course of the work.

Eventually, the debate about the nature reserve in the Årsta forest came to focus on issues of housing development and the drawing-up of its boundary instead of ecological values and natural amenities. How did this come to be? An interest group (the Stockholm Chamber of Commerce) had used the opportunity to make available an analysis of land use in the Stockholm County that showed that five times more land had been set aside for nature reserves in the past 20 years compared to that which had been released for new housing developments. Their report was picked up and cited by national media. The angle was that the institution of nature reserves was a means for Swedish cities and municipalities to tie their own hands with regards to the national housing development targets, and that their right to institute reserves should therefore be rescinded by the central government, and instead handed over to the more tightly controlled County Administrative Boards.

It is my view that the analysis of the Chamber of Commerce was founded upon a narrowly anthropocentric view of nature. The Chamber's goal for urban development in Stockholm was formulated as "an attractive metropolitan region needs to be both densified with new dwellings and have recreational areas of high quality." According to the Chamber, natural spaces in Stockholm were solely for recreational purposes. The organization analyzed a number of proposed nature reserves in Sweden and estimated the potential for development based on their size. It was claimed that the Årsta forest would be able to contribute 3,000 new dwellings if it was extensively developed. Many politicians who later voted on the Årsta decision also took part in debates on the subject arranged by the Chamber of Commerce.

One way to understand this push by the lobbyists is that it was founded upon the assumption that city politicians would be wary of being portrayed as anti-development and of using the nature reserves as a way to block urban development—and as a consequence they would be more disposed towards releasing more land to commercial developers. But a less farfetched reason might be that they sought to ensure that in any future discussions regarding the institution of nature reserves the need for land to be allocated for housing development must be taken into consideration. The report also clearly stated that the position of the Chamber was that "the institution of new nature reserves, in every individual case, should balance the need to protect nature against the need for land for housing development, whereby the latter should always be assigned considerable weight." However, the whole argument to me comes across as illogical, since it rested upon assumptions concerning the amount of space that was reserved for each of these uses. Nonetheless, natural spaces are—unlike dwellings—difficult to pile up and will therefore always require more space. Even so, an apparent but nonetheless surreptitiously claimed commensurability between the two types of land use was established in public opinion, which made a great difference in how events later unfolded. As "considerable weight" came to be placed on housing development, the initial concern for protecting the value of the green space became deprioritized.

The dilution and heightened ambiguity related to the concept of sustainability that follows from different actors invoking it with very different meanings makes commitments controversial that should be self-evident. With the Årsta reserve in mind, it should not be a difficult decision to advocate for the protection of ancient forestland located in the heart of a big city, particularly when housing construction is already taking place at a rapid rate (an estimated 8,000–9,000 dwellings are being built per year) and which is approaching the limits of what the local infrastructure can reasonably carry (around 10,000 dwellings per year). But when interest groups politicize the issue and, furthermore, deliberately confuse the discussion, the risk is immanent that the outcome will be an awkward one. As is commonly known, if an issue is undecided and there is an opportunity to put a political spin on it, politicians are keen to put it in the eye of the storm as a means of profiling themselves and generating attention.

In the Årsta case, this meant that once the issue had been politicized by the Chamber of Commerce among other bodies, politicians were forced to respond to the growing but conflicting demands that they would be able to facilitate the development of both new housing *and* a nature reserve, in the same area. This was not a result of ignorance, but simply that also promising new housing was the only possible way forward towards instituting a reserve. For some of the leading parties in the coalition, who had pushed hard for new housing in their election campaign, it was simply no longer possible to only institute a reserve. The position that housing could be built 'somewhere else' would then have come across as irresponsible and a betrayal of their electoral promises.

In the debate about the Årsta forest, the concept of sustainability was then employed to claim that housing development was indeed a (socially) sustainable solution, which no one in their right mind would disagree with. What in effect happened was that a concern for ecological sustainability was trumped, rather than complemented, by a concern for social sustainability. In the rhetorical competition with municipal incomes, housing for youth, and more employment the ancient deciduous forestland simply did not stand a chance. When the social dimension of sustainability is raised against ecology politicians are faced with the type of absurd dilemmas that I mentioned at the beginning of this chapter; i.e., pitting the protection of a frog habitat against the potential construction of new and urgently needed housing. Any direct answer to that question in an either/or format will stultify the political process, which the example of Årsta forest also evinces. At the same time, such questions—once posed—require a response from politicians, and in this case many politicians will be tempted to go for the more populist option of providing more housing and accessible neat parks, rather than preserving less 'sexy' wild natural spaces. The broader support for social sustainability in the City of Stockholm was evinced by the bipartisan support for the Commission for a Socially Sustainable Stockholm. A ramification of this is that in the cases where the substance of 'sustainability' is not clearly spelled out by the politicians and where there are potential goal conflicts between the different dimensions, it can be tempting for civil servants to favor a social perspective on sustainability, since by default this is seen to have broad political backing.

Nonetheless, not every case plays out like Årsta forest debate. In some instances, the decision-making process has been better prepared and executed. For instance, in Stockholm there has been a recent push to remove physical barriers and to connect adjacent neighborhoods with different socioeconomic profiles. In these cases, a conscious decision was made to produce careful surveys of natural values in the project areas prior to planning. For instance, in the work behind the development program for Skarpnäck, a neighborhood in Stockholm, a survey was performed of existing natural values, which were then valorized in relation to their local, regional, and national significance. This generated a more nuanced discussion regarding the concrete land use allocations, in which ecological sustainability was put on the same footing as social issues, and it was much easier to explain to the public the principles behind the consequent trade-offs between social and ecological values.

Concluding Discussion

Conflicts about land use exist in most cities. In Sweden, such issues generally tend to come to a head when the concrete use of particular parcels of land is decided in local development plans. The associated legally binding land use decisions tend to generate strong sentiments at the local level. The example of the Årsta nature reserve demonstrates the potentially powerful impact of opinion-forming interest groups, which combined with a strong local engagement can have a heavy influence on such matters. It may well be that there might have been a more cool-headed and clearly formulated decision on the issue had it been considered at a more overarching, city-wide level, rather than piece by piece in relation to concrete local projects. In the end, when it comes to Årsta forest, I think that the grounds for instituting the reserve in the form it took became very opaque for the general citizen. Furthermore, this led to mistrust of the competence of the elected representatives, city administration as well as for democratic principles.

The political discussions regarding the Årsta forest are a good example of the political nature of the concept of sustainability. The advantage of employing the three-dimensional conceptualization of sustainability (economic, ecological, social) is that this can lead to the prioritization of interventions in the urban environment that simultaneously contribute to not only one of these aspects. It may for instance be that the problem of run-off management would not have been as high on the political agenda if surface solutions to the problem had not also been a potentially aesthetically pleasing feature of the urban landscape in the form of park development. Well-managed urban lakes contribute with many ecosystem services and can also provide recreational amenities that can be considered to contribute to social sustainability. Thus, social sustainability becomes an argument that can actually support environmentally friendly decisions instead of thwarting them.

However, unfortunately, this is not how things play out in many cases. When politicians debate an issue in the city council, and all of them invoke the concept of sustainability to support their radically different standpoints, it becomes very difficult to follow the logic of the arguments. What is obvious to see, however, is that at least in the case of Stockholm in recent years, the dimension of social sustainability has been gaining a relatively stronger position than ecological sustainability, if the two are pitted against each other. The production of new housing is supported by strong lobbying groups and has broad political support. In addition, in a city like Stockholm, the construction of dwellings generally occurs on municipally owned land that is sold off, thus providing an income for the city that can be argued to also tick the box of 'economic sustainability.' In these cases, the concept of sustainability is employed to sharpen conflicts between housing development and the protection of natural values that some actors are keen to foment.

A hope-inspiring aspect of the case of Årsta forest is that a group of civil society activists were prepared to take a stand and question the terms upon which the goal conflict in the Årsta forest was posed, as well as casting doubt on whether the plans for housing development would actually in any way support socially sustainable development. This intervention put the spotlight on the existing confusion regarding the way the whole problem was formulated. Following this, some of the politicians appear to have begun to question whether they had not overvalued the social sustainability gains of developing housing on unique inner-city greenfield land. The final debate in the city council regarding the decision for the local development plan also evinced that some second thoughts appear to have begun to creep into the minds of leading politicians. How much this was due to the activists' campaign is difficult to assess, but my feeling is that their arguments certainly held some sway in the final stages of the debate, even if they did not in the end totally reverse the decision.

In practice the three-dimensional approach to sustainable development opens up endless debates and the risk of a 'pick and choose' attitude. Of course, there is a broad consensus that sustainability is important, but this also provides possibilities for any special interest group to mobilize the concept of sustainability to support any conceivable position or proposal. In my experience, in recent years social and economic sustainability concerns in the City of Stockholm have been prioritized over ecological sustainability. Consequently, interventions that aim to secure ecological sustainability must also be argued to provide economic and social benefits if they are to stand any chance of gaining political backing, which is not always easy. Nature reserves are intended to protect unique natural values and are nonetheless sometimes instituted, but only if it can be argued that they also provide social amenities such as recreational facilities. However, when the argument for a nature reserve's ecological functions—such as serving as crucial green corridors for flora and fauna— is not placed at the heart of the decision, this might lead to the shrinking of planned protection zones, or to scarce attractive inner-city greenfield land simply being developed regardless, with promises of compensating off-sets somewhere else—as a result of which unique natural values in the urban environment risk being lost forever.

At this time of writing, a new political majority comprising the conservative and liberal parties, as well as the Green Party, has taken office in city hall. In the 2018 election campaign, one of the liberal parties pledged to expand the Årsta nature reserve if it won election and a decision to do precisely that was also part of the subsequent coalition policy platform. If this promise is made good, it may be possible to declare a victory for ecological considerations in the specific case of the Årsta forest. However, the broader fundamental question of the essential meaning of sustainable urban development—and indeed whether the decision helped to achieve sustainability in Stockholm and Årsta in particular—will nonetheless remain open to debate.

Chapter 3

Concretization
Sustainability in City Management and Urban Planning in Gothenburg: From Vague Vision to Social Inclusion Activities

Petra Adolfsson and Sara Brorström

In the center of the rapidly growing city of Gothenburg, Sweden's second most populous city, there is a tall building by the river Göta Älv called 'the Lipstick' due to its shape and color. The top floor of the Lipstick is designated for conferences and meetings and provides a view of the city that is difficult to find elsewhere. From here you can see both the inner city and Hisingen Island, areas with very different characteristics (Figure 3.1). You can see the old disused port areas, and from up here it is obvious that the heavy infrastructure that circles the inner city—in the form of roads and railroads—makes it difficult for the city's residents to gain access to the riverbanks. The story goes that when the local public building committee held a meeting at the Lipstick, the chair of the Planning and Building Committee at that time gazed across the area and proclaimed, "This area needs a vision." When the chair later became mayor of Gothenburg, a project was established with the aim of formulating a vision and strategies for the area, an effort that faced the challenge of fostering agreement across administrative boundaries about what the city, as an entity, wanted to do with the area.

Only a few years after the above recounted episode is supposed to have transpired, the area overlooked from the Lipstick had become crowded with young people on the waters in sailboats, having lunch at food trucks and enjoying a new riverside swimming pool in this old and previously derelict port area. Are there any connections between that visionary politician and the young people in a sailboat? In this chapter, we set out to answer that question. As we are interested in understanding how a vision is concretized into new activities in a city, our story is about the travel of ideas: from the vision expressed by politicians in the city council, to negotiations among city managers, and further to urban planning activities realized by visionary staff in one of the city districts.[1]

The city of Gothenburg is a port and industrial city with a long tradition of a social democratic political leadership. However, over several decades, the city has been transformed into a more mixed, business-based city with a focus on tourism and special events, such as athletics championships. The 2018 local election indicated that the traditional social democratic strength is fading. Gothenburg's past as an industrial city with the largest port in the Nordic region has greatly influenced the city. Large former port areas in the inner city

Figure 3.1 Gothenburg: View from the Lipstick
Source: Petra Adolfsson.

are nowadays rather empty or have been transformed into new, expensive housing areas. The river, still an important part of the regional infrastructure, divides the city. Historically, Hisingen Island, on the north side of the river, has been the residential area for many newcomers and people of limited means.

The city's long history of manufacturing and petroleum handling in the port has generated considerable accumulated pollution. By the 1980s, this situation was highlighted nationally by the Swedish Minster of the Environment, who cited the city as a negative example of environmental consciousness and expressed a need for change. In response, the city conducted a pilot project to enhance cooperation between business interests and the city administration to create better environmental conditions in the city. At the same time, Local Agenda 21 initiatives were being undertaken following the United Nations' call for measures to create a more sustainable world. 'Sustainability' has since become a frequently used catchword in the city administration. In recent years, the social aspects of sustainability have increasingly attracted attention, but one of the city's sustainability managers recently stated that as sustainability is a general concept, it means different things to different people and that the economic dimension of sustainability seems to have been neglected:

> We need to talk more about economic sustainability. Now it is often mixed with economic viability, but it is not the same thing. More of us need to

better understand economic language and financial tools. I think that is the key to moving from vision to decisiveness.

(Civil servant, working on sustainability issues for a municipal corporation, http://alvstranden.com/den-otaliga-hallbarhetstalangen/, retrieved December 19, 2018, translation by the authors)

Towards this background, we explore how sustainability, as part of politicians' visions, has become part of urban planning activities. To describe the *travel* and *concretization* of sustainability, from a visionary ideal to local practice, we use the concept of *translation* [2] as an analytical lens. This concept was developed in response to the diffusion perspective, which implies that an idea can move among actors without being completely transformed. Instead, a translation perspective suggests that an idea will be translated, or slightly transformed, when new actors pick it up and apply it in their daily work. Such translation can result in limited or extensive adaptation of the idea to fit into established professional routines. Consequently, translation can result in changes to both the idea and established routines. Actors might also find the idea uninteresting and reject it. In our case, applying the translation concept means that we are interested in understanding how sustainability is translated to fit daily routines in the context of the city administration in Gothenburg.

In what follows, we begin by describing the process of drafting the RiverCity vision. We take this point of departure because it allows us to follow the translation of the vision into concrete form, and it helps us to understand how sustainability features as a central theme of the vision—from the boardrooms where the vision was developed to the construction of a park and housing area in one city district. We will discuss challenges related to this translation: how to create a shared understanding of sustainability, and how to interpret a vision and translate it into new planning activities.

A new vision for the city 'RiverCity Gothenburg: open to the world; inclusive, green, and dynamic' was adopted by the city council of Gothenburg in October 2012. Municipal actors expressed various reasons why the city needed such a vision. First, the city-owned riverside harbor land could be used more effectively and developed for housing. Second, there was a desire to connect the different parts of the city in order to make it easier to move around within the city, for example, and to mitigate the geographic and social barrier effects of the river Göta Älv. Many observers described Gothenburg as one of the most segregated cities in Europe, and this was perceived as a situation that could not continue unchecked. Third, there was a desire to restructure the municipal administration, so that municipal departments and corporations could work together across boundaries. Fourth, corruption scandals discovered within the city administration were explained by the organizational culture, in which decision-making was not transparent. As reforming the organizational culture was an underlying reason for drafting a vision, how to organize the work of making that vision a reality became crucial. The vision-drafting process took two years, involving actors from inside the city organization and external stakeholders. In addition, workshops were organized in which invited participants discussed ways in which Gothenburg could become more sustainable in the future.

Organization of the Drafting Process

A project leader was appointed and tasked with organizing and managing the vision-drafting process for what was called 'RiverCity Gothenburg.' The project organization was placed directly under city council control, and the steering committee consisted of key political representatives. The structure of the process served to illustrate its importance, that it was not a matter for just one department, but for the whole city. The project organization consisted of a directors' group and a working group. The directors' group was formed on the basis of the three dimensions of sustainability, and actors were invited to join it based on their relevant knowledge of social, economic, or ecological sustainability. Another organizing principle was that the directors' group should include external stakeholders as well. This meant that for the economic dimension, the representative was from the West Sweden Chamber of Commerce and for the ecological dimension, the representative was from Chalmers School of Technology. To represent social sustainability, two city district directors were appointed, one from the city district where considerable development was to take place in the future and the other from Eastern Gothenburg, a socially fragmented district. However, the project leader realized that if the vision was to be accepted within the city organization, the implementing departments and municipal corporations needed to be represented in the directors' group. For this reason, the directors of the traffic, housing, planning, and culture departments and the chief executive officer (CEO) of the municipal RiverCity corporation were invited to join the directors' group. Similarly, the working group was assembled across traditional organizational boundaries, comprising actors from internal as well as external organizations. The working group did much of the preliminary work of the drafting process, writing drafts and organizing workshops.

Invitation of Interest Groups to Workshops

Workshops were organized to define what sustainability meant for Gothenburg. In 2011, the process began with thematic workshops, each treating one of the three dimensions of sustainability, and one workshop involving participants from other Nordic cities with experience of developing waterfront areas. The workshops ended with the participants giving recommendations to the project management team. At the workshop on ecological sustainability, the emphasis was on technical solutions such as green roofs, hybrid cars and buses, and how to decrease emissions. At the workshop, economic sustainability was mostly seen as the purview of trade and industry. The message was that in order to attract more businesses, the city needed to offer good locations and better infrastructure.

At the social sustainability workshop, the discussions were about inclusiveness—creating a city for everyone—and about sometimes leaving things as they are. One recommendation from this workshop was to evaluate how other cities have made it possible for low-income groups to live in attractive areas. The directors' group meetings discussed the outcomes of the thematic workshops, but without considering how the dimensions could be combined. It was evident that the actors had different ideas about what was most important in making a city sustainable and, therefore, what should be prioritized. Here are some examples showing how the members of the directors' group discussed the three different dimensions of sustainability:

> What is most important is that we create conditions that make the city attractive for a diversity of people.
>
> (City district director)

> Social issues about peoples' everyday lives are also dependent on infrastructure and the business sector. Everything is depending on everything else.
>
> (Head of department)

> We know what we mean by ecology, there are regulations. The economical dimension is often dealt with at some point. The social dimension is suffering; no one knows what it is.
>
> (Representative from academia)

An International Perspective

Importance was placed on having an international perspective on Gothenburg's future, so, in 2011, an international workshop was held in the city to which 10 teams of planners, architects, and other experts were invited. They held discussions over a five-day period and then made suggestions for the project. The workshop was described as an innovative way of obtaining new ideas. For example, one member of the directors' group hoped that the teams would go beyond problematizing and find solutions to the city's problem of segregation.

Many staff from the city administration were satisfied with the workshop, both with the results and with the fact that so many prominent people had come to discuss the city's future. Some of the advice that was included in the workshop conclusions was to start work immediately, to work on the traffic landscape, and to involve the citizens. However, the fact that the local politicians did not attend the international workshop as expected was a disappointment.

Civic Participation

In addition to the workshops described above, the city arranged a civic participation process. The aim was to reach as many citizens as possible, and about 2,800 people participated by contributing with their ideas about present and future life in Gothenburg. The citizens' ideas were regarded as a basis for upcoming work on the vision and strategies, but also as a means to develop methods of civic participation. Workshops were held in all 10 of the city's districts with the aim to attract people from different parts of the city. At these workshops, the citizens were asked to identify qualities, problems, and potentials in the existing city. Most interviewees described the civic participation process as exciting, but many underscored how difficult it was both to attract participants and to make use of the generated information. One of the interviewees involved stated: "The most important part is that we take care of what the citizens have expressed. That is not always easy—it is easier to start projects than to finish them" (head of department and member of the directors' group).

The citizens' input was analyzed, sorted, and presented in a report. The report summarized that the citizens wanted the city to be located closer to the water; it should be green and inclusive for all; it should be a city for walking, bicycling, and public transport; it should consist of attractive, mixed-use, human-scaled urban spaces, and the city planners should be careful to preserve the existing identity of the city. These results were described as 'unsurprising,' though some found it interesting that what was discussed during the civic participation process was similar to that which had been discussed previously by the experts in the international workshop and in the directors' group.

To address the youth of the city, 'Young RiverCity' was organized as means to involve young people and children. Young people were invited on a boat trip along the river to discuss what they would like to see in the area. One director described how some children from socially fragmented areas had never seen the river before, and did not even know that Gothenburg was located on the waterfront. This 'reality check' put the challenges to becoming an inclusive city in another light.

Concretize a Vision into Priorities, to Overcome Traditional Ways of Working

Concurrently with the various workshops, work was going on internally in the city. The directors' group met once every month for about three hours. These meetings were busy, with many issues to discuss and decisions to make. The directors and the CEO in this group were not used to working together on a common task, and these meetings offered opportunities to discuss diverse issues that, more or less, concerned the vision. The organization of the project, across boundaries and with the politicians as a steering committee, was described as innovative, but also led to ambiguity when it came to the role of the directors' group. The group members were supposed to enhance one another: they were not at meetings to represent or fight for their individual departments, but to work together. This was difficult in practice, and group members described how the meetings turned into negotiations between interests.

Regarding some issues, many actors wanted to voice their concerns, while other issues were regarded as so problematic that they were hardly discussed at all. This is illustrated in the case of infrastructure and social concerns. The traffic department was generally regarded as powerful in the city administration, and the fact that infrastructure took up so much space in the city was said to be due to this department's power. Actors in the process took the opportunity to interfere in infrastructural issues and to ensure that the vision and strategy document addressed the infrastructural situation. At the time, a new bridge over the Göta Älv was being planned. For the directors' group, it was important that the bridge was built as low as possible to create a more inclusive city by making it easier to cross the river without a car. This became a symbolic issue, and considerable time was devoted to discussing how to ensure that the bridge would be low. When it came to social sustainability, on the other hand, the group members agreed on one particular problem: the city was too segregated and socially fragmented. The group agreed that RiverCity Gothenburg should be for everyone, calling it 'the city for all.' What exactly this meant, however, was unclear: some group members argued that this meant that anyone should be able to *live in* RiverCity, whereas others argued that anyone should be able to *visit* it. One of the members of the directors' group reflected thus:

> I asked the question: what do you mean by a city for all, do you mean everyone? Do you mean the homeless addicts, the newly arrived immigrants—do you mean them as well? Or are they only welcome as visitors? Or are they just low-income persons who are there to work?
> (City district director)

Approved Documents: Vague Formulations

The directors' group also suffered from the effects of the inactive politicians on the steering committee. Moreover, the politicians had different views of the importance of the vision document. Whereas the mayor described the document as the one on which all future planning would be based, the opposition leader said that, in the "document hierarchy," it was situated below the annual budget and other "important policy documents."

In the absence of guidance from the politicians, the directors' group had to 'feel their way forward.' Initially, they presented information about the envisioned future city and the importance of building a low bridge; however, the politicians did not react in the way that the directors' group had hoped, but instead requested more information. Although the politicians did agree on the overall concepts of the vision, i.e., the city as inclusive, green, and dynamic, they did not agree on the details that the group presented. This led the directors' group to remove concrete numbers and facts from their presentations, and instead to show illustrations of a future envisioned city on which the politicians could agree. In October 2012, the city council finally agreed that the vision should be entitled 'RiverCity Gothenburg: open to the world; inclusive, green, and dynamic,' and decided that the three strategies should be to 'connect the city,' 'embrace the water,' and 'reinforce the centre.' Some parts of the document are concrete: every section concludes with 'we will' points, such as 'we will establish a test-bed for socially sustainable housing' and 'we will create a number of large parks,' one being Jubilee Park along the waterfront at Frihamnen. Even so, the document does not specify exactly who will be responsible for the realization of these objectives.

Concretize Visions into a New Organizing Solution: A New Organization to Overcome Silos?

Following the adoption of the RiverCity vision, many of those involved said that it was positive that they had talked so much about social sustainability. There were, however, concerns that their efforts would not lead to real change: "How do we do this so that we do not only talk about social dimensions and then do the opposite because it is too expensive to do something else?" (head of department and member of the directors' group).

The problem was described as a lack of accountability: no one was responsible for realizing the aims of the document. The city council appointed a coordination function to disseminate the vision and strategies throughout the municipal organization. About six months later, the coordination function was transformed into a project organization with the leading directors and CEOs from the city departments and municipal corporations acting as a steering committee. A work group including middle managers from the same departments and corporations was established. Seven subprojects, one for each city district, were created below these two management groups. This organizational model entailed increased collaboration within the city organization. The idea was that the steering committee should agree on how to deal with specific issues by consensus, and then the committee members' different home organizations would make decisions accordingly. One of the directors described the role of the steering committee thus: 'In practice, the steering committee wields considerable influence. We would cause all manner of problems if we did not act according to what is decided upon at meetings' (CEO, municipal corporation).

However, the project organization was not given a budget of its own, but all resources were kept in the line organization. The idea was that this would increase the engagement of different parts of the city and foster collaboration across boundaries, although this also created inertia concerning how to finance issues as they arose.

Regarding the seven subprojects, there was discussion of how they complemented and/or competed with each other. Frihamnen, an area with few existing businesses and activities, was described as a place where major urban construction projects were to be implemented. Two such proposals in the vision, namely to create affordable housing and conduct 'place-building' activities in a new park that was being planned, were soon cited as signs of the impact of the new vision and strategies.

The Concretization of Visions into Actual Solutions: The Traditional Meets the Experimental

Above, we have seen how sustainability became part of the vision and was transformed into strategies and seven proposed subprojects, which were the outcomes of negotiations between the different interests represented by the directors and politicians. From there on, the question of how to handle these outcomes of the process outside the directors' room arose. To continue our story, we will look at one of the seven subprojects, Frihamnen, in closer detail. The social dimension of sustainability was formulated as an important part of the project. Frihamnen is an inner-city area, and the plan was to alter this former port area to create a sustainable urban space where people could live and interact.

Concretize Visions as Projects

The Frihamnen area is not only covered by the RiverCity vision; it is also part of another large city initiative, Vision 2021. In 2021, the city of Gothenburg will be 400 years old, and Vision 2021 articulates various ideas about what should be accomplished by then to celebrate the anniversary. This project is based on civic participation, making the planning timeframe crucial and prompting discussion of new ways of working to handle parallel processes, for example.

By 2035, housing for 20,000 people is to be built and the same number of people are to work in the Frihamnen area. The plan was to complete 1000 housing and 1000 work units by 2021, the year of the anniversary. Dialogues with citizens, several city administration units of the city, and building companies have been important parts of the planning process. New ways of cooperation in the planning process for Vision 2021 earned a prize from the Swedish Architects Association (Sveriges Arkitekter) in 2016. The first plan for the area articulated several strategic issues, for instance to bring together both sides of the river and creating access to the water for all citizens.

Frihamnen is planned for not only residents but also visitors who would like to experience the meeting of land and water. Parts of the area is planned for housing, but there will also be an urban Jubilee Park, which, due to its location by the water is called a 'blue park' area. Part of the housing is intended for students and refugees, and the temporary housing units planned for are to be moved elsewhere in the city in the future. In that sense, the area can be seen as a test bed for new ways of planning not only housing but also public space in Frihamnen.

As mentioned, the area was derelict and nearly empty, especially at night, and the former port area had few visitors. The idea with the Jubilee Park was to create activities to attract visitors and to build a new city area from the bottom up. In 2013, city administrators were assigned to plan for the park and specifically initiate 'place-building'. Two people with parallel roles were responsible for the process; one based in the planning department and the other in one of the municipal corporations that was to implement the RiverCity vision starting in 2012. Also, a team of local actors was created and a local office was placed in the actual park area. Two visions guided the work: the RiverCity vision and Vision 2021. Vision 2021 included the idea of a park, Jubilee Park, and the possibility of swimming in the harbor area. The RiverCity vision emphasized, for example, planning methodology and civic involvement. Putting the two visions together revealed a time gap when the area had to stay empty while awaiting plans, building permits, and housing construction.

Two Visions Meet Locally: To Transform Visions into Concrete Activities and Objects

For the members of the place-building team the generation of ideas was not an issue since previous workshops had provided considerable input from citizens. Instead, the challenge was to find ways to involve people and help them to find their way to the currently empty place. In other words, it was the *how* that especially occupied the team. The team was supposed to influence the plans, implementation, and future results by working with prototypes. 'Prototyping' was a concept taken from the design field emphasizing a different way of working from traditional urban planning: instead of first making a plan and then acting, there was a focus on testing prototypes that could generate insights for future planning. Prototyping can be seen both as a means to explore new ways of working and as the construction of physical objects that may or may not be part of the area in the future. With support from the politicians and the vision documents, the place-building team continued to build a 'relational map', to attract people to an empty asphalt-paved area and connect the area with the rest of the city. When establishing Jubilee Park, the team assigned for the place-building initiative was to discuss ideas for the area—although, as mentioned above, there was no lack of ideas. For example, the team had reams of documents describing ideas that citizens had suggested during previous urban planning workshops. The challenge was to sort through these ideas and find ways to put some of them into practice.

An initiative from another part of the city was presented to the team: a fully funded plan for a roller derby track. The team liked this idea since it fitted the overall goal of being less traditional, and not featuring conventional activities such as football, but instead making room for non-traditional activities that could attract traditionally marginalized groups. Thus, the roller derby plan was realized in the park. Eventually, several initiatives that were similar to the roller derby plan were identified. Meanwhile, a pilot project was initiated to see what basic needs had to be met to render the area safe and useable for the public. The team called these needs 'urban basics,' such as facilities for visitors (e.g., toilets), street lighting, transport, and a bus stop.

A central idea for the future city that the citizens and politicians had highlighted was that of being able to swim in the city's river. This was something that had been impossible for many years, since the quality of the water was too poor. Still, the team thought that the proximity to water must be used somehow and that it should be integral to activities planned for the park. Before the swimming idea could be realized, sailing was brought up as an activity that could be accomplished in the 'blue park.'

That the idea of having a sailing school in the park could be implemented was due to a meeting between the place-building team and a non-profit association with previous experience of sailing and other activities promoting social inclusion. Certain arrangements were necessary before the sailing school could start. One was to have a permit to make it possible for the small sailing boats to share the water near the park with large ships. At the same time, the need for 'urban basics' had to be met. No one involved in the preparations for the sailing school knew whether the idea would succeed, but the focus was on doing something and attempting to make things happen. Ultimately, the pre-ordered sailing boats arrived on time and the local newspaper was there to mark the opening of the school. A representative of the non-profit association that had managed the activity received numerous phone calls from teachers who wanted to provide their pupils with an opportunity to try their hand at sailing. The first season of the sailing school was rapidly fully booked, and pupils from all over the city came to Jubilee Park to sail, probably for the first time in their lives.

One competence that the association brought to the park was the ability to organize activities at short notice. At the same time as the sailing school was getting started, a sauna had been established in the harbor as part of the 'blue park.' The association recommended that the place-building team implement a booking system to create some sort of organization around the sauna and to make the visitors feel that it was something special, a 'limited edition' activity that needed to be booked in advance. The booking system was modified in line with input from the visitors and the sauna was well attended. Other activities were initiated as well. Locals came to the area and, together with the place-building team, built a playground for children. A sandy beach and a picnic area were constructed, and a food truck cooperative came to the area.

The first year's activities, all of which were arranged on an ad hoc basis, went well. However, the association and the place-building team needed a longer-term solution for their relationship, and they decided that the way forward would be a non-profit public partnership. The second season saw another idea from the vision documents influence the organizing of activities in the park, that of involving the youth in the implementation process. Accordingly, young people from different parts of the city were hired to maintain the park. Social inclusion was not only important for the choice of activities in the park, but was also an organizing principle. Consequently, it was important that the young employees represented different parts of the city. If the employees did not know how to sail, the association provided the appropriate training. The work in the park was not only supposed to benefit the visitors, but also to strengthen the competence of young people with limited work experience. In this way, social inclusion became integral to testing the new planning process activities in the area.

An open-air swimming pool adjacent to the river was opened to the public in 2015. As one person involved in the process said, "the pool was like a human with health issues. It needed constant attention and treatment." The struggle of working with prototypes was evident, as were the rewards when the (rather specific) water processes and work routines eventually were settled. The pool was not large enough to allow the whole city to go swimming at the same time, but it served as proof of a concept that could inform future planning activities. In other words, although the temporary prototype might not yet physically exist, the experience that has been gained in relation to work processes for achieving technical solutions, organizing day-to-day activities, and openness to citizens' ideas and involvement, can be useful in future planning.

One actor involved in the park emphasized that "we *do* sustainability with a specific focus on social dimensions," via involving citizens in the 'doing' of the park and by applying an inclusive approach to visitors and employees. This stance was reinforced by the non-profit public partnership with the non-profit association, which does not take detours via pilot studies, but instead goes directly from idea to implementation. For example, a group of visitors thought they were coming for a bicycle activity, but arrived to find sailing on the schedule. The group did the sailing, but said that they would also really like to try bicycling. The park organization discussed the idea, embraced it, and started to call stores to see if they would sponsor a bicycle activity. No sponsor was available, but it turned out that the budget allowed the purchase of a few bicycles. The next week bicycling was among the activities on offer in the park. This illustrates the attenuated timeframe of the prototyping approach, supported by the non-profit public partnership, which allowed visitors to take part in new activities very quickly. Such prototyping involves the testing of ideas close to and in cooperation with citizens, via down-to-earth activities modified based on learning, and facilitating feedback to the city on ways to address social inclusion in urban planning.

Discussion: From Vision to Social Inclusion Prototypes

This section discusses the challenges of creating a shared understanding of sustainability and of interpreting visions and translating them into new planning activities; from strategic documents into temporary and experimental activities for social inclusion.

In its official documents, the city had for several years referred to the three dimensions of sustainability. However, one matter apparently related to the challenges of working with sustainability is finding ways to work across traditional professional and administrative boundaries in a political organization. Like other organizations, the city uses projects to overcome its functional silo organization in which each unit has its specific budget, responsibilities, goals, and skills. Part of the initial work connected to the vision formulation was to organize dialogues not only between city administration units, for example, within the framework of the RiverCity project organization, but also with other actors such as citizens and businesses. Based on the stakeholder workshops, sustainability seemed well aligned with the formulated visions and ideas about the future city. The directors could agree on a vision that included sustainability—i.e., a sustainable city that is open to the world—and the workshop discussions could be translated into three very broad strategies referring to the three pillars of sustainability—social, economic, and ecological—earlier presented by the city. What this study shows is that sustainability was a good basis for dialogues on complex and difficult issues related to the future city. The final form of the vision was somewhat vague, so the discussions among the directors and others did not have to go into details or practical arrangements. The discussion of the vision and the path to a sustainable city could proceed without threatening the organization of the city planning or other city administrative goals.

Considerable challenges arose when the vision had to be translated into local actions, by concretizing the vision as project activities and budget priorities within the city administration. The dialogue among the directors and other actors now needed to explore details and responsibilities in greater depth, and priorities and proposed solutions had to be part of the discussion. Differences between the units' goals and responsibilities became more obvious than in the initial discussions. although this is perhaps not surprising, it indicates why a second challenge was to find ways of working that transcended the established city administrative organization and perhaps even changed traditional planning processes. Our case shows that this challenge may call for boldness and innovation and, not least, can be time consuming. In some cases, the expectations of the planning activities to realize the vision could not be met. The clash between the ordinary planning process and the extraordinary process of the RiverCity vision and Vision 2021 sometimes created delays. The plans and goals gave rise to unintended consequences that could not be resolved at that time due to legal procedures, for example. However, the story presented here shows that the plans and goals of the RiverCity vision nevertheless found their way to realization and new organizational solutions even when unintended consequences became part of ongoing translations. Such unintended consequences can facilitate learning and innovative ways of thinking and organizing. The translation of visions and strategies included learning related to civic participation and social inclusion in local activities in which planning met other communities and practices.

Sustainability seems to be a rather difficult concept to translate into action as it is confronted with traditional ways of working, and with negotiations between interests that are part of traditional city administrative work. At the same time, it has inspired various city actors who have taken part in the process of finding a shared vision of the future city, and has prompted new ways of working with an inclusive approach in urban planning. Even though traditional ways of working in the city do not seem to support further translations of sustainability, concretizations of the vision are found in both larger city projects and local daily activities. The various challenges and opportunities connected with sustainability efforts in this city context are presented in Table 3.1.

Sustainability as an idea has been part of both the problem definition and the work to find solutions. As part of the problem definition, sustainability has been considered when identifying which relevant actors and interests need to be addressed when the future city is discussed. As seen above, the organization of workshops with administrators, experts, and citizens was one way of being innovative in planning processes. Here, for example, the citizens were not only the receivers of the planning decisions, but were also the formulators of the problems that the city planners had to deal with, and also of the solutions to those problems. Despite the difficulties of incorporating the visions into daily activities in the city administration, new activities have been initiated. One of these concretizations is in the facilitation of dialogue between functional units to solve urban planning problems and to challenge the organizing principle of the city administration in general. Another example of

Table 3.1 Translation of sustainability: part of various contextual outcomes in urban planning

Issues	*Organizational Dimensions*	*Time Frames*	*Sustainability and its Outcomes*
Visions and strategies	Workshops Many actors and voices included	Future focus	Discussions: sustainability is vague (elastic) Inclusion of interests
Management systems and routines	Budget Political and unit goals Silos and administrative systems	Yearly focus	Goal conflicts: sustainability is ambiguous Conflict of interests
Local (planning) activities	Planning work deals with other communities and disciplines	Daily focus	Actions: sustainability addresses social inclusion Merger of interests

Source: Table compiled by the authors.

concretization was related to the social dimension, as new ways of working together and incorporating new competences have been introduced and developed in Jubilee Park.

The story of Jubilee Park, or the 'blue park,' shows that even the temporary planning activities tested in the park area need some continuity of organizing principles. The meeting between the RiverCity organization and a non-profit association with competence in organizing activities promoting social inclusion made it possible to try out new activities that it was hoped would attract visitors to the empty space and to fill it with activities for a wide audience. A long-term commitment between the organizations in the form of a non-profit public partnership, instead of short-term ad hoc activity-based agreements, made it possible to add competences to the city planning process, thus further developing ideas of social inclusion. This allowed some ideas incorporated in the RiverCity vision and Vision 2021 not only to be recognized but also to be actualized. The long-term relationship made it possible to fine-tune activities and to apply a learning approach to social inclusion in planning. This meant that sustainability as a concept was translated into social inclusion and transformed into planning activities as visitors and local youth were brought together. This also meant that the experimental aim of Jubilee Park was realized and new activities could be fine-tuned over time using a new organizational form. The temporal and financial limitations sometimes built into project organizations could thus be accommodated, and experience could be transferred back into the ongoing development of the city by highlighting organizational solutions that permitted the evolution of an inclusive planning process in the city.

In sum, the Gothenburg case illustrates the difficulties of concretizing a vision in the form of urban planning activities, following the travel of sustainability concepts through vision documents to urban planning prototypes. The story reveals both challenges and opportunities in connecting city management to sustainability and the aim of making the city sustainable. Many actors have taken part in identifying the city's current and future needs, and these needs, even (or perhaps, particularly so) if vaguely formulated, can be part of a vision upon which many actors can agree. In other words, sustainability is not controversial when it is part of a vaguely expressed vision. It was when the three still rather vague strategies connected to the vision were to be translated into concrete ways of working and local planning projects that differences between interests and actors needed to be addressed.

Although sustainability as a concept is flexible, and many different activities can therefore be referred to as sustainable or as leading to sustainability, the traditional way of organizing planning processes and of organizing the city administration into functional silo units does not facilitate the necessary continuous dialogue and associated continuous translations. The need for dialogue to advance the striving for sustainable activities is crucial, but time pressures, especially those introduced by the city's upcoming 400th anniversary, has made it difficult to achieve the initial goals of the RiverCity vision. Sustainability has so far been a strategic matter. However, the present organization of the city administration seems to have prolonged the process, as the traditional way of organizing by functions seems to create barriers to dialogue and collaboration. These barriers may be based on professional perspectives or administrative solutions concerning how budgets are managed in the city, impeding ongoing dialogues among divergent interests, for example. This seems to have partly influenced the realization of new planning activities for a sustainable city, as efforts in which sustainability is translated tend to be local, and sustainability is not a full-featured coordinating concept among all city actors in their daily work. However, we should emphasize that the city has also introduced tools into daily urban planning to enhance social inclusion, as was the case with the city's work on children's perspective in the planning process.

The translation of visions and strategies is an ongoing process that does not necessarily start with a document and end when the planned project is completed. The concept of translation permits detailed exploration, highlighting the importance of a micro perspective in enhancing our understanding of how variations in ideas and visions can unfold in local practice. It is important to recognize both the intended actions and consequences of work related to the concretization of vision documents, as well as the unintended consequences. These may cause problems in terms of deadlines and financial results, but they can also constitute learning situations generating new organizational solutions that can benefit the organization; in this case the work on social inclusion in urban planning. Our story shows that innovative local initiatives can become part of translations of sustainability. However, only the future will tell whether these new ideas about working with sustainability in urban planning will travel and be translated into new ways of addressing sustainability elsewhere in the city of Gothenburg, or whether they will remain local solutions that are decoupled from the regular city urban planning process.

Notes

1 This chapter is based on a longitudinal study carried out in 2011–2019. It is based on field materials comprising interviews, observations, and documents from the city administration. Brorström followed the strategy work from 2011 to 2019, observing meetings and interviewing politicians and city administrators. Adolfsson studied social inclusion efforts from 2017 to 2018 using interviews and observations (financially supported by the Swedish Research Council and Formas).
2 Bruno Latour (1986) suggested using the translation concept to understand change as the result of negotiation among interests. Barbara Czarniawska and other management scholars have used the concept in the city context to explore change within city management (e.g., Adolfsson, 2005; Brorström, 2018; Czarniawska, 2002; Czarniawska & Joerges, 1996; Zapata Campos & Zapata, 2014). These studies shed light on how the same idea, the same management concept, can be applied very differently in different cities. Using the translation concept means being interested in

understanding such local differences, applying a micro perspective to how ideas that travel globally are used and can influence local ways of working if the idea is seen as useful and is legitimated by local actors. In our case, translation has guided the analytical work, as we have tried to reveal how ideas are negotiated and articulated in documents and how various documents give rise to local actions.

References

Adolfsson, P. (2005). Environment's many faces: On organizing and translating objects in Stockholm. In B. Czarniawska & G. Sevón (Eds.), *Global Ideas: How Ideas, Objects and Practices Travel in the Global Economy*. Copenhagen: Copenhagen Business School Press.

Brorström, S. (2018). How numbers of the future are shaping today: The role of forecasts and calculations in public sector strategic thinking. *Financial Accountability and Management*, 34(1), 17–29.

Czarniawska, B. (2002). *A Tale of Three Cities, or the Glocalization of City Management*. Oxford: Oxford University Press.

Czarniawska, B., & Joerges, B. (1996). Travels of ideas. In B. Czarniawska & G. Sevón (Eds.), *Translating Organizational Change*. Berlin and New York: Walter de Gruyter, pp. 13–48.

Latour, B. (1986). The Powers of Association. In J. Law (Ed.) *Power, Action and Belief*. London: Routledge and Kegan Paul, pp. 264–280.

Zapata Campos, M.J., & Zapata, P. (2014). The travel of global ideas of waste management: The case of Managua and its informal settlements. *Habitat International*, 41, 41–49.

Chapter 4

Strategy
What Is More Important than Getting Things Done? Learning from Sustainable Sydney 2030

Martin Kornberger

When I began my investigation into the Sustainable Sydney 2030[1] strategy in 2006, the leadership team in Sydney's Town Hall echoed a commonsensical view of strategy. As one senior manager stated, Sydney 2030 was "the blueprint for the future." Strategy was conceived as a linear, rational process. First, ideas would be developed and discussed, then they would be agreed, and eventually they would be delivered. Think first, then act—that was the Cartesian premise of the strategy project. Of course, in between there would be some adjustments, perhaps even setbacks as "realities will always impinge," as one interlocutor reflected; but by and large Sustainable Sydney 2030 was the roadmap with which Sydney was supposed to move towards a green, sustainable future. The strategy document itself was well crafted, encompassing, and evocative.[2] It defined *green, global,* and *connected* as attributes of a sustainable future. It proposed strategic directions for urban development and 10 'big project ideas' envisioning these directions.

In 2016, a decade later, I returned to the City of Sydney to gauge the effects of Sydney 2030. This was an enticing project as Sydney 2030 was univocally heralded as a success story. The city administration, as well as critical journalists and external observers, agreed that the strategy was indeed a "success." As a researcher, the interesting point was less about trying to judge success objectively (if that was possible), and more about understanding the constructed and shared view of what success actually means. My aim was, through the eyes of the local actors, to better understand why, or what, made Sydney 2030 a "success." Sydney 2030 provided the electoral platform for Clover Moore, who since coming into office in 2004 has won four consecutive elections, making her the longest serving Lord Mayor in the city of Sydney's history. In this sense, a vote for the Lord Mayor was also a vote for Sydney 2030. As one senior city executive stated in an interview, "I think a lot of people would say, 'I'm going to vote for Clover Moore, so I'm actually voting for Sydney 2030.'" Meanwhile, an external observer commented: "I think it [Sydney 2030] was the catalyst for everything that the Lord Mayor has done. I mean any of the positive initiatives that you might attribute to her administration are due to the fact that she had a strategy that had integrity and rigor."

Here comes the puzzle: when looking at implementation as a measure of a strategy's success (as received wisdom suggests) Sydney 2030 could hardly be called a success story. For instance, only one out of the 10 'big project ideas' was realized in 2016, and that was the George Street light rail. But this project was owned and operated by the New South Wales Ministry of Transport and none of its communications even mentioned Sydney 2030 as being the inspiration for the project. It was perhaps even more troubling that my interview partners in 2016 doubted whether the light rail actually delivered against Sydney 2030's objectives. While it was clearly a welcome transport solution, the new train terminal at the harbour would cut off the city even more from the water, and given its design and planned frequency to achieve capacity, the light rail trains would cause a 'tram jam' along George Street. As one of my interlocutors put it, in a seemingly paradoxical way: *if they deliver light rail, they will not deliver*. However, this only looked like a paradox in a superficial sense. In reality, Sydney 2030 had interwoven goals and actions, seeking to leverage ideas and integrate solutions. This meant that a project such as the introduction of light rail was not only a transport solution but also an urban renewal project, an economic development project, a sustainability project, and so forth. When it came to delivery through an agency focused on transport, the focus zoomed in on light rail as a means of transportation, hence losing sight of the other interwoven goals outlined in Sydney 2030. Put metaphorically: in order to cut the ribbon of the light rail project, the valuable ties that the strategy had created had to be cut again.

What Is More Important than Getting Things Done

I found these results theoretically surprising and practically puzzling: if strategy does not fulfil its purpose—commonsensically defined as delivering its intent—what else could possibly make it a success? As demonstrated above, judging implementation as a measure of a strategy's success, Sydney 2030 could not be called a resounding success. So, what could be more important than getting things done? I reduced this formidable puzzle to a question that I asked my interview partners in a round of conversations held in February and September 2016. What was it that made Sydney 2030 a success story despite the lack of execution? Having analyzed their reflections, I identified three effects of Sydney 2030 that were not linked to direct implementation, but nonetheless were crucial. These three effects describe what I call 'impact beyond implementation' (see Kornberger et al., 2019).

New Sensibilities

First, Sydney 2030 brought about what one interviewee called a "new sensibility" for the urban environment. Sydney, once described as an "accidental city" (Ashton, 1993), has been shaped by its colonial past, and that means, so my interlocutor said, that the city is focused on property rights and ownership. In contrast, Sydney 2030 shifted the conversation, thus highlighting the experience of the city. The questions discussed as part of the strategy process were not who builds which building how high, or who owns that building? Rather, the conversation revolved around issues such as how does the space between the buildings work? What makes an attractive urban experience for those moving between the buildings? Or, in short and in slightly more abstract terms, what makes a city?

In this sense, Sydney 2030 brought into the public consciousness what Jane Jacobs (1961) had written half a century ago, namely that the city is the macro effect of many micro actions which have, in themselves, very little to do with city making. Walking the dog, chatting to a neighbor, shopping locally—Jacobs identified a myriad of those mundane, quotidian practices that together result in an urban commons (Borch and Kornberger, 2015) or a social infrastructure (Klinenberg, 2002) that makes the city a vibrant, resilient place. The strategy introduced this "complex idea of what makes a city" (as one interviewee said) and instigated a public debate about the nature and value of the urban environment.

In this process, the city administration saw its role as the "custodian of context", as one senior executive of the city said to me. Realizing that the 'value' of the city was indirectly achieved through the interplay between activities, people, and buildings, the city focused on managing this in-between, or the context, rather than individual projects. This meant thinking about relations, linkages, and unintended consequences—in short, drawing an ever more sprawling map of how the built environment, cultural development, economic growth, social policy, and sustainability were related to one another. To use a metaphor from one of the interviews, the city was a jigsaw puzzle whose parts were distributed across different levels of government, citizens, businesses, and other actors. The city's job was to bring the pieces together, but not necessarily to design, own, or control them. The city administration changed its self-understanding from being an author and hence director of the future towards being a curator or part of a conversation that would bring about the city. One strategist captured this notion in a conversation as a 'change of mentality' not only of the administration, but also of citizens, developers, and property owners.

Therein lies one key effect of Sydney 2030. It changed the mentality of those engaged in city making, equipping them with a 'new sensibility' that foregrounded context, experience, and the complex nature of the city. The strategy process introduced a new language to capture this new way of seeing the urban environment. One interlocutor jokingly said that a few years ago the term 'fine grain' was understood as flower seed mix, but today it is part and parcel of the vocabulary of planners to articulate the 'new sensibility.' To summarize, the German sociologist Georg Simmel posited that the urban environment does not just comprise bricks and buildings but is first and foremost a state of mind. Sydney 2030's approach to changing the city started right there—seeking to change the mentality of those engaged in making the city.

Collective Discovery and Learning

A second effect of Sydney 2030 was that it instigated a deep learning process across the city. Several of my interviewees emphasized that the strategy process itself was not a neutral instrument to describe how to get from A to B. Rather, the process itself was 'educational,' changing those involved in the strategic conversations as they unfolded. One of the city's senior strategists explained, "[Sydney 2030] had a very big role in educating the councilors about how the city actually works. I mean because they've been elected on various platforms in their local constituencies and do not necessarily understand how things work." It also was an educational experience for the public as the consultations, roundtables, town hall meetings, exhibitions, and online engagement were "not only about hearing from people what they thought was important" but concerned getting people "to talk differently about the kind of issues that we were confronting," as a senior policy advisor elaborated. Sydney 2030 was about "lifting people's thinking" and "breaking their patterns of interaction" in order to establish new ways of thinking about the future of the city. The strategy process was crucial because it sequenced and choreographed that learning experience (see Kornberger and Clegg, 2011).

Sydney 2030 was also a learning journey for the city administration in its quest for sustainability. One senior manager explained that the process of crafting the strategy was not only a "technology deep dive" but also an important relationship building exercise with other cities and experts working on the topic. He continued thus:

> [Sydney 2030] allowed us to get into a network of cities that are really leading the way which for us has been hugely beneficial in just having exposure to and contacts with or within those cities as well about how they're looking to address climate change. ... [H]aving really frank and open conversations with those cities really helps to allow us to understand what are the best actions that we can take. [It] allows us to build strong business cases and also allows us to fast-track our actions. So, if we can learn from someone else's mistakes or learn from someone else's successes then that's a great thing. I just don't think we would have got a seat at the table with those conversations had we not done [Sydney] 2030.

The above-mentioned quotation emphasizes the importance of a network of peers in which learning takes place, and Sydney 2030 was the ticket to a seat at that table. It instigated a process of search and discovery. Again, we are in contradiction with received wisdom of strategy success: it claims that a strategy is a plan through which to accomplish a given objective. In our case, the outcome was less important than the process (something black-boxed by orthodox strategy); rather, strategy was a mechanism through which to actually discover interesting preferences and networks. This was especially important in the case of sustainability—an emerging field with many innovations. For instance, the manager related that the city was in favor of 'trigeneration' as the technology to support the sustainability agenda. However, as technology evolved, trigeneration turned out to be less attractive and has been superseded by other technologies. "We went down some rabbit holes," the manager explained, but that was not a problem because the strategy process equipped the strategists, citizens, and city-makers to climb out of the "rabbit hole" and to collectively search for other, better solutions. This capacity to learn collectively was the second major effect of Sydney 2030.

Building Community, Creating a Public

Strategy usually assumes that a strategist is in charge and that there is an audience that is more or less involved in the strategy-making process. It is a typical subject-object relationship. Sydney 2030 was different: it constituted a community through its process. Thus, strategy constructed its subject, so to speak—a public that would be the author of Sydney's future. In the context of Sydney, this community- and identity-building aspect of strategy was particularly crucial. The default state in Sydney was a lack of shared identity. Horizontally, the strategists were only too aware that "everyone is an author in the making of the city," as one interviewee told me. He continued: "the success of Sydney 2030 won't be the grand plan; it'll be thousands of decisions about infrastructure priorities, about investment decisions by firms, or decisions that universities make about investing in affordable accommodation [and so on]." This horizontal distribution of authorship was amplified by a vertical distribution of authority. In the Australian governmental system, city government plays a rather minor role. One informant evaluated the situation thus:

> I've never met such disempowered city government as I've met in Australia because it doesn't exist. ... So, we are in the presence of a democratic deficit and a governance deficit that is leading to random projects, essentially. I think it's catastrophic ... Essentially, we haven't got the governance we need to manage the city.

Facing governance gaps and horizontally dispersed individual decision-makers posed a twofold challenge for Sydney 2030: the city would ultimately be shaped by the actions and decisions of people that were outside of the city administration's direct sphere of influence. In other words, the city had no formal powers over many of the things that needed to happen for Sydney to develop towards a sustainable future.

Strategy's solution to this intricate governance problem was to "corral the voice and represent the identity" of the community to other levels of government, as one interviewee told me. Using Anderson's (1983) felicitous phrase, another interviewee explained that Sydney 2030 had created an "imagined community" around the shared concerns of citizens and other actors who had an interest in Sydney's future. Through its conversations, gatherings, and public events the strategy process established a shared repertoire, a common set of concerns that strengthened the sense of identity in the community. In fact, as our interviewee argued, the strategy process created that community in the first place; as every community that transcends the number of people a room can physically hold, it needs shared symbols through which it can identify itself. The strategy offered such a symbol around which people could develop a sense of 'we-ness.'

For the challenging governance gaps, this meant that the strategists could speak 'on behalf of the people' which legitimated their claims. As one senior policy advisor explained, the strategy process forged and delivered 'public support' for policies and actions. Using the example of the light rail, he argued that the state government possessed the necessary competencies (or could easily obtain them) to rip up the street, lay down the tracks, and buy the rolling stock needed to move people from A to B. In other words, the scare resource was not technology—but public support for the project. According to my interview partner, Sydney 2030 was the process of creating this scare resource, thus lending legitimacy to policy.

So What? Souvenirs to Take Away from Sydney

We can now address our puzzle and answer the question: what is more important than getting things done? First, strategy introduced a 'new sensibility,' suggesting that the city was not the sum total of property rights, but the experience resulting from the movement of people between buildings. It shifted the focus from the individual project to the context, and, perhaps most significantly, it instigated not a change of building codes but a 'change in mentality,' echoing Simmel's already quoted bon mot that the urban environment is a mindset. Second, strategy was a dynamic, transformative learning process. It was not a neutral tool describing the blueprint for the future (as a plan would); rather, through its process, strategy engaged people in a conversation, and this conversation changed people's mentalities. The specific ideas proposed in the strategy document might turn out to be "rabbit holes" (as one interviewee put it in relation to trigeneration); but the search that led people down these rabbit holes, and the network of peers they created on the way represented invaluable learnings. In other words, through strategy, the city enhanced its collective capacity to learn. Third, the strategy engendered a sense of identity among those living and working in Sydney. The governance gaps (specifically significant in the Australian context) and the horizontal distribution of civic decision-making created a scattered *body politic*. Strategy provided a platform for the collective to find itself, to articulate its thoughts, and to form an (imagined) community. This was significant, as one interviewee explained, because it is public support and legitimacy that are the scarcest resources, when it comes to urban development. Strategy, in this sense, was a process through which to create and utilize this scarce resource.

So why was Sydney 2030 regarded as a success? Not because it delivered what it proposed, but because through what it proposed, it engaged city-makers and the public alike in a process that changed their mentality, equipped them with a new language to talk about the urban environment, and instigated a collective learning journey. It is like children playing with Lego®: although their entire focus is on building a specific object, what they are really doing is stretching their imagination.

This has implications for strategy practice: if strategy's impact is a result of its process (i.e., if the journey is the destination, so to speak), then obviously we ought to put more focus on the strategy-making process, and perhaps less on the final outcome. The strategist's role is that of a convenor or curator, orchestrating a conversation with many voices. While the bigger picture emerges out of these conversations, it needs to be framed by the strategist. For the strategist, this means leaving behind the old idea of the strategist as model builder. In *Republic*, Plato suggested that the strategist should strive to achieve the geometer's precision:

> For in pitching a camp, or taking up a position, or closing or extending the lines of an army, or any other military manoeuvre, whether in actual battle or on a march, it will make all the difference whether a general is or is not a geometrician. ... the knowledge at which geometry aims is knowledge of the eternal, and not of aught perishing and transient.
>
> (Book 7)

Like the military camp, the strategy model remains an abstraction. Jullien (2004) reminds us that the model reduces reality to those forces it identifies as significant while eliminating the others. This is the model's strength: its focus is also an organized and legitimized form of ignorance. But, as soon as the model interacts with reality, circumstances impinge—literally meaning those things that stand around ('circum-stances'). Circumstances sabotage the model's purity. The strategists of Sydney 2030 engaged in a different task: they were not model builders but 'custodians of context'—i.e. they would relentlessly bring in relations, linkages, and interactions (*circum*-stances!) between projects, ideas, and people.

In this sense, strategy's power to accomplish change was less obvious. Indeed, it became clear to me during interviews in 2006 and a decade later that the executives of the city of Sydney remained very aware of the fact that they actually had few formal powers. They only knew too well that the vast majority of the actions that a sustainable future demanded were beyond the city's direct control. They engaged in the strategy process because they were relatively powerless. As one senior strategist told me, it was precisely because the city did not control major transport projects that Sydney 2030 focused so much on transport. The strategy was a way 'to warm the room' as another interviewee posited; a way of changing how people think about the urban environment, and how they make decisions in relation to the city. Thus, strategy is an indirect way of influencing those in power. Strategy is, to conclude with a more apt definition than that of the blueprint for the future, the "art of creating power" (Freedman, 2015).

Notes

1 The research commenced in 2006 and included interviews with strategists and decision-makers in the city administration as well as consultants hired to work on Sydney 2030. Observation and participation in events complemented the data collection. In 2016, a decade later, I returned Sydney and conducted a further round of interviews to gauge the actual effects of the strategy. The research approach and method are described in more detail in Kornberger and Clegg (2011) and Kornberger et al. (2020).
2 See www.cityofsydney.nsw.gov.au/vision/sustainable-sydney-2030.

References

Anderson, B. (1983). *Imagined Communities: Reflections on the Origin and Spread of Nationalism*. London and New York: Verso Books.

Ashton, P. (1993). *Accidental City: Planning Sydney since 1788*. Sydney: Hale & Iremonger.

Borch, C., & Kornberger, M. (Eds.) (2015). *Urban Commons: Rethinking the City*. London: Routledge.

Freedman, L. (2015). *Strategy: A History*. Oxford: Oxford University Press.

Jacobs, J. (1961). *The Death and Life of Great American Cities*. New York: Vintage Books.

Jullien, F. (2004). *A Treatise on Efficacy: Between Western and Chinese Thinking*. Honolulu: University of Hawaii Press.

Klinenberg, E. (2002). *Heat Wave: A Social Autopsy of Disaster in Chicago*. Chicago and London: University of Chicago Press.

Kornberger, M., & Clegg, S. (2011). Strategy as performative practice: The case of Sydney 2030. *Strategic Organization*, 9(2), 136–162.

Kornberger, M., Meyer, R., & Hoellerer, M. (2020), *Exploring the Long-Term Effect of Strategy Work: The Case of Sydney 2030*, Working Paper, WU Vienna.

Chapter 5

Best Practices
Contradictions of the 'Green City' in Germany

Samuel Mössner and Rob Krueger

Two Tales of Best Practice Planning

On November 20, 2018, the city of Münster, Westphalia, was awarded the title of Germany's most sustainable city. This university city of approximately 310,000 inhabitants, situated north of the Ruhr area and close to the Dutch border, is famous for its high share of bicycles in its modal share (City of Münster, 2018). With a bike share of about 40%, the judges argued, the city has clearly taken the lead as the informal German bicycle capital and provides excellent infrastructure and facilities for cyclists. And, indeed, cycling in Münster has a long tradition. Following the demolition of the inner city in the bombings of World War II, politicians and administrators decided to rebuild the city along its mediaeval road system. As a result, the city is compact and walkable, a forerunner of the mobility transition.

What the judges failed to mention, however, is the fact that 80% of the 360,000 daily work-related commuter journeys are still made by car. Approximately 300,000 car journeys are made in and out of the city of Münster each day. Statistically, these cars are occupied by just 1.2 persons (City of Münster, 2018). And while the academic discourse argues that petrol-powered and car-centered mobility is expected to come to an end soon (Gössling, 2013), the city's transportation department still considers the car an important means of transport in its new master plan that outlines the city's transportation policies up to 2035 (Stadt Münster, 2018). This car-orientation is legitimated by a "responsibility that results from 50 years in which we promised people that the car is important. We cannot ignore that and change now" (city planner, 2018, authors' translation).

Münster has many parallels with Freiburg im Breisgau, a city with 220,000 inhabitants located in south Germany. Freiburg is internationally hailed as a 'green city' and a role model for sustainable urban development. In 2000, the city presented its green city achievements in the German pavilion at EXPO in Shanghai, China. Like Münster, Freiburg won the German Sustainability Award in 2012. Academic publications consider Freiburg "a lonely pinnacle of European urban excellence: the city that took on every challenge ... and did best in it"

(Hall, 2013, p. 89). Every year, numerous researchers and practitioners assemble in the city in order to discover and learn from this 'best practice.'

While Freiburg continues to uphold its sustainability agenda in the city, including developing sustainable neighborhoods, institutionalizing strict low energy standards, improving the tram network within the city, and supporting more sustainable lifestyles, supported by a vigorous branding and marketing program, meanwhile, in the hinterland, towns and cities such as Münster continue to cling on to the dream of living in suburbia, with its (semi)-detached single-family housing, car dependency, social homogenization, and daily commute to the green city. While at the first glance, Freiburg might appear as a green island in an ocean of unsustainability, families are in fact quitting the city and moving into the hinterland because they can no longer afford the cost of living and high house prices in Freiburg. The hinterland communities benefit from the economic downsides of living in the green city, and welcome these middle-class 'renegades' who have been 'displaced' by Freiburg's sustainability agenda: those citizens, who are in search of relatively affordable housing or who are willing to spend more on larger plots than on strict energy regulations (for an interview with Mayor Endingen, see Miller & Mössner, forthcoming). The lack of regional governance and the non-existence of any serious regional planning cooperation between the green city and the surrounding municipalities is explained by the mayor of a smaller municipality in the Black Forest, located approximately 25 km from Freiburg: "The green city Freiburg ends where the train ends" (city planner, 2018, authors' translation). This smaller municipality is de facto excluded from the regional public transportation network.

The academic literature and countless expert groups who visit Freiburg or Münster rarely recognize the regional context, namely the city's relationship with its hinterland. Despite researchers' blindness to this reality, there are interesting relationships that need to be addressed in order to fully understand Freiburg's sustainability agenda. The dominating focus on the city itself that leads sustainability research comes with a desperate hunt for the best practices that are required in order to find ostensibly better solutions that might transform our cities into more sustainable places (Roseland, 1997). We argue in this chapter that this search for best practices is highly problematic. It overlooks spatial contexts and ignores the complexity of urban development. And while it is still tempting for politicians and those who are looking for quick and easy solutions, one should act with caution when declaring that a city has adopted best practices.

Best Practice and the New Green Competitiveness

So-called best practices have been widely circulated among cities for a generation. Since the Brundtland report, the importance of cities and local initiatives have been at the forefront of the sustainability debate. In 1992, for example, the Rio Earth Summit advocated for 'acting locally' and by doing so opened up the new competition to search for and find the best practices (Nagorny-Koring, 2018). Through the Aalborg Charter, an urban sustainability initiative approved in 1994 by the participants at the first European Conference on Sustainable Cities & Towns, leading European Union (EU) municipalities committed themselves to adopting more sustainable approaches to urban planning. The follow-up to the Aalborg Charter, the Basque Declaration announced in Lisbon in 2016, emphasized and institutionalized local agenda initiatives and thousands of European cities and communes are now 'Local Agenda 21 communities' aiming at the implementation of sustainability at the local level (Mössner & Krueger, 2018). More recently, C40 cities, which came out of an initiative of former London Mayor Ken Livingstone, focus on climate protection at the urban level (Lee & van de Meene, 2012). There is a 'green capital' program by the EU, a 'sustainable city index' in the UK, France is promoting its 'EcoCité' program, and the USA is searching for the 'greenest city' (Rosol et al., 2017). Some of these initiatives are public interventions, others are sponsored by private companies such as Deutsche Telekom, Siemens or other technology-oriented firms which link these initiatives with commercial interests. The names of these cities make up a 'who's who' of green cities to be plastered on our favorite newspapers (Mössner & Krueger, 2018).

Since the 1980s, many cities around the world have established green policies that promised to successfully mitigate climate change. Policy-makers, practitioners, and researchers have traveled far and wide to explore the various dimensions of the 'sustainable city' as a coherent and effective concept (Hall, 2013; Newman et al., 2009; Roseland, 1997). These actors have made extraordinary efforts to discover indicators and models that could help to transform our cities into more sustainable places (Roseland, 1997). Sustainability policies focus on and connect multiple policy fields such as housing, transportation, lifestyle and consumption, energy, and ecological renaturation with the aim to provide "urbanites with a clean environment, a growing economy, and a society that promotes harmonious citizen interactions, while simultaneously limiting carbon dioxide and other GHG emissions" (Zhou et al., 2015, p. 448). There is hardly any city in the world that would reject sustainability for its own agenda and the results and achievements seem to be promising. So far, it looks as if we are on track to make the transition to sustainability.

But the hunt for the greenest city has already turned into a new global competition that is fueled by the search for best practices, the identification of a best example which is based on a competitive and quantitative rationale (Rosol et al., 2017). The focus on best practices has a long and well-established tradition in urban planning and theory. However, it is not without its contradictions and ambiguity. It depends heavily on the respective geographical scale one looks at; it fosters economic competitiveness instead of sustainability; it tends to ignore local specifics, contradictions and particularities; and it presupposes that the complexity of urban policy-making can be reduced to quantitative indicators which, of course, lack such objectivity. Epistemologically, the best practice approach is based on the ideas of comparison and the transferability of urban policies from one place to another. This tradition of policy transfer is not without its criticisms. Research into policy transfer often understands actors and institutions in a rationalistic way (Silomon-Pflug et al., 2013) following a "rational-formalist tradition" (McCann & Ward, 2012, p. 325) and consequently ignores the fact that policy-making is a cultural and social process.

Given the political nature of all these indicators and models, they are often rejected or simply ignored by politicians. This raises questions about the role of urban politics and the way in which sustainability is interpreted, understood, discussed, implemented, mobilized, and eventually obfuscated. Contrary to the countless awards and competitions that have been won by cities for their sustainability agendas, and the best practices that they have adopted, we argue that in reality the green city does not exist, and that awards obfuscate the real problems that accompany this paradoxical form of 'actually existing sustainability' (Krueger & Agyeman, 2005). A closer look suggests that perhaps cities are not as sustainable as they might seem at first glance. All around the world suburbanization is increasing, and much of this growth takes place at the urban fringe outside the declared growth boundaries. In December 2014 *The Economist* declared that "those who argue that suburbia is dying are wrong on the facts."[1] Due to the lack of affordable housing policy in inner cities, suburbanization and exurbanization have emerged as de facto affordable housing policies pushing lower-income groups and the middle class towards the outskirts of the cities and beyond. As urban sprawl continues, work-related commuting distances increase. And for many suburbanites, the car remains the only means to overcome the rural/urban gap. The technological innovations of hybrid and electric cars promise that a change from fossil-fueled transportation to more sustainable forms of mobility is possible and indeed very close. Car and bike sharing sustain this idea. But the opposite is also true. Car-dependency is stronger than ever before. In Germany, for example, the rate of car ownership increases every year,[2] and the proportion of electric or hybrid powered vehicles is marginal. Yet despite the 'diesel-gate' scandal, the number of Volkswagen diesel automobiles sold in Germany in 2018—despite political insecurities about a possible ban on diesel models in inner cities and awareness of the damage that they inflict on the environment—is increasing. At the same time, the public transport sector suffers from a lack of investment and technological lock-ins. The debate about the need for free public transport in cities, which would contribute to the transition to sustainable transportation, was recently rejected by the argument that public transport has already reached its limits and further demand cannot be met.[3] Soil-sealing and land consumption are serious issues all around the world. In Germany—the "greenest nation" (Ueköttter, 2014)—every day approximately 65 hectares of native land is consumed for streets and settlements. In North Rhine-Westphalia, Germany's most densely populated region with the highest number of inhabitants, and average daily land consumption areas of 10 hectares—the equivalent of 10 football pitches lost nature every day. The regional government's aim to reduce this number down to 'only' 5 hectares a day by 2020 is improbable—a truly sustainable approach to land consumption is totally unrealistic. This has little to do with population growth, as many politicians and developers want to make us believe. Rather, land rents are high and reflect economic growth opportunities.

In the following section, we will try to unmask the contradictions of best practices. Referring to the two introductory vignettes of Münster and Freiburg, we argue that there are inconvenient facts that come with the implementation of green political projects. Specifically, we query the nature of transition when it comes from stabilizing (economic) growth, and we criticize the territorial container within which green policies are usually embedded. Finally, we question just who is selected in order to represent the 'social' aspect of the sustainability triangle. This chapter seeks to destabilize the desirability of emulating the best practice example if one is serious in aiming towards urban sustainability.

Sustainability Transition and Growth Trajectories

In terms of path dependency, Münster is no different from many other cities. The car is the opium of urban planners. The automobile is needed to support traditional growth and the urban and regional job market. Although officially aiming at decarbonizing urban transportation, transportation policies still avoid thinking about and planning for a transitory mobility plan that would exclude cars and include a debate about a "profound structural transformation of capitalist consumer societies" (Blühdorn, 2017), while also still not understanding the transportation transition as a coherent and holistic concept. There is a need to recognize the new possibilities and to include support for alternative economic spaces (Krueger et al., 2017). The city thus persists on rather traditional narratives and growth logics. This, despite the fact that the sustainability transition is widely demanded. It is, perhaps, the marketing strategies that propel transitions as the predominant growth paradigm is often neither questioned nor discussed by policy-makers and planners. The judges of the German Sustainability Award recognized the difficulties that confronted Münster's transportation system. But they explicitly praised the city's response to this challenge with the city's plan to implement high-speed bike lanes for e-bikes to the hinterland. From a transitional perspective, these bike lanes (despite the fact that their construction is still far from reality) disguise the adherence to traditional norms and values that are outdated. At the same time, the planning of such 'e-bike lanes' favor a socially fragmented understanding of sustainability. Münster's transportation transition appears, from this perspective, as a "highly path-stable dynamic" (Isaksen & Trippl, 2017) which is embedded in spatial imaginations and narratives of technological innovation and growth that will eventually block and impede the transition. Path stability presents another set of issues.

Economic geographers have researched path stability for some time now (Bathelt & Boggs, 2003; Feenstra & Hamilton, 2006; Isaksen, 2014). They focus on the articulation of (economic) development in regional settings, and the continuity and change that is made by institutional arrangements. They try to explain how regions do or do not transform and react to internal or external threads and challenges. Path dependency, stability, and elasticity are framed by imaginaries, narratives, and convictions. Path stability is often achieved by what Blühdorn calls "narratives of hope" (Blühdorn, 2017) that pretend that the continuity of growth-oriented trajectories of the status quo are an immanent part of the transition. Good examples include smart and new technologies, such as the e-bike, that promise to overcome the problems of carbonized work-commuting, or the digitalization of the society that makes us believe that we can tackle climate change through technology without changing our social and cultural norms and our beloved consumption patterns. Solar panels transform suburban detached houses into shiny examples of sustainable living, while hybrid cars appear to offer a sustainable means of transportation. What they have in common is their contribution to manifesting and transforming traditional norms and values into a new outfit of sustainability. Path dependency and stability provide insights into issues of sustainable urbanism in that they show how transitions are often not a break from previous socio-technical relationships, but are in fact continuations of them. All too often, however, the post-politics (see below) of urban sustainability capture the concept of transition and make it into something more that it is. As a result, policies are seen as an end in themselves, rather than pathways into new futures.

The Territorial Trap: The Green City as a Spatial Container

Like many other cities around the world, Freiburg acts as a territorial entity that ostensibly possesses a degree of autonomy and self-determination that allows it to effectively manage sustainability. While the city mobilizes its agenda to other municipalities, very little cooperation exists between the green city and regional municipalities. There is a weak level of cooperation and governance. Regional planning is regulated and governed by local politicians, and there is a need for a higher-tier institution that could regulate sustainable policies. Cooperation and co-ordination between the city and the regional municipalities are low, and so is the flexibility of sustainable urban policies. The city administration maintains a strong focus on sustainability but this is not without its problems.

The Intergovernmental Panel on Climate Change has argued for a greater urban focus on sustainability research and practice (IPCC, 2007) and a considerable amount of research and literature has been published in support of this argument. Wachsmuth and colleagues write that in contrast to previous decades when "cities were seen as sustainability problems rather than solutions" (Wachsmuth et al., 2016, p. 391), they now appear as key actors and crucial sites through which we try to address climate change and sustainability: "Manhattan skyscrapers, rather than rustic rural towns, are quickly becoming the picture of sustainable living in the twenty-first century" (Wachsmuth et al., 2016, p. 391). This critique of the urban imperative (Miller & Mössner, forthcoming) highlights the territorial enclosure of sustainability policies and practices, which have surprisingly limited range and remain within the urban administrative boundaries. While sustainably is a relational concept par excellence, urban policies supporting sustainability are often territorially bounded. The mismatch between these two concepts becomes very evident when looking at the consequences. Public transport networks often stop at the city borders, while connections to the hinterland of green cities are comparatively poor and relatively infrequent. City councils have a political mandate for the city but not for the hinterland. German planning law, for example, has made subsidiarity one of its most important principles. The principle of subsidiarity holds that political and planning issues and decisions should be decided at the lowest administrative level. In the German planning system this is interpreted as the urban scale that is at odds with the various flows and relationships that urban policies have to deal with.

The perspective of green cities is still detached from the development that occurs at the regional level and consequently excludes the surrounding municipalities. However, problems for commuters, transportation, traffic flows, and the displacement of mostly younger families from expensive cities to relatively cheaper suburbs do not stop at the municipal borders, as urban policies do. All too often, green city policies are promoted within discrete territorial containers, making it a prominent example of what political geographer John Agnew in 1992 called a "territorial trap' (Agnew, 2010). Even in the academic literature, a spatially relational focus is missing that shows "how policies travel from the sites of innovation to become common practice across the territorial reach of entire systems, or not" (Miller & Mössner, forthcoming). Only a few studies criticize this "city-centric focus" (Brenner & Schmid, 2015) as a "localist ontology" (Macleod & Jones, 2011) or a "methodological cityism" (Angelo & Wachsmuth, 2015). With regard to best practice, urban research and planning needs to move away from "understanding cities as discrete, self-enclosed, and analytically separate objects" (Ward, 2008). Instead, a sharp, open, and transparent debate is needed that takes into account the planning principle of subsidiarity of municipalities, the role of regional planning, and the spatial range of urban policies. Cities never exist in isolation, but rather in a web of relationships and flows which are territorially constituted and regulated through a variety of inter-related state scales.

> If urban arenas are identified as appropriate scale for the analysis of sustainability transitions, they need to be understood in the sense of inter-related and internationally embedded spatial settings in which actors of interest are located and visible innovation in the respective sector occurs rather than contiguous territories.
>
> (Affolderbach & Schulz, 2016, p. 1953)

Urban planning practice and research needs to be aware of this.

Participation for Exclusion: Green Post-Politics

During the awards ceremony for the German Sustainability Award in December 2012, Lord Mayor Dieter Salomon famously proclaimed that it is the active citizenry that continues to push politics and administrators towards a greener way of planning (see Mössner & Krueger, 2018). Although this narrative has made its way into numerous (international) publications arguing that Freiburg has brought together "politicians, urban planners and residents in a highly constructive participation process" (Hambleton, 2014, p. 228), it is only half the story. A large part of society has not been able to participate in Freiburg's desirable sustainable development. When it comes to profits, social tolerance and participation in the green city are clearly less important.

It has often been stressed that the process of transforming cities into ecocities should be an inclusive and participatory process that includes all citizens. There seems to be a broad consensus in urban society about the political strategy of implementing sustainable development. Sustainable urban development ought not be subject to political disputes or antagonistic positions. Rather than an all-embracing consensus, the implementation of sustainable urban development is far from being free of ideologies, political interests, and the exercise of power. There is a stage-managed consensus (Macleod, 2011, p. 2632), including those parts of society that are in line with conservative green politics while others are excluded, including those who cannot afford to maintain a technologically improved and sustainable lifestyle, the poor, and those who do not want to share the ideals of this kind of sustainability (including suburbanites and SUV-lovers); such people are excluded and displaced by market mechanisms (Mössner & Krueger, 2018). Developing, promoting, exporting, and implementing models of urban sustainability must be understood as a process of gaining political power to decide, exclude, and construct hegemonies, and to create and maintain social inequalities (Mössner, 2014). It is neither neutral nor objective, but—as politics always is—it is subject to societal negotiations that reflect and produce social conflicts, class differences, inequalities, and occasionally exclusion. For us, it is problematic that planning for sustainable cities is no longer considered a political question in any fundamental sense but is instead reduced to a (post-political) managerialism and to a technical and administrative planning-related question of simply finding and applying the best models and practice.

As Metzger points out,

> postpolitics and planning aims at pinpointing and flagging up new forms of politics in planning processes which function to suppress or preemptively foreclose possibilities towards dissent through bypassing, short-circuiting or circumscribing difficult and contentious issues concerning the specification of desirable futures.
>
> (Metzger, 2018, p. 181)

This 'foreclosure of possibilities' leads to the exclusion of opinions not for their specific argument but rather for ostensibly 'unpolitical' reasons: this includes managerial processes, legal regulations, and other 'consensual' agreements (jobs, wealth, health, or nature related reasons). Growth trajectories are legitimized by jobs and well-being, the green city agenda by a reference to awards or academic literature.

Conclusion

Sustainable urban development is difficult to achieve. This is because planning for sustainability opens up new possibilities and enhances citizens' quality of life but is accompanied by deep and severe societal conflicts and disagreements about which kind of sustainability is being proposed. And even those who do not question this important task for our common future, and who accept the need for change for the benefit of generations to come, differ in the perspectives, understandings, and strategies that will lead us to a sustainability transition. As much as academics and practitioners alike have been talking about blowing up silos or siloed thinking in recent decades, these seem stronger than ever. The cases presented offer not only a rebuke for the green city but show clearly how planners must dismantle silos if we are to take green urbanism seriously.

In this chapter, we argue that there are four key processes that characterize the difficulties of current urban sustainability strategies. We argue that best practice and the search for the best solution ignore the particularities, specific local circumstances, and contradictions that are immanent to all planning and practice. It fosters the competitiveness of cities and eventually falls short on contributing to a transition towards sustainability. We have further outlined that transitions that emerge out of the search for best practice do often not break with previous socio-technical relationships but instead enforce and perpetuate them. The strong city focus that comes with the aforementioned processes—the search for best practice and path dependency—is based on an urban imperative that contradicts the idea of sustainability as relational. There are epistemological problems with such 'cityism' and the understanding of cities as containers. We conclude with the thesis that consensus and consensual decision-making processes are leading to social and political exclusion. We argue that the technocratic focus on sustainability ignores the political nature of sustainability. In this sense we argue that the real green city is not a result of international competitions and wins no awards. The real green city is perhaps not even a city, but instead takes the form of a politics that recognizes relationships and flows and connections among agglomerations. It understands the connectivity between policies here and there, whether at the global or the local/regional level. The real green city is a forum of debate, and is contested and rejected. The real green city is a thought and a debate about an argument and a discourse.

Notes

1 See www.economist.com/suburbs.
2 www.kba.de/DE/Statistik/Fahrzeuge/Bestand/bestand_node.html.
3 *Zeit* online, February 18, 2018.

References

Affolderbach, J., & Schulz, C. (2016). Mobile transitions: Exploring synergies for urban sustainability research. *Urban Studies*, 53(9), 1942–1957.
Agnew, J. (2010). Still trapped in territory? *Geopolitics*, 15(4), 779–784.
Angelo, H., & Wachsmuth, D. (2015). Urbanizing urban political ecology: A critique of methodological cityism. *International Journal of Urban and Regional Research*, 39(1), 16–27.
Bathelt, H., & Boggs, J.S. (2003). Toward a reconceptualization of regional development paths: Is Leipzig's media cluster a continuation of or a rupture with the past? *Economic Geography*, 79(3), 265–294.
Blühdorn, I. (2017). Post-capitalism, post-growth, post-consumerism? Eco-political hopes beyond sustainability. *Global Discourse*, 7(1), 42–61.
Brenner, N., & Schmid, C. (2015). Towards a new epistemology of the urban? *City*, 19 (2–3), 151–182.
City of Münster (2018). *Verkehr in Zahlen*. Retrieved March 23, 2020, from www.stadt-muenster.de/verkehrsplanung/verkehr-in-zahlen.html.
Feenstra, R., & Hamilton, G. (2006). *Emergent Economies, Divergent Paths: Economic Organization and International Trade in South Korea and Taiwan*. Cambridge: Cambridge University Press.
Gössling, S. (2013). Urban transport transitions: Copenhagen, city of cyclists. *Journal of Transport Geography*, 33, 196–206.
Hall, P. (2013). *Good Cities, Better Lives: How Europe Discovered the Lost Art of Urbanism*. London: Taylor & Francis.
Hambleton, R. (2014). *Leading the Inclusive City*. Bristol: Policy Press.
Intergovernmental Panel on Climate Change (2007). *Climate Change 2007: Mitigation of Climate Change*. Cambridge: Cambridge University Press.
Isaksen, A. (2014). Industrial development in thin regions: Trapped in path extension? *Journal of Economic Geography*, 15, 585–600.
Isaksen, A., & Trippl, M. (2017). Exogenously led and policy-supported new path development in peripheral regions: Analytical and synthetic routes. *Economic Geography*, 93, 436–457.
Krueger, R., & Agyeman, J. (2005). Sustainability schizophrenia or "actually existing sustainabilities?" toward a broader understanding of the politics and promise of local sustainability in the US. *Geoforum*, 36(4), 410–417.
Krueger, R., & Gibbs, D.C. (Eds.) (2007). *The Sustainable Development Paradox*. New York and London: Guilford Press.
Krueger, R., Schulz, C., & Gibbs, D.C. (2017). Institutionalizing alternative economic spaces? An interpretivist perspective on diverse economies. *Progress in Human Geography*, 42(4), 569–589.
Lee, T., & van de Meene, S. (2012). Who teaches and who learns? Policy learning through the C40 cities climate network. *Policy Science*, 45(3), 199–220.

McCann, E., & Ward, K. (2012). Policy assemblages, mobilities and mutations: Toward a multidisciplinary conversation. *Political Studies Review*, 10(3), 325–332.

Macleod, G. (2011). Urban politics reconsidered: Growth machine to post-democratic city? *Urban Studies*, 48(12), 2629–2660.

Macleod, G., & Jones, M. (2011). Renewing urban politics. *Urban Studies*, 48(12), 2443–2472.

Metzger, J. (2018). Post-Politics and Planning. In M. Gunder, A. Madanipour, & V. Watson (Eds.) *The Routledge Handbook of Planning Theory*. London and New York: Routledge, pp. 180–192.

Miller, B., & Mössner, S. (forthcoming). Urban Sustainability and Counter-Sustainability: Spatial Contradictions and Conflicts in Policy and Governance in the Freiburg and Calgary Metropolitan Regions. *Urban Studies*.

Mössner, S. (2014). Sustainable urban development as consensual practice: Post-politics in Freiburg, Germany. *Regional Studies*, 50(6), 971–982.

Mössner, S. & Krueger, R. (2018). Deconstructing Modern Utopias: Sustainable Urbanism, Participation, and Profit in the European City. In Andy Jonas, Byron Miller, Kevin Ward, & David Wilson (Eds.) *Handbook on Spaces of Urban Politics*. London and New York: Routledge, pp. 1–15.

Nagorny-Koring, N. (2018). *Kommunen im Klimawandel: Best Practices als Chance zur grünen Transformation?* Bielefeld: Transcript Verlag.

Newman, P., Beatley, T., & Boyer, H. (2009). *Resilient Cities: Responding to Peak Oil and Climate Change*. Washington, DC: Island Press.

Roseland, M. (1997). Dimensions of the Eco-City. *Cities*, 14(4), 197–202.

Rosol, M., Béal, V., & Mössner, S. (2017). Greenest Cities? The (Post-)Politics of New Urban Environmental Regimes. *Environment and Planning A*, 49(8), 1710–1718.

Silomon-Pflug, F., Stein, C., Heeg, S., & Pütz, P. (2013). Die unternehmerische Stadt als Gegenstand von Urban-Policy-Mobilities-Forschung. *Geographische Zeitschrift*, 101(3/4), 201–217.

Uekötter, F. (2014). *The Greenest Nation?* Cambridge, MA: MIT Press.

Wachsmuth, D., Cohen, D.A., & Angelo, H. (2016). Expand the frontiers of urban sustainability. *Nature*, 536(7617), 391–393.

Ward, K. (2008). Editorial: Toward a comparative (re)turn in urban studies? Some reflections. *Urban Geography*, 29(5), 405–410.

Zhou, N., He, G., Williams, C., & Fridley, D. (2015). ELITE cities: A low-carbon eco-city evaluation tool for China. *Ecological Indicators*, 48(1), 448–456.

Chapter 6

Mobility
Promises of Intermodality for Sustainable Mobility in Bordeaux

Patrice Godier and Guy Tapie

July 2018 marked a turning point for Bordeaux Métropole[1] with an announcement that came as a hammer blow for car commuters: the city's oldest bridge, built in 1822, was henceforth to be dedicated solely to pedestrians, bicycles, and public transport. Crossing the Pont de Pierre by car would no longer be possible following its transformation into an infrastructure node entirely dedicated to 'active mobility options.' This measure taken by the president of the Métropole completed a one-year experimental temporary closure of the bridge that serves the historic heart of Bordeaux and connects the city across the Garonne river. Each day the bridge is traversed by 9,000 cyclists, 7,000 pedestrians, and 800 joggers, and the system put in place to assess and analyze the practices of the residents of Bordeaux during the temporary closure obtained results that were convincing enough to lead to a permanent decision (Figure 6.1). In addition, the local media was quick to highlight the importance of the event, which symbolically manifested the priorities that the elected Metropolitan Council members had endorsed since the early 2000s. Even though the stone bridge only carried 3% of the river-crossing traffic prior to its closure, it was included as one of several planning decisions that all had a common goal in mind: to drastically reduce the number of cars in the city center. The four tramway lines that have been constructed over the past 20 years are still considered the most important means of reducing car circulation. Nevertheless, the words that the president of the Metropolitan Council chose to use to defend the decision to ban cars permanently from using the bridge marks a particular dramaturgy in which the event is situated: "We are living in a key moment in the history of humanity. To give the signal to regress in terms of changed behaviors and our ways of living in the city [by allowing cars to use the bridge again] would mean going backwards in time."[2] This decision thus relaunched debates about the question of mobility and travel conditions in the city center and beyond, from a perspective of sustainability and 'civilizational' challenge due to climate change.

However, the decision was far from unanimous. The local shopkeepers and the mayors of the peripheral suburban municipalities were swift to express their concern by stressing the unequal treatment that this choice implied for residents in the peri-urban areas who, owing to a lack of public transport options, are forced to use their cars to get around. The mayors called for accompanying measures (including awarding a bonus to carpoolers, a more developed bicycle plan, and the possibility of constructing a metro line) which they deemed to be lacking in the current policy approach. Nonetheless, while doing so, they did not call into question the long-term validity of the decision to close the bridge to car traffic. Indeed, many inhabitants of the Bordeaux region confront mobility problems and the interdependence of municipalities' mobility planning throughout the metropolis on a daily basis. In line with this, public mobility policies face a dilemma of how to address the different transportation issues that residents experience in the central and peri-urban areas, respectively. In the metropolitan city center, expectations are set for radical changes of habits, to the advent of an enlightened user who privileges soft modes of transport and supports actions in favor of energy efficiency. In the outskirts, the aim is rather to support car-sharing in order to counter the tendency for car owners to drive alone. Meanwhile, there is a tension between mobility and the flux of populations between the city center and surrounding small towns. This chapter focuses on and discusses the challenging endeavor for an urban agglomeration to cater for more sustainable mobility habits.

Figure 6.1 The Pont de Pierre in Bordeaux after it was closed to car traffic.
Source: Patrice Godier.

Building a Sustainable Mobility System at the Metropolitan Level

The definitive closure of the stone bridge, which was only one of four crossing-points over the Garonne by car within the Bordeaux metropolitan area, represents only one step in the process of a vast ongoing project on mobility in Bordeaux. The major challenge for the metropolitan administration, which is aware of the risks for increasingly congested arteries and of the current limits of its tram network, is to review more generally its metropolitan mobility offer in a sustainable way. The aim is to redefine an offer that can change travel and transport habits by discouraging, or at least reducing, car use. The measure taken to reserve the venerable stone bridge for soft mobility is only one element of the overall mobility system that is being revamped. Another central element is to create a functioning network at the urban level, of which the metropolitan Réseau Express Régional (Regional Express Network—RER), similarly to the RER in the Paris region, is a major component. The objective is to improve connections between residential and economic spaces by integrating small towns and villages located on the fringe of the metropolis, thus pushing the urban-rural border further back. Bordeaux's geography and its urbanization in the form of a sprawling city require other combinations of public transport than those currently available. Indeed, the metropolitan area is one of the least concentrated conurbations in France, with a density equivalent to only a quarter of that of Paris. This trend towards urban sprawl and peri-urbanization is explained by the presence of a vast and available territory and also by a tradition of housing that favors single-storey dwellings and properties with gardens. Another of its characteristics is that the capital city, Bordeaux, is located at the heart of this conurbation which has been designated a UNESCO World Heritage Site owing to its 18th-century architecture. This makes it an exception (with its vineyards) favored in recent years by developments in the historic center that have largely contributed to the renewal of the city's image and to the ongoing metropolitan "awakening" (Godier et al., 2018), which has been remarked upon by international travel guides that contribute to tourist flows.

In this context, public policy in the field of mobility aims to achieve a form of organization that is at the same time more "fluid, reasoned, and regulated."[3] This includes finding a compromise between linking areas in the sprawling city that are dense enough to be connected together by efficient transport systems, and the cost of extending the tram network that is unsustainable when serving more sparsely populated areas. The objective is to take into account the way in which the various parts of the city use transport, and the lifestyles that this transport supports, which go beyond the limits of municipalities and the metropolitan area, as demonstrated by the analysis of current mobility practices.

Interchange Stations: New Components of Urban Transport Networks

The reasoning advanced by the metropolitan government in its proactive mobility strategy embodies the idea of linking centralities (from the largest to the smallest) through a public transport network that promotes multimodality and facilitates intermodality. The driving force behind this change in focus is a spatial arrangement of interchange stations conceived as connecting points between different urban transport networks and modes of transport. The figure of such spatial arrangement is present in many cities around the world, widely developed by the technical literature, and constitutes the "new universal components of urban transport networks" (Amar, 2004). The metropolitan government defines a *pole d'échange* (interchange station) as "a place of passage from one mode of transport to another, which includes the park and ride facilities of the Transports Bordeaux Métropole (TBM) network,[4] railway stations and the connection points of the various public transport networks" (Bordeaux Metropolitan Council, 2007). The concept is part of Bordeaux's mobility planning framework that considers the shift between different modes of transport to be the most credible alternative to car use. It implies that the user must be able to move continuously via a network that is well connected throughout the area. The aim of this organization is to offer as many people as possible complementary modes of transport facilitated by exchange hubs designed as network nodes for the traveller. Although they are intended to optimize the passage of users, the creation of exchange hubs is also likely to trigger urban development projects in their proximity and around the metropolis.

Bordeaux has six railway axes, of which five converge in the central railway station, the Gare de Bordeaux-Saint-Jean, and they have become valuable in the recent mobility policy. A total of 72 km of railway is used for inter-urban passenger traffic. Although in recent decades trains have been used less frequently for regional travel, the railway has been rediscovered as an asset that can strengthen the attractiveness of public transport. This is demonstrated by an increase in the number of passengers per km travelling on all routes served by regional trains (transport express régional (TER) to Bordeaux. However, representatives from the regional government (région Nouvelle-Aquitaine) have pointed out that given the capacity of the existing infrastructure and the hierarchy of rail flows, which prioritize journeys to Paris via the train à grande vitesse (TGV—high-speed train), the potential of the railway to serve local public transport needs is hampered. Through the planned rejuvenation of the railway, the redevelopment of stations into interchange nodes, the modernization of trains and carriages, and the move towards a single pricing formula, the TER is destined to become the backbone of the regional mobility system when its operation is expanded in the near future. As a member of the public transport users' association pointed out, "our reading of the urban area is that it takes 40 minutes to travel by tram from the outskirts of Bordeaux to the historic center, but only 10 minutes by TER." An increase in the number of railway lines and the frequency of services are also part of this pattern. Through the improved TGV network, all the main cities of the Nouvelle-Aquitaine region (Bayonne, Poitiers, La Rochelle, and Limoges) would benefit from having better connections that put them within two hours of travelling time to Paris. In the Bordeaux area, peri-urban residents would benefit from much more frequent connections between the residential areas and places of employment. From this perspective, city centers would be accessible to a geographically wider population either directly or in connection with the lines of the urban network. At peak times, the frequency of these lines could approach every half- or quarter-hour, and the regional government has expressed the ambition that even rural areas with a railway line would be served more regularly than they are at present. These objectives mean that the regional Nouvelle-Aquitaine mobility system would meet the objectives of the metropolitan mobility system by instilling more sustainable mobility habits for residents living beyond the urban cores.

Operationally, the sites for an extended transport network are being structured around connection points to different modes of transport, i.e., tram, bus, and train, between the transport network of Bordeaux and the regional area. There are plans to introduce an additional metropolitan commuter train, similar to the Parisian RER, to run between the central station and the airport, and to connect the Bordeaux university campus which is a major place of work and study-related activity, the main hospital which is the city's largest employer, and other important economic areas. The target users are commuters who are forced to commute daily between their homes and places of work, and consequently the network is planned to connect the region broadly to the non-residential areas that are generally concentrated around urban and peri-urban Bordeaux. The reasoning that guided this planning was structured around a triple integration of locations, temporality (trains that run every 10 minutes) and pricing, as well as attempts to think of the peri-urban and rural sites as part of the metropolitan area.

However, reflections on transport planning are closely intertwined with urban planning and the design of urban public spaces. The mobility offer does not only involve a reflection on the type of networks and the choice of means of transport, the densification of the city through large-scale urban projects has also been factored in as a central concern in the mobility policy. This can be seen in several major ongoing development projects in Bordeaux, such as a program to construct 50,000 houses along the transport axes over the next decade, and the implementation of the Euratlantique project that is financed by the national and metropolitan governments and covers 740 hectares around the central station, the Gare de Bordeaux-Saint-Jean. In the weaving of the metropolitan network, the renovation of the Gare de Bordeaux-Saint-Jean and its extension to develop TGV links have a singular status. The objective is to make it a business district with public amenities, creative industries and the centrality of the central train station, which have gained importance for the growth of the area through the selling point that Bordeaux is just 'two hours from Paris' following the recent introduction of the TGV.

The Promises of Intermodality

Several challenges to the promise of intermodality remain. The development of contemporary station districts still needs to combine the symbol of a modernity associated with the industrial city, movement for work, travel, the rhythms of the city during the day and at night, with the expectations of many residents in the middle-sized urban area that there will be a tram stop right outside the front door with the neighborhood supermarket not far away. In terms of urban forms, their design also raises many questions, some of which are frequently debated in Bordeaux, such as the density and height of the buildings located around or near them. Similarly, the decisions about what kind of services should operate in and around the station have remained open for many years. A change that has been made to railway stations in France in recent years has been that of opening them up to a variety of commercial functions, not only those directly concerned with transport. The urban station is now a hub for organizing traffic flows, information, and social relations.

The discussions held between Bordeaux's Metropolitan Council and the SNCF about the development of the Gare Bordeaux-Saint-Jean illustrated the conceptual diversity of what the 'urbanization' of a station can mean. The SNCF's preference was to construct a 20,000-sq-m shopping mall within the station. However, many experts in the council wanted to focus on the station's functionality—i.e., the use of platforms, ticketing systems, and an ad hoc signal system—in consideration of its mission to transport passengers and freight. They urged caution about adding to the already increasing flow of passengers as a result of the introduction of the TGV, and the potential attendance of visitors coming to the station solely for shopping purposes. What Roland Barthes wrote about Tokyo's stations, that "each district is collected in the void of its station" (1970), resonates with perceptions of the central station in Bordeaux. Many planners and mobility experts in local and national policy arenas expect the station to embody the social values of society at large. An official in the metropolitan mobility service commenting on the commercialization of the station space declared that "the station is very republican, it is a public service, and it shouldn't be Americanized." Nonetheless, the SNCF has partly succeeded in imposing its managerial model of promoting the concept of hub services to develop commercial operations that have become accessible thanks to the TGV.

For experts, the recent idea of the exchange center implies a change in the design of the sites, as well as in the architecture and signage with the aim to better organize the service offer and to integrate the exchange center into its environment. A study on preferences among travelers in France published by an inter-ministerial research program about transport innovation reveals that users prefer functionality over architectural prowess (PREDIT, 2000). The most highly ranked quality criteria were the speed and comfort of pathways. Travellers appeared to appreciate aspects such as escalators that facilitate swift movement through stations, and they are sensitive to the quality of passenger shelters, e.g., waiting rooms. While travellers are satisfied with the limited facilities offered in smaller stations, they appreciate being able to conduct micro activities in central stations, such as drinking coffee and visiting the newsagent. The study showed that they are also sensitive to the organization of spaces that avoid conflicts between busy commuters, those who use the cluster's services (ticketing, shops) and passengers waiting for transport connections.

However, if habits relating to public transport are to be changed, it is not enough merely to focus on the creation of places and infrastructures. It is also a matter of cognitive perceptions affecting inhabitants' choices of different modes of transport. In the social representations of means of transport in the urban area of Bordeaux, the car holds a dominant place. The development of the suburban cities around the city center designed for cars maintains this privileged relationship between metropolitan residents and their vehicles (80% of all trips carried out in Pessac and Mérignac, two cities adjacent to Bordeaux, are made by car). This is even more so for local business owners. According to the head of a small business, "people prefer to use the car when obliged to travel in the morning and evening, so that they can enjoy a comfortable lifestyle adapted to economic constraints," since public transport cannot compete with the car when a business is dependent on people moving around. Meanwhile, transport specialists Kaufmann and Paulhiac (2006) have identified a mechanism whereby often "[t]ravel times by car are significantly underestimated, while those of public transport are significantly overestimated" by users. This is proof, among other things, that travelling can be experienced and understood as moments of social friction, whereby image and usage constraints play a decisive role for practices.

In Bordeaux, the image of public transport has been regenerated over the past 15 years following the development of the tram network that was built in the early 2000s. It has been interlinked with a partial geographical redistribution of cycling and walking practices to include the perimeter beyond of the city center, including the right river bank that previously was largely disconnected in terms of soft mobility from the left bank. As for the public bus system, it is perceived as a slower and more constrictive mode of transport, and as socially more stigmatizing. The transformations engendered by the tram network system and an increase in the number of bus routes have significantly modified people's perception of the bus, without completely doing away with the view of the bus as constraint.[5] In the daily perception of users, it still fails to provide a reliable alternative in the event of disruptions to tram services, as actual bus arrival and departure times seldom correspond with published schedules.

The term *gares et pôle d'échanges* (stations and exchange hubs) was popularized among the general public in Bordeaux via the tram network, before it became widespread through the SNCF's media campaign. Nevertheless, the meaning of the concept remains unclear and the experience of intermodal transport among the locals living in Bordeaux is still recent. This can be exemplified with the suburban commuter train stations that in general have a strong Parisian connotation. This connotation is, however, distant from the local reality of the sites in Bordeaux, which relates to the process of metropolization. The *bordelais* surburban station certainly cannot compete in terms of size, service, or frequency of trains, with those of Paris. While the mobility system throughout the region is developed through the conceptualization of a metropolitan area, local inhabitants say that they do not feel that they belong to the metropolitan area. Local inhabitants' qualitative perception of the metropolitan area is measured by the obstacles and hardships that they encounter when travelling through the urban agglomeration by car. Meanwhile, the municipality is the primary sociopolitical entity that should encourage in the populace the idea of belonging to the metropolis. Potentially, the end stations of public transport lines could mark the edge of the metropolis, and thereby give to those living within this boundary a sense of metropolitan belonging.

Lived Intermodality

Intermodality is an emerging practice in metropolitan France: comparative data with other major cities shows that the population in Bordeaux Métropole stand out owing to their frequent use of private car-tram and tram-bicycle exchanges (La CUB, 2009). The tram has become important for securing access to mobility for people residing on the periphery of the metropolis, and the introduction of park and ride facilities in connection to the tram network have reduced uncertainty factors and other hazards that constrain mobility. Hence, this significant difference with other French agglomerations that have a stronger collective transport infrastructure whereby the intermodal transfer offer is often a more sophisticated transport network including exchanges between the metro, tram, and bus. Besides the 80,000 commuters residing outside Bordeaux, of whom half live within a distance of 30 km from the metropolis (INSEE, 2016), and for whom hypermobility is a forced necessity, other categories remain poorly identified. This is the case, for example, of the 'mobile precarious,' which includes inhabitants whose daily life is heavily dependent on transport for getting to work and who have neither guaranteed employment nor home ownership. Similarly, residents in large social housing areas and in territories located some distance from the metropolis are categories whose mobility practices receive little attention.

Studies have shown that intermodality should be considered in tandem with 'travel loops,' i.e., the succession of trips that a person makes during the day, with the home as a start and end destination. The car is the dominant mode of transport when a succession of trips is required, since in Bordeaux it is the most flexible option for carrying out a sequence of activities that need to be achieved daily, such as taking children to school, going to work, and shopping at the supermarket. Analyses have also suggested that the distance between activities carried out during the day tend to increase, that a growing number of persons use several modes of transport during the course of a single day, and that multimodal practices are increasing in France (CERTU, 2012; Le Breton, 2008). A student's description of her choice of mode of transport resonates with the tendencies observed in the studies: "for me, mobility means being able to use the means of travel that is most suitable for any given situation. It's convenient to live in Bordeaux; in the morning you can take the tram, and then happily return calmly by bike." Intermodal transfer is a strength for network accessibility but also a fragility for people's mobility. Several studies have highlighted the stress experienced by travellers when it comes to changing between connecting transport modes (Barrère & Rozenholc, 2018; Massot, 2010). For transport experts and behavioral psychologists, three important efforts are required of the traveller: physical, cognitive, and emotional. The consideration of these aspects and the fragility related to changing connections have induced predictability as a central concern among managers of traffic flows in Bordeaux. The concern with predictability has led to efforts focused on developing an information system that makes travellers aware of time schedules and any irregularities in the transport network.

In addition to the concern with information systems, a new offer has been added to the more traditional multimodal means of transport (car/train/tram/bus). Like many urban areas in France and Europe, the public administration in Bordeaux has developed the provision of self-service bicycles planned in connection with carpooling initiatives to favor this additional change of transport mode. The increase in communications systems and mobile phone applications has also been key to making the new modes of mobility available and efficient. Real-time information about demand, timetables, schedules, arrivals and departures gives users greater flexibility to manage their journeys. In Bordeaux, this signifies a revolution in terms of how people move through the metropolis.

To summarize the implications of the promise of intermodality, the functioning and the perception of the role of stations and exchange centers is part of a profound change in the urban mobility model. After having negotiated the transition from planning for car use to trams in the city center at the turn of the 21st century, the current issue in Bordeaux is how to move to another level of public transport across the metropolitan territory. For the metropolitan authorities, the planning of stations and exchange centers is embedded in the idea of a 'networked city,' where intermodality plays a role in introducing a modified user logic of transport modes and systems that corresponds to the policy ambition of the metropolis to provide 'a high level of services.'

The concern with intermodality is a way of reconnecting with the model of a city made up of numerous smaller town centers without being gigantic in itself, which was the French model of urbanization until the Second World War. Meanwhile, there is a tension between the living conditions in the larger region and in the metropolitan area. It is necessary to find a political compromise between elected officials in the metropolis, and the elected officials in the department of Gironde. The latter are defending the idea that the metropolis cannot aspire to encompass all activities and all populations at the expense of smaller regional cities located outside the metropolis. For some elected officials in the metropolitan periphery, Bordeaux Métropole's stated ambition to become a city of one million inhabitants has come to represent an image of the metropolis as emptied of its local particular identities that are connected to the different municipalities. The engineer who was the former head of the mission to construct the tram network in Bordeaux Métropole pointed out in an interview that this debate is fundamental, even if it "remains silent, because it is a subject of strong ideological and political opposition." The debate about this tension, which opposes the trickle-down theory (which implies that the wealth accumulated in the metropolis spills over to the less wealthy municipalities) to the drain of wealth theory (which implies that the metropolis dries out the peripheral territories), is manifested in the discourse of mayors of smaller municipalities in the region that oppose the 'metropolitan giant.' The demands of the *gilet jaunes* ('yellow vests') social movement, which rose to prominence in 2018 initially as a response to the national government's plan to increase taxes on fuel, amplify the unease about territorial inequalities in the distribution of wealth by calling territorial distribution into question. The movement, which has a strong presence in Bordeaux, is largely represented by the inhabitants of the peri-urban area who are confronted, among other things, with the mobile precariousness mentioned earlier. In order to ease the tension between smaller municipalities and the metropolis, in early 2019 the mayor of Bordeaux and the president of the Metropolitan Council was forced, under pressure from departmental elected officials, to abandon his support for the national government project that aims, as part of an increased act of decentralization, to accord to the metropolitan areas the same powers as those of the departments. Since then, the president of the Metropolitan Council has agreed to organize a round of discussions with his counterpart in the department of Gironde to search for complementarity and cooperation between departmental and metropolitan services, with a strong emphasis on establishing contractual collaborations.

Going Forward: The Challenges of Intermodality

The need for elected representatives in all municipalities to find political compromises and alternatives to the unsustainable car-centered urban development that has dominated in Bordeaux has become all the more urgent in times of climate change when there are environmental issues to address. The expectation that the continuous extension of the tram network would increase the acceptability of denser land use developments in the peripheral metropolitan municipalities quickly vanished. In the face of inhabitants' consistent demands for single-family housing and, because of the inability of the tram network to perform as well in sparsely populated areas as it does within the more densely populated areas, the promise that the trams would provide greater mobility options has not been met. The public's expectation of detached housing upsets professionals in the urban development business, as a representative of a major construction group signalled during a debate on mobility: "One day, the people of Bordeaux must stop believing that you can live in a house deep in the forest, while having as many transport options as there are in Châtelet-Les Halles [a major metro station] in Paris, and as many public facilities as there are in Berlin." If the tram has been able to assist in making the city what it is today, it is incapable on its own to meet the requirements of sustainable development at the metropolitan level.

Faced with the impossibility of offering all areas within the metropolis their own tram station, the elected representatives of the suburban municipalities have developed a joint interest in a Bus Rapid Transit (BRT) system. This bus system, which will cost half the price of the tram, still requires a heavy infrastructure with platforms, stations, and passenger information systems. The BRT system is an alternative to serve certain parts of the metropolis that the tram network does not reach. However, the phenomenon of urban sprawl, as well as the urgent need to address environmental concerns, extends beyond the metropolitan area that the reach of the planned bus system is confined to. The car continues to be used for 70% of all trips in the Gironde department (80% of kilometers traveled) while it is limited to 60% of all trips in the metropolitan area, according to figures from the Gironde department. Reducing greenhouse gas emissions requires at least limiting car traffic to the current usage. However, additional journeys necessarily result from any increase in population. In the metropolis, where it is both expected and desired that the population will increase by approximately 250,000 inhabitants by 2030, this growth will result in nearly one million more daily trips, none of which ought be made by car. Population growth also concerns the rest of the department of Gironde whose residential attractiveness is strong enough to dispel doubts that Bordeaux's desired population growth will absorb Gironde's overall growth.

The environmental imperatives and mobility needs of the inhabitants of the Gironde emphasize the interdependence between territories as daily commuting and journeys take place across territorial borders, and across the different transport authorities organizing the mobility offers.[6] The most obvious aspect of this interdependence can be seen in the distortion between the location of homes and of jobs. The geographical distribution gap between places of residence spread throughout the department and the concentration of jobs in the metropolitan area, a situation characteristic of a metropolitan context, leads to an increase and extension of work-related commuting. This situation implies rethinking the organization on a larger scale than that of planning instruments such as the metropolitan plan for urban transport conceived in 1996 with reflections limited to creating tramway corridors. In 2008, the urban planning agency drafted a report proposing for the first time taking a shared approach to the transport strategy in the Gironde metropolitan area by 2020.[7] The structuring of various transport offers is based on a shared vision of the organization of the larger urban metropolitan area. The challenge is to better connect the major urban centers in the area, but through the consideration of the area as a joint metropolitan area rather than as a selection of urban centers. However, a central debate is emerging among actors in the domain of urban planning: should residential areas be brought closer to places of employment or should efforts be focused on organizing a mobility system, including public transport and road networks, that is better able to facilitate all individual travel to the main places of employment?

In terms of road traffic, the saturation of the ring road that surrounds Bordeaux Métropole is considered one of the most urgent traffic problems in the Bordeaux urban area. The ring road occupies a major place in the movements within and through the metropolis; 64% of all vehicles use the ring road for journeys within the urban area, while transit flows along the ring road represent only 8% of all journeys made, all transport means included. Current reflections on work to maintain the ring road exemplify a rationality aimed at making better use of the existing infrastructure rather than investing in a new one. But since the state and the metropolis are currently the only financers, it can be assumed that the necessary work that needs to be done, such as widening the roads, will remain incomplete until the next decade, despite the calls from city officials that the state must speed up the realization of the work in order to expand the capacity of the ring road. However, it can also be assumed that widening the ring road will not eliminate traffic jams unless the extension is coupled with regulations about the use of new car lanes to discourage those whose travel is not, for example, of a business nature. As for a new major bypass road around the metropolis, which is a political debate that has resurfaced recently in Bordeaux despite the official abandonment of the idea in 2008, it seems today to be precluded not only due to the current political agenda, but also due to the lack of financing. The saturation of the ring road is connected to recent measures taken to reduce traffic in the inner city. Increasing parking fees, a reduction in parking places, the increase of underground parking and limited access to historical areas for non-residents coupled with the absence of road tolls—a measure that has been locally studied but which is opposed by city officials—have directed more traffic towards the ring road.

Conclusion

The main challenge in developing a sustainable mobility system for the Bordeaux metropolitan area concerns travel habits between the most urbanized, densely populated central parts, and the municipalities located outside the ring road. A persistent choice of certain means of transport, particularly the stubbornness among many travelers to continue to use their cars despite the alternatives that are on offer, is a major challenge in terms of getting people to change their habits.

To meet these challenges, the railway—tram and train—is included in the strategical outlines of the various transport authorities today, and it is presented as the framing structure of mobility networks at a metropolitan level. The establishment of a rapid rail transport offer, such as metropolitan commuter trains similar to Paris's RER, appears to be a major challenge that will need to be addressed in future. The consensus reached among the elected representatives of Bordeaux Métropole on this subject at the end of 2018, with a unanimous vote of the community assembly, gives a solid legitimacy to the political orientation towards expanding the railway. Wishing to demonstrate a shared political will, Bordeaux Métropole and Nouvelle-Aquitaine have aligned their respective positions in order to present a united front in discussions with the state and the SNCF. However, the encounter of technical problems and the delicate issue of financing has curbed enthusiasm to bring this plan to fruition. Although claiming to be "aware of the very high expectations of the population," the regional director of the SNCF considered that, in view of the technical problems that need to be resolved, it was necessary to "have the clarity to say that there will not be a network dedicated to serving the metropolis comparable to that of Paris in the future."

The acceleration of the process to create a more developed regional rail service, in the context of high social expectations and the urgent need to address environmental concerns, has not prevented a continuing debate about the development of mobility options. In particular, the scenario of equipping Bordeaux with a metro system has resurfaced. Following extensive planning for the introduction of a metro system during the 1980s, and abandonment of this project after many political-urbanistic episodes in the 1990s, the idea has again been reawakened. In light of the saturation of tram lines in the hyper-center, the question of a metro network, even for those who denounced it as inefficient and costly during the previous rounds of preparation, is being reconsidered. Furthermore, the mayors who accepted the closure of the Pont de Pierre to car traffic only after assuring compensation for their constituencies in the shape of additional bus lines and increased efforts to build a fifth bridge over the Garonne, are calling for action to advance the metro project. Local policy analysis suggests that neither the tram network, the BRT, nor a metropolitan RER provide the functions that a metro can: i.e., to quickly and safely transport a large number of people with high frequency and speeds. The examples in France (e.g., Lyon and Toulouse) and elsewhere in Europe (e.g., Karlsruhe and Nuremberg) of cities that have combined systems of public transport, metro, tram, and bus testify to the efficiency assured by a metro network. Bordeaux is lagging behind in terms of the mobility offer, which demands swift action in a context of intensified environmental demands. Besides global reports, local alerts are multiplying regarding poor air quality, quality of life and urban heat island effects, as well as strong social tensions associated with actions addressing environmental issues, as evinced by the gilet jaunes movement. This urgency for action is making itself felt at a time when infrastructure projects are sluggish, and financing difficulties make public authorities very cautious about investing unless the state provides effective support, while public opinion is putting pressure on demands for action.

Notes

1 In 2018 the intercommunal structure of Bordeaux Métropole comprised 28 municipalities and 776,000 inhabitants (being the fifth largest metropolitan area nationally), of which 252,000 reside in the city center. The wider urban area that the Métropole is part of, as defined by the National Institute of Statistics and Economic Studies (INSEE), is home to more than one million people. Today, with annual demographic growth of 1% (achieved partly through attracting seniors and Parisians to the region), the metropolis has set for itself an ambition to become an attractive urban region at a European level.
2 www.sudouest.fr/2018/07/05/pont-de-pierre-a-bordeaux-il-restera-ferme-aux-voitures-a-dit-alain-juppe-5206643-2780.php.
3 To borrow the title of a report about mobility in Bordeaux Métropole published by the Urbanism Agency A'urba in April 2013.
4 The TBM network is managed by the Keolis group, which is a subsidiary of the Société nationale des chemins de fer français (SNCF), the French national state-owned railway company.
5 Use of the public bus system increased by 25% between 2009 and 2017.
6 Bordeaux Métropole is responsible for the city bus and tram network, the Gironde department for coaches covering longer distances throughout the region, while the Nouvelle-Aquitaine region operates the regional train network.
7 This approach was shared between Bordeaux Métropole, the Gironde department, the region, the joint authority of Bassin d'Arcachon Sud, the joint venture between various public authorities known as the Syndicat mixte du schéma directeur de l'aire métropolitaine bordelaise (SYSDAU), and the state field service for transport equipment.

References

Amar, G. (2004) *Mobilités urbaines: Éloge de la diversité et devoir d'invention*. Paris: Editions de l'Aube.

Barrère, C., & Rozenholc, C. (Eds.) (2018) *Les lieux de mobilité en question: Acteurs, enjeux, formes, situations*. Paris: Karthala.

Bordeaux Métropole Council (2007) *Délibération n°2007/0216 Les pôles d'échange multimodaux: Modalités d'intervention de la Communauté urbaine de Bordeaux*. Retrieved March 23, 2020, from www.bordeaux-metropole.fr/Metropole/Organisation-politique/Deliberations?annee=2007&q=0216.

CERTU (2012) *Les typologies de gares. Quels enjeux? Quelles méthodes? Fiche n°2*. Éditions du CERTU, Collection Dossier. Retrieved March 23, 2020, from http://outil2amenagement.cerema.fr/IMG/pdf/Typologie_des_gares_cle027daa.pdf.

Communauté Urbaine de Bordeaux (2009). *Note de synthèse des principaux résultats Enquête Déplacements*. La Communauté Urbaine de Bordeaux. Retrieved March 23, 2020, from www.bordeaux-metropole.fr/var/bdxmetro/storage/original/application/317c36bae301b411bee81c67376729aa.pdf.

Godier, P., Oblet, T., & Tapie, G. (2018). *L'éveil métropolitain: L'exemple de Bordeaux*. Paris: Éditions du Moniteur.

INSEE (2016). *De plus en plus de personnes travaillent en dehors de leur commune de résidence*. N°1605. Retrieved March 23, 2020, from www.insee.fr/fr/statistiques/2019022.

Kaufmann, V., & Paulhiac, F. (2006). Transports urbains à Montréal; évolutions des référentiels et enjeux d'une politique durable. *Revue d'économie régionale et urbaine* 1: 49–79.

Le Breton, É. (2008). *Domicile-travail: Les salariés à bout de souffle*. Paris: Carnets de l'info.

Massot, M.H. (Ed.) (2010). *Mobilités et modes de vie métropolitains: Les intelligences du quotidien*. Paris: Éditions l'Oeil d'Or.

PREDIT (2000). *Intermodalité et interfaces: Comprendre les usages pour guider les décisions*. Retrieved March 23, 2020, from http://isidoredd.documentation.developpement-durable.gouv.fr/documents/CETTEXST005063/CETTEXST005063.pdf.

Roland, B. (1970). *L'Empire des signes*. Geneva: Skira.

Chapter 7

Complexities

Construction Sites of Sustainable Low Carbon Transition in Paris: Snapshots of Internal Organization, Energy Plans and Technical Infrastructure

Jonathan Rutherford and Sylvère Angot

Presenting the outcome of long-term work towards the production of a detailed local energy plan for a sustainable and low carbon Paris, the director of the Atelier Parisien d'Urbanisme (Paris Urbanism Agency—APUR), emphasized that "the city of tomorrow will not be so different from that of today." Summarizing the approach that the Agency was taking in its work, she argued that "What we are proposing is a delicate, non-binding transition through the implementation of a multitude of small, very simple, articulated, grouped and shared actions that together will combine their efficiencies" (quoted in Moutarde, 2015).[1] This approach is strikingly practical and processual in the Parisian context, where a recent succession of national debates and policies around environmental issues and various transitions ('the energy transition,' 'decarbonization,' 'the ecological transition') still tends to play up the big objectives, rigid instruments, and huge amount of effort required to help the whole of France (and its local territories) make the transition to greater sustainability. The APUR director thus gives voice to a pragmatic view of building up from everyday work towards sustainable and low carbon transition, thereby situating the complexity of the changes that are required in the many small and tangible practices that are engaged by people across the city in different settings. This chapter takes up this perspective by locating the low carbon transition of Paris in the daily work and ongoing challenges of various local actors as they try to make gradual advances towards achieving sustainability objectives.

A processual and pragmatic view makes the overall aims of low carbon transition more immediate and arguably less daunting. Figures suggest that CO_2 emissions in Paris are stable rather than declining (see Mairie de Paris, 2012), and that, whether these are viewed in the context of a target of achieving a 20% reduction by 2020 at a European level, the Factor 4 reduction by 2050 at a national level, or the 25% reduction by 2025 at a municipal level, Paris is not decarbonizing fast enough. This is all the more the case when comparisons are made with other cities using actual sustainability results. The problem is that this leads to a narrow focus on the factors or reasons for the relative lack of success of a particular city on some generic global low carbon trajectory which takes a singular quantitative end point, result, or desire (drastically reduced CO_2 emissions) as the sole measure of accomplishment. For those working on energy and climate issues on a daily basis, this may be too distant and indirect as a gauge of what they are doing, and potentially disheartening if regular achievements are not visible in headline figures. In an uncertain context replete with shuffling positions, tentative actions, and unexpected outcomes (see Callon et al., 2001), we need to avoid foreclosing debate around what might constitute a productive site, arena, or practice of sustainable urban change. While highlighting the challenges and tensions involved, the aim here then is to track the ongoing construction of low carbon sustainability transition in Paris through a focus on three distinct sites of practice and engagement. The three sites—internal organization of public authority action, production of energy plans, and reconfiguration of technical infrastructure—are emblematic of the kinds of issues facing local actors on the ground as they attempt to turn Paris into a sustainable city.[2] After discussing each site in turn, a concluding section examines their wider analytical and practical significance.

Internal Organization of Public Authority Action

A first site of low carbon sustainability transition practice in the Paris region concerns the challenge of organizing public action in territorial authorities in this domain. Research has constantly emphasized that one of the major challenges in addressing environmental, energy, and climate issues at a local level is how these issues are taken up by departments and individuals within public authorities. A great deal of effort is thus expended on shifting capacities for action, internal political negotiations, budgets, resources, and work more generally to produce meaningful policy implementation (see, for example, Gabillet, 2015; Rohracher & Späth, 2014; Rutherford, 2014).

The uptake and organization of sustainable transition in the work of a departmental local authority in the east of the Paris region[3] illustrates the challenge in more detail. Under French decentralization, the departmental authority has a mandate covering a wide range of policies, including social assistance and integration, education and childcare, health, culture and tourism, as well as roads, transport, and economic development. From the 1990s increasing environmental awareness led to the deployment of long-term voluntary Agenda 21 initiatives, aimed at the integration of different areas of policy intervention to promote cross-cutting local environmental and sustainable development work (Emelianoff, 2005). More recently, the legislator has introduced an obligation for all administrative authorities responsible for populations greater than 50,000 to produce *Plans Climat Energie Territorial* (PCET—territorial energy and climate plans) involving both mitigation and adaptation objectives. At the same time, work has also been done on a broader strategic plan (the Territorial Project— Projet Territorial) for the department that places these issues in a wider development context. The work on the ground of the local authority and its officials has shifted from a broad-based Agenda 21 to the more recent and precise energy-climate focus and has been complex and difficult, as we discuss here.

The mandatory production of a PCET,[4] with the formulation and implementation of concrete policies, was a new step in relation to the territorial environmental policies and sustainable development agenda that were developed largely on the basis of local political will during the 2000s. The work of the local authority on energy-climate issues for the PCET fell under the remit of a newly created service within the existing environment department, and produced a number of issues, tensions, and changes in the nature and conduct of that work and in the relationships between the various people involved in it.

One of the main issues was the reconciliation of distinct objectives, chiefly the definition of 'transition' and how this should play out in ways of working towards this. The objective of implementing an energy-climate transition on the territory of the department (through the PCET) did not exactly insert itself into a political and institutional vacuum. It became a reconfiguration of other already existing objectives and plans (including Agenda 21 that was initiated in 2004, and an annual sustainable development report, the Territorial Project, that was published after this). These already had their own officials working on them, and their allocated resources, as well as their interconnections, their political legitimacy, their modes of governance, and their own indicators. Interviews conducted by the authors with officials revealed the competition that existed within the local authority's organization between the various plans, and in particular, the rise of the Territorial Project with which the other plans were meant to be coherent. Moreover, despite a broad desire for transversality, the new service within the Environment Department which was managing and working on the PCET was not very central in the authority's organization chart and had trouble accessing political resources (local politicians) and administrative resources (the main officials in the authority).

The PCET was conceived as the climate component of the Agenda 21. But the PCET as a simple part of a broader Agenda 21 and as part of the wider political objectives related to the Territorial Project appeared rather marginal and positioned in a corner of the organization, "far from the heart" (authors' interview with a PCET official, 2014) of the territorial transition desired by the political decision-makers. As proposed by another official:

> Indeed, there are a lot of plans and schemes, and eventually the PCET suffered greatly from that and it finds itself considered, I was going to say like another vulgar scheme whereas this is not at all what it must be. ... They [the officials working on the PCET] have trouble developing their multi-year action plans because the directorates consider that it is not a priority, that there is not really any impulse.
>
> (Authors' interview with a sustainable development official)

Furthermore, the link between Agenda 21 and the PCET was not obvious, even to people within the authority, thus leading to some confusion about the two plans:

> The PCET has recycled the climate energy actions of the Agenda 21. Agenda 21 is like a rake, so that we go very wide and shallow, while the PCET goes in with a spade. That's what happened here. So many people think that the PCET has replaced Agenda 21, even our communications team. But it still exists. Agenda 21 still has a number of cross-cutting projects.
>
> (Authors' interview with a PCET official)

A second issue was how to shift from an distinctive policy and set of objectives and to implement transversality across the functioning of services within the authority. This was partly about the limits and the problems of securing financing and other resources allocated to energy issues and policies, as has been proven in countless other cases. But more specific to the authority was a view that the move from an initial policy to its 'institutionalization' across the organizational body paradoxically met with a loss of urgency and marginalization. The approach adopted under the PCET had been initially to focus on an internal approach before building and implementing a territorial component. But a fundamental difficulty was that the PCET was the latest in a series of cross-cutting policies. It required the integration of different components of the authority in its implementation (e.g., technical committees, tracking of actions, evaluations). This integration was confronted with the daily priorities and workloads of people who were supposed to participate in the work. It became necessary for the energy-climate service to find ways of avoiding increasing the workload of other services, the managers of which "were there, cold, silent, saying to each other that they will come to annoy us!" (authors' interview with a PCET official). The energy-climate service was thus forced to adapt to ways of doing and find a means to involve other people in the process without creating a further burden.

The imposed transversality of the Territorial Project did not produce different results. The officials were not consulted by politicians prior to the commencement of the project. Instead, they were faced with a fait accompli and were expected to carry out the project. The Territorial Project defined eco-building as a key aim for the department, but without providing much details on what this meant:

> The first thing we asked ourselves was: what are the sectors of eco-construction? Because every time we asked this question, we weren't sure what we would hear. We had a little trouble putting sustainable development back in there, we don't all speak the same language ... here we can sometimes have an elected official who only thinks strictly about economic aspects or environmental associations who think of energy.
>
> (Authors' interview with a PCET official)

In other words, the 'concrete operational' work always follows and adjusts to the prevailing level of discourse and strategy, rather than the other way round. The position adopted by the officials was that of pragmatism. The goal was not to force links that did not exist at the time, but to work gradually to bring approaches and people closer together.

A third issue was simply the limited political interest in energy-climate issues and ways to overcome this. Policy-makers generally struggle to make these issues a priority and there are many well-known factors behind this, including a lack of money for their implementation, a lack of awareness and training on environmental issues, the problem of political temporalities (a reluctance to deal with long-term policies compared to policies that are more immediately visible to the electorate), and a lack of widespread public interest in green policies and therefore little incentive or obligation to act on them. Energy and sustainability policies more generally were clearly seen as 'second division' policies when it came to implementing them in the department. For officials in the local authority, there was a politician responsible for sustainable development who was supposed to work with them on these questions. But the relationship between him and the people working on energy issues was poor: "We haven't seen him for a year. That's a long time. So, we go ahead, we meet some actors, we do things, but because it is not on the roadmap of the politician ... This is a real problem" (authors' interview with a PCET official). The PCET service was not prominent in the administrative hierarchy, and the politician did not relay the concerns and needs of the service, which might have raised awareness more widely about what was being done and what was required.

Furthermore, while sustainable development requires strong mobilization and support across the board, a single politician was necessarily quite isolated on these themes, and other local politicians were less interested or less competent. The lack of interest of politicians in the energy and sustainability themes was one of the main problems confronting the project leaders. One of them indicated that this called into question the basis of their own job (authors' interview with a PCET official). Plans such as Agenda 21 or the PCET are not management policies or regulatory or procedural plans, but project policies, which are also supposed to involve a degree of local civil society participation. This transversal 'project mode,' conveying a certain method of action (prefiguration, construction, implementation, evaluation, improvement), requires the support of politicians who are defending a strong 'political line.' The time spent informing ('training') politicians about the issues and trying to interest them did not allow them to be wholly involved in the implementation of the project and its operational energy and climate aspects. One result was the transformation of policies that were supposed to be systemic into purely technocratic policies:

> We really started with a technocratic logic. This means that, as we began by mobilizing services around an energy-climate approach, it was then very

difficult to pick up the politicians. They said at the outset, 'we will move forward within the framework of the PCET, and we must structure a real environmental policy.' But today, we are in a traditional operation—in other words, we produce summary documents, which are sometimes seen to politicians, but without any feedback.

(Authors' interview with PCET official)

More generally, these points refer to the complexity of maintaining political and administrative commitment beyond the moment of the construction of a plan itself. While the work of drawing up a plan gives rise to mobilization and a display of consensus about the project, the implementation phase typically receives less investment and some of the dynamic fades away as people move on to other themes and issues and political attention is diverted elsewhere. As a result, while initially viewed as open vehicles for integrating sectoral policies, both Agenda 21 and the PCET gradually became just another policy tool which could not generate and sustain the political awareness required (Angot, 2013).

However, officials in the local authority gradually got to grips with what was required by looking more widely for the commitment needed. They set up a coordination network to bring together those working on policies at different levels across the department. The idea was to propose structures for the exchange of information and experience, feedback and learning for technicians. Even though the activity had just started at the time of our research, those who attended meetings found them beneficial to learning and mutual acquaintance. They also mobilized a series of intermediary actors to carry out certain tasks and to build up a network of relationships, which could be complimentary to the authority's own work. This offered flexibility, reactivity, ways around administrative and legal constraints, wider coverage of the territory of the department, and the testing of new ideas.

The local authority is not a single actor, but its actions are formed from a wide variety of individuals (such as officials or technicians, decision-makers, politicians, and intermediaries) who possess different skills, motivations, and very varied powers. Analyzing the relationships between these different individuals, the daily work they do, the tools, and the charts and the other devices they use becomes crucial to understanding the dynamics at work and how actions and policies are created and maintained. Sustainability practice here involves a panoply of people, interpersonal relationships, routines and organizational devices, and that is just internally within the authority.

Energy-climate issues remain off the radar of many decision-makers right now, and the will to make substantive efforts is not always present. It remains very difficult to maintain a consistent level of political commitment in favor of transversal approaches, as well as to develop guidance for their implementation. Funding of different actions is not guaranteed and the officials and technicians who work on them are obliged to make do with limited resources and support. There are problems, negotiations, and conflicts—but local officials are responding, testing, adjusting, and learning all the time.

Production of Urban Energy Plans

A second site of low carbon sustainability transition practice in the Paris region concerns the challenge of producing knowledge that can inform sustainability interventions. This takes us beyond the scale of internal organization from the previous section to the wider challenge of 'grounding' and making visible the stakes of energy and climate in the urban fabric so that they become actionable for those who are concretely reworking the city.

A number of agencies in and associated with the City of Paris in recent years have been involved in 'territorializing' national, regional, and local energy and low carbon transition objectives by attempting to create the (knowledge) space for concrete interventions. Prior to the signing of the Paris Agreement on climate action and other strategic documents, there was very little awareness of and scarce information about the varying environmental 'performance' of existing building stocks, neighborhoods, and urban morphologies. Over the last 10 years or so, the planners of the APUR are one group that has been crucial to making visible the stakes, issues, and potential sites of action in this domain.

A succession of analytical reports have been produced during this time, 'grounding' ambitious objectives in the existing urban fabric of Paris, and using a variety of methods (such as cartography, thermographic measurement, modeling, and scenario-building) to translate technical knowledge into policy choices (APUR, 2013). But the 'performance' of the urban fabric in climate and environmental terms is heavily contested, so even this fine-grained technical analysis has not produced consensus.

One recurring issue has been what (or not) to do about the high proportion of historic Haussmannian homes and buildings in central Paris, 40% of which have electric heating. Electric heating concentrates a number of debates about nuclear power (which comprises almost 80% of the French electricity mix); inefficiencies in producing and transporting electricity from abroad; and high levels of electricity consumption at particular times (in winter, for example) which force the bringing online of fossil fuel-based generation or the importation of German electricity which does little for environmental goals. Analysis by APUR planners showed that buildings with individual electric heating systems to be quite good from a CO_2 emissions perspective compared to buildings with collective gas or fuel systems. Such homes are fitted with easily adjustable radiators, and their inhabitants are often young professionals who tend to be environmentally aware and switch systems off when they go out to work, plus there is the technical and heritage issue of how to actually go about renovating these historic buildings (APUR, 2007). Reports by APUR thus endorsed electric heating over other forms of heating and suggested that individual meters should be installed in apartment buildings heated by fossil fuels as it was argued that this would stimulate more virtuous behavior from residents compared to when heating was just part of a general collective charge (authors' interview with an APUR planner). Yet the reports ended up being censored and their publication delayed by green party politicians in Paris whose priority was contesting nuclear power—and therefore electric heating—rather than CO_2 emissions.

Interventions in energy systems in France always involve negotiating with powerful sectoral actors and vested interests due to the long-held monopolistic organization of energy in the country. This brings into view competing perspectives on sustainability transitions. Even just engaging in mapping actual or potential energy resources, flows, and networks brings planners into debate with energy companies, local authorities, and building owners. A solar energy potential map implies that home owners would readily agree to the installation of solar panels on their roofs. Extending district heating networks goes against competing sources and companies for heat. Even work on thermal insulation with a prospect of reducing building energy consumption is contentious in an energy system which is still oriented towards growth and revenues derived from increased consumption.

As part of its work on the local energy plan for the Greater Paris metropolis, APUR has focused on studying three scenarios for the thermal renovation of residential buildings in Paris by 2050 (APUR, 2014). These scenarios are respectively termed as ambitious, median, and minimal. In the first case, external thermal insulation has been applied to the walls of all Parisian buildings that were constructed before 1990, with the exception of the street façades of the oldest buildings (constructed before 1949) which are insulated from the inside. In this case, energy consumption is reduced by a factor of 2.7. The median scenario takes into account the difficulty of renovating some of the historic buildings, especially the lodges and street frontages. Only the walls of the courtyards and the gables would have external thermal insulation. Considerable effort was made to insulate buildings constructed between 1949 and 1975, resulting in a decrease in energy consumption by a factor of 2.4. Finally, the minimal scenario uses the assumptions of intervention on old buildings. Only half of all buildings constructed between 1949 and 1990 have been renovated, which takes into account some specific difficulties in intervention (with regard to thermal bridges in particular). Only simple energy gains are sought and in this case the energy reduction is by a factor of 2, which still meets the objectives of the Paris regional climate, air, and energy plan (Conseil Régional d'Ile-de-France & Prefet de la Région d'Ile-de-France, 2012).

Whether specifically with regard to electric heating or as a broader contribution to urban energy planning, the purpose of APUR's work is to provide decision-makers with territorialized tools that rationalize and guide planning, construction, and renovation choices. Fine-grained highly technical work is required to produce this 'objective' knowledge to inform decisions, but these decisions are always likely to be contentious either generally as in the case of electric heating or on a case-by-case basis as is likely with respect to building renovation. Such elaborate technical expertise and production of information is oriented towards retaking control of energy consumption and its consequences, but the process does not necessarily create consensus because sustainability knowledge is never neutral.

Reconfiguration of Technical Infrastructure

A third site of low carbon sustainability practice in the Paris region is the challenge of reconfiguring the infrastructure. Following on from the two previous sites, the challenge here is about manipulating the 'below ground' technical aspects of sustainable cities that often defy immediate control. Heat pipes, production plant,s and resource flows and mixes, as well as contracts, meters, and other material objects, become part of the constant daily negotiation of sustainability transition practice.

Paris has one of the oldest and most extensive district heating systems in Europe. There is an explicit policy objective both at a city and a regional level to expand and interconnect the district heating system in order to increase economies of scale and to diversify and improve the flexibility of the system (e.g., render it more resilient by using more than one resource). Parisian municipal plans and actors make reference to using its position as owner of the heat infrastructure and co-owner of the Compagnie Parisienne de Chauffage Urbain (CPCU) distribution company to extend the network to other parts of the city currently heated by less efficient fuel or electricity (even if the latter is better from a carbon viewpoint). The schéma régional climat air énergie (SRCAE—regional-level climate air and energy master plan) of December 2012 outlined an ambitious goal for a 40% increase in connections to heat systems by 2020, representing 450,000 extra buildings, to be achieved through the extension of existing systems and the interconnection of networks (Conseil Régional d'Ile-de-France & Prefet de la Région d'Ile-de-France, 2012). But how these objectives are to be met, and how the current heating system can be reconfigured for transition, are complex issues.

It is not clear to many actors how the goal of 40% more connections to heating systems by 2020 is to be achieved. As of 2015, growth in connections was around 1.5% per year, which is a long way from the goal, such that a real connection policy needs to be outlined and implemented (authors' interview with a heating company official). It is not evident either which is the best level for investment and heat load. Many observers have suggested a collective and mutualized approach, albeit across different territories (Paris and the inner ring of municipalities, or the new Paris Métropole intermunicipal cooperation structure, perhaps), but this would require somebody to take the lead and to organize things, and urban governance has been in a state of flux in Paris in recent years.

Furthermore, heating systems are heterogeneous and contentious strands of urban materiality. Objectives of interconnection, mutualization, and economies of scale require overcoming the technical and contractual difficulties of linking together different systems. The CPCU Paris-centered network is a steam system, while systems in surrounding municipalities use hot water. There are thermodynamic limits to the extent to which energy can be transferred between a hot water system at 80°C and a high-pressure steam/vapour system at 230°C. These different technologies were one of the reasons (along with local political tensions) that prevented the Batignolles planning project in the north-west of the city from sending heat "easily and cheaply" across the municipal border into neighbouring Clichy Levallois (authors' interview with a City of Paris official). The interconnection of heat systems is also problematized by the different types of existing contracts through which municipalities have conceded their own systems to various operators, e.g., separating distribution only as in the case of Paris, or also production as in other municipal contracts. The length of each contract and the dates when they are up for renewal also vary greatly. French public contract regulations (the *Code des Marchés Publics*) prevent municipalities from modifying or stopping a particular contract, so combining or mutualizing separate systems across municipal boundaries would require, in theory, separate contracts to be up for renewal at the same time and to have similar conditions of operation. Interviewees referred to the 'tangle' or 'minefield' (*maquis*) of contracts stopping what would appear to be commonsense technical connections such as the use of recovered heat from EDF's Ivry electricity plant to the east of the city which at the moment is wasted (authors' interview with a City of Paris works department official).

Heating pipes are also presented as a political nightmare. They are laid under the road rather than the pavement (due to their diameter) and therefore necessitate costly major street works for their repair and maintenance. These works also require permits from local authorities who are rarely keen for streets to be regularly dug up due to the fact that this is unpopular with local residents. The City of Paris works department cites such local opposition as an important factor with regard to the extension and maintenance of the CPCU system, which can lead in some areas, where there has been an accumulation of works, to local politicians blocking any new street works (authors' interview with a City of Paris works department official). Digging up roads, even for urgent maintenance, is "almost impossible" during the 12-month run-up to local elections (authors' interview with a heating company official). A major biomass plant project in the north-east of Paris, which formed a major part of plans for further decarbonizing the Parisian heating system, was abandoned when it was estimated that laying the pipes linking the plant to the existing CPCU network would have been as costly as building the plant itself due to the fact that the pipes would have to traverse five municipalities. For at least one interviewee using the analogy of a hard cheese full of holes, this inherent degree of permanent contestation typifies the substantial difficulties of working with the Paris "gruyère" (authors' interview with a heating company official).

Another area of uncertainty and tension relating to heating systems concerns ways to drastically increase the proportion of renewable and recovered heat in the energy mix of systems. For many actors, it is not clear how this can be achieved. In spite of the use of just over 40% of recovered heat from waste incineration in the CPCU's energy mix, the company has found it difficult to reach the level of 50% renewable and recovered heat. This threshold triggers both a decrease in the rate of value-added tax, from 19.6% to 5.5% (thus permitting a reduction in customer tariffs), and a process of so-called classification of networks which would allow the City of Paris to force new builds and planning projects to connect to existing heating networks, thereby achieving a better return on infrastructure investments.

Biomass resources have represented around 3% of the mix in the region (or 0.1 Mtep), yet this was supposed to increase to 30% of the mix (or 1.2Mtep), according to the SRCAE. This increased use of biomass is a primary instrument to meet local climate and energy plan objectives. It is planned to use an existing plant and replace half of the coal with wood pellets that are not humid and burn quite easily, and can be used in the same boilers. However, this demands an increase in logistical capacity for transport and storage necessitating substantial investment given the current limits of local availability and access to biomass resources. The wood will therefore initially be imported from Canada and Ukraine because these countries have an established supply chain and industry that France still lacks. Some observers unsurprisingly have questioned the carbon efficiency of long-distance imports of wood to meet climate and energy goals. Furthermore, in the longer term other regions beyond the City of Paris are expected to orient their climate and energy plan around biomass, potentially leading to competition for resources given that French producers are unlikely to be able to produce enough wood for the whole country (authors' interview with a City of Paris works department official). Another regulatory constraint is the fact that some biomass components such as wood from construction projects and wooden pallets are classed as 'waste' by French legislation, and therefore are subject to a restriction on their treatment. Some actors have denounced the contradictions of a system which is supposed to be trying to create a biomass industry (authors' interview with a senior advisor to a Parisian politician), and yet is exporting perfectly usable wood pallets to Sweden.

According to the SRCAE, it was intended that geothermal energy as a proportion of the regional energy mix was to increase from 3% to 13% by 2020. This is unlikely to be achieved at time of writing. Geothermal energy requires a lower temperature heating network than CPCU's vapour network (authors' interview with a City of Paris works department official). There can also only be one geothermal well or sink within a certain area to avoid over-extraction problems which can create intermunicipal problems if the area crosses boundaries (authors' interview with a City of Paris official) or even competition over what is actually a limited resource even though Ile-de-France sits on the large Dogger aquifer (authors' interview with a City of Paris works department official). The initial heavy investment required for either large-scale biomass or geothermal production appears to be a significant barrier (authors' interview with a heating company official). Networks using these resources would need to connect to thousands of homes to guarantee any kind of heat load and a return on investment, and this lack of demand has led to the abandonment of possible projects (authors' interview with a City of Paris official).

In sum, infrastructure adjustments, resource flows, contractual and regulatory issues and their techno-political interpretation and mobilization constitute major areas of debate over how to organize the provision of low carbon heating for Paris to meet its climate and energy objectives.

Concluding Reflections

The aim of this chapter has been to use three sites of practice to explore how actors on the ground in the Paris region are grappling with the ongoing challenges of effecting a low carbon sustainability transition across the French capital. We moved from the internal organizational struggles of mobilizing and maintaining energy-climate action within a local authority to the work of Paris planners in producing urban energy knowledge with a view to literally 'grounding' objectives in the urban fabric of Paris, and finally to work going on around infrastructure with a variety of actors toiling to reconfigure pipes, production plants, and resource flows to extend and optimize the availability of low carbon affordable heating across the region, viewed as the primary means of delivering decarbonization. The production of organizational capacity, actionable knowledge, and maneuverable infrastructure constitute key ongoing challenges at the frontline of sustainability practice.

To conclude, we make three brief points about the challenges studied and their wider practical implications for understanding the complexity and dilemmas of urban sustainability. While this appears in some ways to be a story of inertia and path dependency (and indeed 'non-transitioning') from which actors are struggling to extract both themselves and (collectively) the Paris region as a whole, it can be argued that this view relies on an unhelpful imaginary of an end state somehow representing or defining a 'perfect' situation of sustainability/low carbon transition from which we should be backcasting to assess progress along a linear pathway. If we shift perspectives and view sustainability/low carbon as an ongoing, plurivocal process of actual and possible transformation, then the kinds of incremental work practices studied here appear more valuable as they contribute to constituting less fixed and rigid pathways along which we may want to travel, and which can be adjusted and debated more directly. Practical achievements in low carbon transition work can be measured in ways other than direct and quantifiable CO_2 emissions reductions, by 'shared actions' or 'combined efficiencies' of the kind we have seen here.

A first point then is that the persistence of struggles and of a lived politics of sustainability on the ground suggests more of a presence of healthy discussion, deliberation, and dispute over urban futures than an emergence of some kind of post-political shared vision or dominance of technocratic management (Krueger & Gibbs, 2007). There are possibilities of transition here if we argue that political debate is how this change may come about. It may not always 'feel' positive to those living it daily on the ground, but this might just be ecological democracy in action.

Second, there is much to be said for the potential of a more distributed sense of collective action towards sustainability. The sites in this chapter were practiced or managed under shared responsibility, with no real dominant individual, actor, or group, which downplays any idea of choices, decisions, powers, and thus accountability, of any single agent. Furthermore, each site brought up the issue of multiple sustainabilities. Processes and practices were not just around low carbon transition but developed around a parallel mix of wider issues (authority, control, nuclear power, energy dependence) which emerge through contests over particular objects or materials (resources, pipes, contracts, reports, radiators). These often escape control, and thus contribute to shaping possibilities through the shifting contingent positions they occupy within wider relational networks. For practitioners, this means being open to entanglements with an increasingly diverse material world, becoming "compositionists who gather things together while respecting their heterogeneity" (Beauregard, 2015, p. 225).

Third, it is clear that by struggling or muddling through actors are nevertheless engaged in an incremental learning through doing process, and that the importance of this cannot be understated. Indeed, what else can we ask for? Sustainability transition practitioners are dealing with big issues and translating them into local contexts by attempting to increase capacities, diversify knowledge, and make infrastructure more flexible for their actions. Many practitioners are very aware of the tensions, contradictions, and limits of particular measures and initiatives, and a degree of reflexivity and evaluation of work being done is surely useful in forging productive ways of reconnecting planetary concerns and local matters. There is no one permanent path to 'getting it right' and making and maintaining associations which might constitute a sustainability process is a fragile and provisional achievement which will always be challenged politically, technically, and socially—and that's surely a good thing.

There is undoubtedly a need for compelling tales of sustainability futures that can guide, promote, and bring together debate as we anticipate and project urban worlds for 2025, 2050, or whenever. These brief reflections foregrounding sustainability in practice in the Paris region showcase and make visible the little steps and struggles through which the 'bringing together' is actually done, and how meaningful responses to big issues are constructed on a daily basis. Rather than external distant despair at the lack of progress towards some ambitious normative goal, this perspective plays up sometimes quite modest work on the ground but which helps to make sustainability or low carbon transition a more achievable goal.

Notes

1 All the quotations in this chapter which were originally in French have been translated by the authors.
2 The discussion in this chapter draws on research done at different times and to different depths around the three sites, so they are uneven in their approach and content

(hence 'snapshots'). Another method would be to explore the overlaps and intersections between organizational change, knowledge production, and infrastructure shifts through the same actors or authorities, but this would require a different form of in-depth empirical material, and the aim here is not to suggest that these themes or areas of action are the only practical routes to sustainability.

3 The Conseil Général for one of the eight administrative departments of the Paris (Ile-de-France) region.
4 Now called a Plan Climat Air Energie Territorial incorporating air quality as well as climate and energy.

References

Angot, S. (2013). Plans climat-énergie territoriaux et Agendas 21: Des outils institutionnels au service de la transition? *Mouvements*, 75(3), 125–134.

Atelier Parisien d'Urbanisme(APUR) (2007). *Consommations d'énergie et émissions de gaz à effet de serre liées au chauffage des résidences principales parisiennes*. Paris: Atelier Parisien d'Urbanisme.

Atelier Parisien d'Urbanisme(APUR) (2013). *Une plateforme pour un PLU thermique (séminaire 10 juillet 2013)*. Paris: Atelier Parisien d'Urbanisme.

Atelier Parisien d'Urbanisme(APUR) (2014). *Un Plan Local Energie (PLE) pour Paris et la métropole (Note N°81)*. Paris: Atelier Parisien d'Urbanisme.

Beauregard, R. (2015). *Planning Matter: Acting with Things*. Chicago: University of Chicago Press.

Callon, M., Lascoumes, P., & Barthe, Y. (2001). *Agir dans un Monde Incertain: Essai sur la Democratie Technique*. Paris: Editions du Seuil.

Conseil Régional d'Ile-de-France, & Prefet de la Région d'Ile-de-France (2012). *Schéma Régional du Climat, de l'Air et de l'Energie (SRCAE) de l'Île-de-France*. Paris: Conseil Régional d'Ile-de-France/Prefet de la Région d'Ile-de-France.

Emelianoff, C. (2005). Les agendas 21 locaux: Quels apports sous quelles latitudes? *Développement Durable et Territoires*, 4. Retrieved March 23, 2020, from http://developpementdurable.revues.org/532.

Gabillet, P. (2015). Energy supply and urban planning projects: Analysing tensions around district heating provision in a French eco-district. *Energy Policy*, 78, 189–197.

Krueger, R., & Gibbs, D. (Eds.) (2007). *The Sustainable Development Paradox*. New York: Guilford Press.

Mairie de Paris (2012). *Bilan du Plan Climat 2007–2012*. Paris: Mairie de Paris.

Moutarde, N. (2015). Un plan local énergie pour la métropole du Grand Paris. *Le Moniteur*, 20 November. Retrieved March 23, 2020, from www.lemoniteur.fr/article/un-plan-local-energie-pour-la-metropole-du-grand-paris.922334.

Rohracher, H., & Späth, P. (2014). The interplay of urban energy policy and sociotechnical transitions: The eco-cities of Graz and Freiburg in retrospect. *Urban Studies*, 51(7), 1415–1431.

Rutherford, J. (2014). The vicissitudes of energy-climate policy in Stockholm: Politics, materiality and transition. *Urban Studies*, 51(7), 1449–1470.

Chapter 8

Values

Valuing Sustainability in Bordeaux: Should the Grass Be Cut?

Jenny Lindblad

Sunlight reflects off the freshly paved road that cuts through the landscape that is being prepared to host approximately 400 housing units. On one side of the road the ground is covered by packed gravel that marks out where buildings will be constructed. On the other side grass is growing, and there are a few trees and bushes scattered across the area (Figure 8.1). A group of a dozen persons, composed of officials from the local government, project managers who work for the property developer, and me, a researcher, are gazing across an overgrown stretch of land that does not come across as very inviting to the kinds of shoes and clothing that the group is wearing. Our visit to this site located in Bordeaux, France, is part of an evaluation process that unfolds as a full-day workshop during which the construction project's achievement of stated ambitions towards sustainable development are examined. Giselle,[1] who works for the developer, informs the other participants that the wetland in front of us is connected to waterways that have important functions for reducing the risk of flooding in this area close to the Garonne River, and that it has values of biodiversity. A limited part of this parcel of land will be developed, and the rest will be protected. The land is owned by the developer, while the local government's land use plan[2] outlines the regulations that apply to the development. The regulations were prepared to allow for a dense construction project on this site that is located in a residential area that mainly comprises private houses. In the light of the modest requirements of the land use plan as applied to the wetland area, Anne, an official, praises the developer's intention to leave parts of the wetland area unbuilt so as to favor its ecological values. Expressing concern about the continuous care for the area, she asks if there are any plans to ensure that the wetland remains protected after the house-building project has been finalized. Giselle is certain that challenges lie ahead, and anticipates that the new residents will question why the vegetation in the wetland area is left untended unlike in other areas in the neighborhood where the grass is cut regularly. "How can we make people understand why we aren't cutting the grass in the wetland area?" she asks, and proposes that organizing excursions with school children to the area could be an intervention contributing to acceptance among inhabitants. Anne shows support for this idea, and they discuss the possibility of using the site as a pedagogical tool to inform residents in the neighborhood about the ecological values of a wetland area in terms of ensuring biodiversity and preventing flooding.

This chapter centers on the dynamics that emerge from the exchange about the wetland area, namely how sometimes conflicting values that can be attached to a mundane element like grass can create difficulties for practitioners working to protect ecological values, and what conflicting values imply for the achievement of sustainable urban development. Sustainable development is certainly a "wicked problem," as Horst Rittel and Melvin Webber famously say about the problems that planners have to deal with. Scholars have previously emphasized the complexity of conflicting values and what this means for planning practitioners (see, for example, Campbell and Marshall, 1998), and they have inquired about the usefulness of evaluation instruments to assess how effective planning efforts are in achieving sustainable development (see, for example, Hull el al., 2011). The present analysis makes use of valuation studies (Helgesson and Muniesa, 2013) to explore how values in the evaluation process are practically dealt with in relation to two related but distinct operations: *evaluation* and *valorization*. These concepts are used to highlight how the practices of

Figure 8.1 View from the construction site overlooking the recently paved road and the wetland area
Source: Jenny Lindblad.

evaluation shed light on the practical challenge of stabilizing values over time and through changing configurations of actors in construction projects. By exploring practices of valuation, I will arrive at the suggestion that acts of evaluating render visible the unstable nature of values, and that this calls into question the possibility that sustainable development is indeed fully achievable.

Evaluating and Valorizing

In recent years I have studied the planning practices of the local government in Bordeaux.[3] The city authority's stated ambition to construct 50,000 new housing units as outlined in the land use plan is coupled with the intention to leave 50% of the territory unbuilt, in keeping with the city's sustainability policies. While the city proudly announced its firm engagement to reduce urban sprawl, I encountered officials in the planning department who were concerned with a broader variety of sustainability-related issues at stake in urban development projects. In response to this concern, a group of officials tested an evaluation process aimed at considering how various dimensions of sustainability are taken into consideration in the city's many ongoing construction projects. The evaluation process addressed a variety of issues: social diversity; affordable housing; mobility options; energy provision; and biodiversity. In the procedures that I took part in, biodiversity took a prominent role through the question of cutting the grass. The officials with whom I worked directed their attention to the question of grass as a challenge in the sense that even if the ecological biodiversity values of wild-growing grass were generally recognized among professionals at the planning stage of urban development projects, it was uncertain whether these values had been adequately thought through, especially as to how these grasslands might appear at a later stage in the project. To situate this issue in the site visit discussed above, while the ecological value of the grass was established among the professionals standing on the paved road looking at the wetland area, the future inhabitants who will also stand on the same paved road may perceive the value of that same grass quite differently. In what follows, I utilize episodes from an evaluation workshop as a focal point to further outline and discuss the challenge that this entails. The question I ask is if, and perhaps how, such values can be stabilized over a period of time. It is a question that ties into central concerns in agendas for sustainable development and urban planning that is an inherently future-oriented activity concerned with "the transition over time from current states to desired ones" (Abram and Weszkalnys 2011, p. 4). In this chapter, I draw on Mark Whitehead's description of sustainable cities as "a complex hybrid of social, economic, political and ecological forms, which are continually articulated and rearticulated within specific spatial contexts" (2003, p. 1186). In the analysis that follows, sustainability emerges through specific evaluation practices in local development projects as a matter of ecological aspects related to values around vegetation.

The conceptual keyword 'valuation' is chosen for two reasons. First, this chapter examines the work carried out by officials in a city administration performing what they frame as an (e)valuation of sustainability achievements in specific urban construction projects. Second, it recalls the theoretical framing which I make use of in the analysis presented here. In the field of valuation studies that I draw on, valuation is understood to be 'a social practice' which, according to Claes Helgesson and Fabian Muniesa (2013), means that values are constructed and produced through practices, in comparison to the idea of values as absolute or inherent in an action or goods. Meanwhile, Martin Kornberger adds that values understood this way are not "preferences of a subjective mind," but rather "effects of valuation practices" (2017, p. 1754). Valuation understood as coming about through practices presents itself as a suitable way to approach the diverging views on grass that were brought to the fore in the evaluation workshops. Based on a similar approach, François Vatin (2013) has pointed out that the distinction made in the French language between *évaluer* and *valoriser* is useful to distinguish between two types of operations of valuation practices. *Évaluer* means to evaluate, as in assessing the value of an existing good, and *valoriser* means to valorize, as in creating or increasing a value (Vatin, 2013, p. 33). If we take the interactions in the introductory vignette as an example, it may be suggested through the lens of these two value operations that the professionals in the workshop *evaluate* the wild-growing grass as an important ecological feature of the wetland area. Meanwhile, the suggestion to use the wetland area as a pedagogical tool means through which to *valorize* the biodiversity qualities of this same grass that may be challenged and even abandoned once the stewardship of the area is passed to the future residents, and subject to their evaluation of its value. In the rest of this chapter, the two operations of valuation practices—evaluating and valorizing—will guide my analysis of the evaluation workshops and the reflections expressed by the participants in order to address the question of if, and perhaps how, values of sustainable urban development can be stabilized over time.

The Evaluation Process

The administration's evaluation process of construction projects in Bordeaux is a fairly recent innovation, and it exists currently for a trial period. Anne, an official in the department of urban planning, experience of developing the procedure.[4] Based on her experience of the planning and realization of an earlier large construction project with explicit sustainability objectives, Anne identified the need to capitalize on lessons learned from this and to find out to what extent similar projects have achieved their goals. She exemplifies this necessity through an anecdote from her previous experience. In parallel to programming a housing development, the city was preparing a nearby extension of the tram network. However, it was not until further into the programming phase that these two parallel projects were merged, because it was realized that having the tramway pass directly through the new neighborhood would be ideal from a sustainability point of view, since the number of car parking spaces could then be reduced in favor of public transport options. With the reduction of accessibility for cars in the neighborhood came the question of waste management. How could the waste collection stations be placed so that they would be accessible to the garbage trucks, but at the same time easily accessible for residents? Instead of attending to such issues early on in the process, Anne notes that

> the concerns among the councilors [*les élus*] were elsewhere. These issues [i.e., the tram network and waste] were said to be too technical and were therefore put to one side. Certainly, they are very technical, but they could have a massive influence over choices in the planning process.

There was only limited interest among the councilors for allocating money to the evaluation process, although at the time no evaluation process for assessing sustainability policies was in place. The local government has, as several officials noted to me, only a limited "evaluation culture," which was reflected in the absence of a structured return of experiences from recent efforts put into major development projects. As a result of a number of engaged councilors attributing importance to following up on the development projects, the evaluation was eventually granted a budget for a trial period of two years.

The instrument used in evaluations is a guide made up of five booklets that each includes around 50 questions. Each booklet targets a different stage in a construction project: programming; the feasibility of the program; conception of buildings and public spaces; the building site; and the management and use of the finished project. The questions in the booklets were based on the local government's planning documents and sustainability policies, without explicitly reproducing the objectives manifested in those documents. The questions are not formulated so as to address specific targets expressed in those documents, but in a manner that stimulates discussion and reflection among developers about those targets. Anne explains:

> The procedure is based on evaluative questions, and questions on methods. The idea is to prompt the project developers to find out if all the elements have been taken into consideration, and to somehow oblige the developer and the councilors to see 'well then, we didn't pose that question, how could we take it into consideration at this stage, or at least address it'?

The 'elements' that ought to be taken into consideration vary between projects, and there is no set list of elements that each evaluation procedure should address. Ultimately, the 'evaluators'—officials from different city departments—put together a set of questions that they pose during the workshop with a developer. The focus is less on covering general objectives set by the local government, and more on improving the specific objectives of a project, for example to create public spaces that are used by residents, to produce apartments that meet certain environmental standards, or to enhance biodiversity. Certain questions are also addressed in the preparation for the workshop when key actors in the development process are interviewed. Anne stresses that the workshop is intended as "a continual evaluation process" instead of a one-off event. The evaluation procedure is thus formative rather than summative. It is described by its creators as being a means to recall the importance of considering sustainability aspects at different stages of a construction project, to function as a pedagogical device to collect knowledge about experiences gained on different projects, and to be used as a basis for future work. An evaluation is concluded with a report that summarizes positive aspects, aspects that can be improved, and examples of 'best practices' that emerged through the evaluation process. In addition to assisting the developers, "there are also all these notions around education in relation to councilors that are extremely important in this evaluation procedure," Anne specifies. A summary of each report is distributed to the councilors, who are an important target group in that ultimately they formulate the political expectations of construction projects.

Beyond reaching the decision-makers, the coordinating group hopes that the evaluation procedure will contribute to "creating a culture of sustainable urban development" among the variety of actors involved in urban development in Bordeaux. The idea that an evaluation procedure can participate in producing a shared 'culture' resonates with what Vatin describes as a relationship between the assessment and production of value: "*valorization* is present in the acts of *evaluation*, in that they are provisional modalities for establishing a value that is under construction" (2013, p. 45, emphasis in the original). In line with this statement, the workshop can be seen to function as a modality both for evaluating what becomes of the objectives set for a specific construction project, and for constructing values, such as when different values are being discussed in the workshop. The evaluation procedure is thus seen as a form of "valuation practice" (Kornberger, 2017). In what follows, I return to another workshop that was similar to the one in the introductory vignette. At this particular workshop, officials from Bordeaux Métropole met with project managers from a construction development, where some of the residents had already moved into the new dwellings. As was the case at the first workshop, conflicting ideas about the management of the grass emerged.

The Workshop

A group of 15 people are mingling in a room on the second floor of the show house for the recently constructed area that I will call Les Arbres. The site covers approximately 12 hectares and hosts over 800 apartments, office spaces, and a hotel. The construction of a biomass heating plant, together with the classification of the apartments as low energy use, a variety of forms of tenure and apartment sizes, and the creation of one-hectare-sized park favoring biodiversity were important parts of the project's stated ambition to be sustainable. Some of the people in the room seem to know each other already, cheek-kissing upon entering, while others are meeting for the first time, shaking hands and introduce themselves by name and affiliation. Croissants are spread out on paper bags from the nearby pastry shop; powdered coffee, tea bags, and hot water stand on a table from which people serve themselves while talking to one another. The walls in the room are adorned with the plans of the area with illustrations of proposed buildings, streets and the park with wild-growing grass, flowers, birds, and trees. On the opposite side of the street, visible from the room where we meet, the final materialization of the plans stand.

Anne invites everyone to take a seat around the table. One of her colleagues has already provided each place seating with a pen, post-it notes, a file containing documents about Les Arbres, and a folder that holds booklets and summaries of outcomes from previous workshops. Catherine, from the consultancy firm specializing in ecological concerns and citizen participation that took part in developing the evaluation procedure, acts as moderator. She proposes a round of introductions around the table which reveals that those present in the room include the project leader from the development company, architects and the landscape architect from the agency that prepared the designs for the project, municipal officials, metropolitan officials, the person managing the show house and public consultations, colleagues from the consultancy agency, and the president of a local housing association.

The day is organized in blocks around four themes—urbanism, nature/ecology, usage, and governance—which are evaluated separately. The officials and Catherine put questions to the developer and architects. The questions are formulated along the lines of "Have you thought about this?" and "Have you considered that?" During a break I speak with an official who has already participated in several workshops and who shares his impression that the representatives from the development company often appear nervous at the beginning of the day because they are unsure about how the evaluation will proceed. Eventually, the charged atmosphere eases up, he continues, when they notice that the officials are also engaging in an evaluation of the practices of the public administration. This happens today too. Officials repeatedly self-critically assess the actions that the public administration could undertake to help to improve the project, for instance in terms of planning for cyclists and pedestrians. The answers and exchanges crossing the thematic blocks are steered only to a limited degree by the moderator, who asks questions to keep the discussion on track. Each block is concluded with a five-minute reflection period during which every participant writes on post-its, based on the precedent discussions, aspects of the project that they think were exemplary, and aspects that could be improved. Thereafter, each participant presents her or his conclusions by attaching their post-it notes on boards affixed to the wall. Catherine recalls that today everyone is "playing the role of an evaluator." As we will see, this also entails being a 'valuator,' in that during the course of the discussions, a number of values are put into play.

Following a site visit, the members of the group takes their seats to start discussions within the thematic blocks. During the block for 'nature and ecology,' the landscape architecture, Javier, presents his designs for a park that was placed in between the buildings (Figure 8.2). The area was formerly used by industries that left behind polluted soil. Javier explains that they mixed the polluted soil on the site with compost and left it to rest for about a year, by which time its microbiological properties had been restored. "It was necessary to give nature time to recover," in order to create a park as "a space for human beings, but really also as a space for nature," he explains passionately. A variety of plants that were indigenous to the south-east of France were chosen, so that when the first inhabitants arrived, the park was already flourishing and provided a welcoming space for the new residents. Javier adds that a maintenance plan has been drawn up for the park, so that the original conceptualization of the space as a lively biotope will be sustained. Several officials say that they are impressed with the amount of effort put into developing the park, and describe it as a good example of a green space that is considerate not only of human recreation needs but also of ecological values. Then the president of the local housing association intervenes and comments that the inhabitants pay eight euros as part of their monthly fee for the maintenance of the park, yet the grass is rarely cut. For what are we paying, he asks? The landscape architect answers that the park is maintained in various ways, and that the grass is left to grow because it increases the park's biodiversity: "If you leave the grass to grow, the flowers begin to grow, and then insects arrive." This, he states, is the course of biodiversity. "But the park doesn't look tidy when the grass is not cut!" the president exclaims in a disgruntled tone. In response, the landscape architecture refers to diverging "cultural visions," namely that it is necessary to change perceptions of what 'nature' and 'tidy' mean, and that also a park with growing grass requires maintenance although not through cutting. An official suggests that it is necessary to take a pedagogical approach to change perceptions and make residents understand *why* the grass is rarely cut.

The intervention of the president of the housing association evoking a view of uncut grass as 'untidy' upsets what appears to be an established perception among the other participants about its ecological values. The official calling for a pedagogical approach to the problem brings the question of valorization into the evaluation; beyond assessing the current state of the park, it calls for a continuous engagement to enhance the ecological value of the park that might in its current state and management be fulfilled, but that remain unstable. Thus, if the workshop is taken as an isolated incident, it is perhaps possible to contend that the park is exemplary in terms of achieving ecological values of sustainability. However, the president's evocation of conflicting appreciations of the grass, and the professionals' concerns about the stabilization of the park with its unkempt grass draws attention to the possibility that the current exemplarity may be revoked in later stages when shifting configurations of actors are responsible for its maintenance. When the house-building phase has been completed and the participants in the realization of the project have

Figure 8.2 A section of the park area in between the recent constructions
Source: Jenny Lindblad.

moved on to other sites, residents, property owners, and municipal representatives will be involved in determining the course of the park. The following section addresses the relations extending beyond the workshop.

After the Workshop

A few weeks after the workshop, I meet with Anne in her office where she recalls that the purpose of the evaluation was not to assess success or failure in some way, but rather to incentivize the developers to reflect on the choices that have been made and those that have yet to be made, and to continuously learn from experiences of doing sustainable urban development for the benefit of future projects. However, the councilors' initially hesitant support for the evaluation procedure was shadowed by skepticism. Anne suggests that this is due to the fact that

> the word 'evaluation' means judgement. It is really badly viewed because they basically understand it as 'you will look at what we have decided, what we have wanted to make, and you will judge that,' although it is not at all that. ... It is not at all about the evaluation, it is about a continuous progress, about a continuous improvement of projects.

Although Anne and her colleagues expressed a view of the evaluation procedure as a moment of continuous learning from what has been done, to improve what is to be done, the response from the councilors regarding the evaluation procedure signals that they understand it as a moment of judgement. The understanding of the evaluation procedure thus differs. Read through the two analytical concepts of valuation processes, the officials involved in designing and implementing the evaluation procedure approach it as an endeavor of creating and enhancing values (valorizing), while the skeptical view of the councilors resonates with an understanding of the same endeavor as being about formulating static judgements with regard to what has been done (evaluation) (Vatin, 2013).

The lukewarm interest from the councilors was a source of concern when I first met the evaluation coordinators. One year and several workshops later, they encountered another difficulty. Several of the project managers who had participated in the procedure requested modifications of the drafted report summarizing the conclusions drawn from the workshop. In a few cases, the project managers requested modifications to the content and the wording to such an extent that some aspects that were discussed as having the potential for improvement, as well as the critical experiences, were omitted. The reports that got held up in draft form tended to regard projects carried out under the city administration's own management. The coordinating team interpreted this as being due to the fact that the project managers, in their role of officials in the local government, were concerned about the way in which the projects were presented to the councilors. What was readily discussed during the workshop, which was not attended by the councilors, proved to be sensitive in a written medium that was to be made public for a larger audience. It appeared that the meaning of evaluating as assessing and judging static value came to the fore anew, from previously being an obstacle to support from the councilors' for the procedure, to later playing into the possibility to distribute the conclusions from the workshops. The absence of finalized reports meant that the outcomes of the workshops could not be communicated to the intended recipients, namely the councilors. This in turn generated further problems for the continuation of the workshop, since the few finalized reports made it difficult to demonstrate—or valorize—the potential of the evaluation procedure in order to receive a budget for an extended trial period. Furthermore, this also meant that the councilors remained uninformed about the challenges identified during the evaluation procedures, which were meant to feed into subsequent construction projects to anticipate difficulties encountered in previous ones.

The importance of reaching councilors relates to the question of how to stabilize the ecological values of wild-growing grass established among the professionals. "Take the park for example. The question of management is not the problem, the colleagues at the service for green spaces know how to manage the park; the problem is that of public acceptance towards it," Anne explains with reference to the workshop in Les Arbres. She continues:

> It's not the developer, nor is it the design of the park that is the problem. The problem is that the design, which was very well done, could be completely ruined if the mayor, under pressure from the residents for example, demands that the park be mowed every month. And then the park won't have the same added values, the same amenities in the end.

The quotation above certifies that the evaluation procedure intervenes at a specific moment in time, and that, in other words, an evaluation implies an assessment of achievements up until that specific point. If it is understood as a static end point in the realization of the project, it could be concluded in the moment of evaluation that the realization of the park as a site favoring biodiversity is a successful achievement of sustainable urban development. However, the views about grass that are brought to the workshop through the participation of the residents interfere with such conclusions. The use of the spaces and buildings produced through a development project continues when the developer and municipality are no longer in negotiation about the design of the area, and the expectations and experiences of residents and property owners are of more importance. In the case of the Les Arbres project, the design and realization of the park was in the hands of the developer. Eventually, when the project is completed, the responsibility for managing many of the spaces between the houses will be allocated to the municipality. While the municipal councilors were satisfied with the conceptualization of the park as a site for biodiversity, as stated during the evaluation procedure, the changing relations that occur when residents occupy the spaces and express expectations about the park may reverse their initial support for wild-growing grass.

An official concluded that what needs to be communicated to councilors is that "you can design the most ecological park possible, but if you do not explain why the park is maintained in this or that way ... it will never work." It is required that councilors "carry the project politically" if contested issues are to be handled in favor of values that counter expectations expressed by residents, and generally mayors and councilors are sensitive to the opinions of the electorate. Therefore, one of the ambitions emphasized by the coordination group was to demonstrate to the councilors the importance of specific actions if ecological values are to be maintained. Giselle's suggestion about the need to educate residents about ecological values, and Anne pointing to the risk that a mayor under pressure from local residents might reverse the decision not to cut the grass are examples of how the professionals are concerned with valorizing, as one example among other sustainability related issues, the presence of unkempt grass. Their concerns correlate with the kind of operation that valorizing implies, i.e., to continuously create and enhance certain values so that the desired values (of professionals) continue to guide decisions about the management of spaces such as a park, and thus are stabilized for a longer period throughout the different phases of a construction project.

Should the Grass Be Cut?

The overarching aim that I set out for this chapter was to explore questions of how, and if, sustainability values established by a group of professionals can be stabilized in the case of a construction project. The experiences from the evaluation workshops suggest that values can be temporarily established among a group of actors involved with the conceptualization and realization of a construction project. However, the lesson from Bordeaux points to how sustainable urban development rests on temporary achievements that always hold the potential of being reversed. Doing sustainable urban development involves aligning efforts, attention, and resources across time and tensions. Although established among one group of actors, values always hold the potential of being altered so that arriving at a conclusion that sustainability has been *achieved* in a construction project is misleading. If it is an achievement, it is one that constantly has to be reperformed as circumstances change—for instance when residents move into an area and start to question why the seemingly scruffy grass is not being cut.

That sustainability is never achieved in an absolute sense brings into question what is at stake in the evaluation procedure: does the challenge lie in the practice of evaluating what became of the specific sustainability objectives set for a construction project, or does the challenge pertain to something more fundamental, potentially ontological, about the nature of values? While both options certainly qualify as challenges, the constant eventuality of value-regimes changing makes the work of doing sustainable urban development a continuous endeavor without a clear end state, which the evaluation procedure makes tangible. The evaluation procedure, built on a formative approach, attends to the unachievable dimension of sustainable development. Developed to evaluate construction projects at different phases of their realization, the evaluation results in praising exemplary achievement from specific project at specific stages of its realization. Simultaneously, it encompasses a prospective view cautioning that although temporarily established, ecological values require continuous valorization, and maintenance, in order to be stabilized. The way in which the evaluation procedure unfolds fosters engagement with questions of how construction projects can *be* sustainable. In this case, *being* is not intended as an adjective, such as when a construction project earns a label or certification of being a 'sustainable neighborhood.' Considered through two value operations, the production of labels may certainly have valorizing effects (Kornberger, 2017), but understood as assessments of how well sustainable development objectives are reached, they can only be considered as telling about the achievements up until the point of the labelling. Being sustainable requires the continuous alignment of efforts, attention, and resources, since an achievement at one point in time may be overthrown and rendered considerably unsustainable later on. The experiences of the difficulties to achieve a park, for example, with stabilized ecological values put into question the possibilities of arriving at the highly placed ambitions. The formative evaluation procedure does little to emphasize success or final achievements. If it can be agreed that sustainability is unachievable in any absolute sense (there will always be conflicts and contradictions between valuations of sustainability among groups of professionals, councilors, and inhabitants), the models for appreciating and evaluating construction projects should allow for acknowledging achievements of sustainability as temporary, but achievements none the less. Thus, instead of being directed at objectives such as achieving a '*sustainable city*,' attention can be directed at *how* ecological values can be established, and stabilized, in specific construction projects with varying conditions.

By exploring the dynamics involved in the question of cutting or not cutting the grass, the study about evaluation practices in Bordeaux demonstrates how work towards sustainable urban development is a matter of micro decisions that are taken during the course of a construction project, as well as in the sets of relations that emerge following the completion of the construction phase. Through the act of evaluating, values are established and assessed, but also negotiated and created (Vatin, 2013). A dilemma made visible through the practices of evaluation is how values established among a group of professionals during a particular stage in a construction project can be valorized and stabilized throughout later appropriations of sites invested with care for specific values. The work done by professionals in the (e)valuation workshop around the multifaceted nature of things as mundane as grass brings to the fore the challenges involved in sustainable urban development. It also brings attention to the fact that this line of work is continuously, although temporarily, achieved.

Notes

1 All names are pseudonyms, for the purpose of anonymity.
2 The land use plan (*Plan local d'urbanisme*) outlines detailed zoning regulations for the territory of Bordeaux Métropole. The land use plan is subordinate to the town planning code (*code de l'urbanisme*).
3 The local government is Bordeaux Métropole, an intercommunal grouping of 28 municipalities. This chapter builds on seven months of fieldwork during a two-year period (2016–2018) that I carried out as part of my PhD research. During the fieldwork I met with officials, planners, and politicians working with metropolitan sanctioned land-use planning. The material is constituted of interviews, participation and observations from meetings among officials, public gatherings revolving around urban development, and complementary studies of documentation from the public administration. I also participated in meetings among officials and developers, such as the workshops presented in this chapter.
4 This chapter is primarily based on exchanges with professionals participating in the evaluation process. Evidently, more persons than those who are introduced in this chapter have stakes in the presented practices. However, since the aim of this edited volume is to explore challenges encountered in practices of doing sustainable development, I chose to focus on the perspectives conveyed by the professional participants in the evaluation process.

References

Abram, S., & Weszkalnys, G. (2011). Introduction: Anthropologies of planning—Temporality, imagination, and ethnography. *Focaal* (61): 3–18.

Campbell, H., & Marshall, R. (1998). Acting on principle: Dilemmas in planning practice. *Planning Practice & Research*, 13(2), 117–128.

Helgesson, C.F., & Muniesa, F. (2013). For what it's worth: An introduction to valuation studies. *Valuation Studies* 1(1): 1–10.

Hull, A., Alexander , E.R.., Khakee, A., & Woltjer, J. (Eds.) (2011). *Evaluation for Participation and Sustainability in Planning*. London: Routledge.

Kornberger, M. (2017). The values of strategy: Valuation practices, rivalry and strategic agency. *Organization Studies*, 38(12): 1753–1773.

Rittel, H.W.J., & Webber, M.M. (1973). Dilemmas in a general theory of planning. *Policy Sciences*, 4(2): 155–169.

Vatin, F. (2013). Valuation as evaluating and valorizing. *Valuation Studies* 1(1): 31–50.

Whitehead, M. (2003). (Re)analysing the sustainable city: Nature, urbanisation and the regulation of socio-environmental relations in the UK. *Urban Studies*, 40(7): 1183–1206.

Chapter 9

Programming
Programming Urban Transitions in Practice

Jonas Bylund

I am a programmer. Like the software tinkering type, I am tasked with supporting and knocking out thematic content and strategic relations for JPI Urban Europe. The latter is spelled out Joint Programming Initiative, so fortunately it makes sense to be a programmer in that context. But programming means research and innovation funding and support means not only serving the community of practice with calls for funding, but also to shape opportunities and an ecosystem in support of the program's objectives. The main objective is to support urban research and innovation to tackle the societal challenge of urban transitions and transformations towards sustainable—and livable—urban futures in Europe and around the world. These types of programs with thematically oriented calls for funding are not uncommon in national contexts. The European Union (EU) also puts a lot of emphasis on Horizon 2020, the current Framework Programme (2014–2020) that specifies EU research and innovation support and funding, on calls, and somewhat less emphasis on programming. Although there are some transnational programming environments coordinated by it such as ERA-NET Cofund actions,[1] European Innovation Partnerships (EIPs) and European Institute of Technology (EIT) networks. Beyond Europe, the Belmont Forum is a similar outfit to JPI Urban Europe. However, the so-called public-to-public (P2P) transnational character is somewhat of a hallmark for the JPIs.

JPIs were borne out of the European Research Area (ERA) along with a plethora of other and European Commission (EC) driven instruments (such as the ERA-NETs, European Innovation Partnerships (EIPs), and European Cooperation in Science and Technology (COST)). This type of action was set up to enable European countries, primarily EU member states but not restricted to these, to cooperate transnationally with national programming funds around societal and grand challenges. Drawing on the Lund Declaration of 2009, this cooperation would be challenge-driven (Lund Declaration, 2009). JPI Urban Europe is thus a member states' initiative for tackling the grand challenge of urban transitions to sustainable and livable cities and urban areas.

Although the approaches to how the challenges each JPI tackles varies among JPIs, they are required to be articulated in a Strategic Research and Innovation

Agenda (SRIA). It is literally a script and is analogous to the software programs. It lays out why, what, and how. Hence, this is also where the programming gets more 'joint' in terms of the member states having to sign off the main objectives and approaches it presents (along with a blessing by the EC).

Programming Dilemmas?

JPI Urban Europe recently updated its SRIA to outline challenges and approaches for beyond 2020 (see JPI Urban Europe, 2019). This chapter draws on experiences of situations typically occurring in and around the drafting of this update.

The drafting of this agenda was a 'difficult doing' when it comes to thematic content in sustainable urbanization. Not for the writing itself, but for the kind of programming JPI Urban Europe set up as its ambition: to tackle sustainable urbanization co-creatively and in a transdisciplinary manner.

It would have been easy to simply commission a couple of renowned professors to generate a text that outlines the state of urban sustainability transitions and what priorities we should aim to include in our program beyond 2020. Easy, but probably not very sensible. It would certainly be scientifically interesting. Unfortunately, this approach does not get us very far, since any single type of actor group affected by urban developments (a 'stakeholder') of course filters and molds these matters according to their perspective. Science, in a clumsy and blunt categorization of a set of specific knowledge practices, is in this sense not exceptional, even if the types of knowledge generated by scientific approaches to research do aim at a specific kind of robustness beyond rhetoric. The point here is that if anything, all types of stakeholders are exceptional. And, of course, programmers filter and mold too! But to simply present the current and (probably) coming urban societal challenge in a framing made by only one of these groups to all the others does not shape the ground for much traction.

It is a bit like the proverb that was popularized by Al Gore and others:

> If you want to go fast, go alone;
> If you want to go far, go together.

JPI Urban Europe needs to make the SRIA make sense for more actors than research and policy. We found out, during the SRIA process of consultations, that in order to 'go together,' a dilemma-driven approach may be the best way to identify and construct thematic priorities. The dilemma-driven approach in the JPI Urban Europe understanding is that dilemmas are commonplace tension gradient spaces, a bit like the paradox-vaults that Bornemark (2019) devised to explore tensions through practical philosophy. Furthermore, they are essentially wicked issues, which means that there is no high ground of facts to simply short-cut the way to resolve dilemmas.

The overall argument on the usefulness in proposing to program the thematic priorities would be that JPI Urban Europe aims to create knowledge and evidence for urban transitions and acknowledges that it has to consider dilemmas as competing targets and strategies due to the complexity of urban matters (cf. e.g., Amin & Thrift, 2016). Hence, dilemmas are also identified and loosely outlined in the SRIA in order to highlight the need for (policy) action and to address such issues through programmed activities, partly in calls for research and innovation, but also through dialogues across stakeholder groups to deal with different interests, and so on. Thus, the focus is on main transition pathways and call for research and innovation to address the related dilemmas, and critical and cross-cutting issues in order to move forward.

In order to describe how this works, I would like to show some of the settings where much of this work is done. These are four vignettes functioning as snapshots of the typical policy and research settings in which the dilemma-driven approach is supposed to work. Through the notion of *programming*, this chapter will be an autoethnography of sorts. That is, it is a short reflection on how urban sustainability is a difficult doing which seems to require, in the case of research and innovation programming—particularly transnational programming—a dilemma-driven approach to shape communication lines between more or less loosely connected urban related fields, issues, sectors, or silos. In line with this, the chapter concludes with the last vignette that is a reflection on academic knowledge practices as exemplified by the setting where the papers this book initially draws upon were presented and examined.

Typical Situations for Agenda Setting

There are at least three working environments I keep returning to in my everyday practice of programming which mainly involves translating policy and strategic lines into operational matter in JPI Urban Europe. Apart from typical institutional and conference center-style meeting spaces, and of course my own office space in Stockholm (well, actually just a borrowed desk in an activity-based office landscape), not to mention my 'mobile office' by working anywhere I can, such as on trains, planes, and in airports. The latter type of working space is not very specific for this line of work. There is some sense of work being done in relatively even proportions among these spaces, but it is also laptop work and less human face-to-face interaction. Rather, I want to highlight a couple of the more specific ones. One such working environment is an EU Committee of the Regions plenary room. The other is a 'grey meeting room' at the Directorate-General (DG^2) Research and Innovation. Both types of work space are located in Brussels. I single out these two spaces since they evoke something of the policy-maker in everyday knowledge practice space. The third and fourth types are more conventional academic conference and seminar situations.

Vignette 1: A High-Level Policy Conference Setting

In the plenary, everyone is focused on the 'panel' with the chair (see Figure 9.1). The space is designed to centralize the chairperson who (supposedly) directs and moves the exchange. Of course, a funneling of perspectives, literally and cognitively, is intended, towards the leader or the chief of the day. This is also supported by 'protocol.' It is a part of the protocol not 'mattered' by spatial attributes. Almost ritualistic, it is not a place for too much creativity on the spot. It is for reporting and negotiation on (usually) known positions. Challenges, such as where to find knowledge and solutions to European economic growth and regional development, are typically elaborated here. Someone may question statements delivered from the 'stage,' mostly using a very diplomatic tone and choice of phrasing. Rarely do we hear statements or articulations challenged per se. Discussions turn more by implicit statements between the lines, like code, like encrypted messages that mean very different things to those 'in the know' and those who are not. Being in the know is of course a main point of this part of policy development and negotiation. For instance, it is almost customary to avoid talking about 'problems,' and problematic issues are consequently re-coded as 'challenges,' something which gives the policy practice a positive outlook rather than wallowing in the negative, so to speak.

Vignette 2: The Policy-Makers' Meeting Room

The EC meeting rooms are typically called something like 7.A149 and they are rather grey rooms usually without windows (see Figure 9.1). Although some of these meeting rooms have windows to the hallways, whose walls are also grey, the windows somehow light up the meetings. You see other people walking and working outside. Inside the meeting room, the grey of the walls is actually accentuated by one or two A2 posters highlighting one or the other policy action line and intensely red chairs are placed around the table. Otherwise, these meeting rooms are typical of those found in the DG Research and Innovation in Square Frère Orban, Brussels. They are located in the heart of the building with two parallel hallways on each side so that the staff offices can have windows that let in the daylight. These are about 20 meters long and perhaps six meters wide, with tables positioned in a U-shape. So, you feel oddly distant from the other side of the table, even if it is actually quite close. Usually, EC staff seems to place themselves on the one side of the room and external people on the other. These meeting rooms are also much more focused on PowerPoint presentations on screens than the plenary kind. Talks revolve around things in the making, about ambitions and activities, about policies and action lines that may or should connect to or even support each other. Or they focus on the bureaucrats' braids of intricate schemes and plans for implementation. In my experience, these talks are usually more informal and outspoken yet still tend to dodge conflicts and friction.

Programming 133

Figure 9.1 Photo (left) taken at the JPI Urban Europe Policy Conference 2019, in the plenary room of the Committee of the Regions, EU. Photo (right) shows a typical meeting room with the EC Interservice Group on Urban Development. Both settings are located in Brussels.
Source: Jonas Bylund.

Vignette 3: An Academic Conference Panel

Another common but slightly different kind of setting is a typical research conference session. Perhaps it is not entirely conventional in terms of how we are seated in the particular sample here. We sit in a circle, or rather in an ellipsoid formation and on swing chairs with wheels. It is a roundtable session, but without a table. The session's panelists are mixed with other participants. Even if this physical-material-bodily organization of sessions is not uncommon today, it is a stark contrast to both the Brussels' plenary and the grey room presented above. The session has been convened to discuss 'whither urban sustainability' with the Association of European Schools of Planning's (AESOP) community of practice.

A huge turnout, there are many participants in the room. There seems to be a vigorous interest in the questions posed during the session around whether urban sustainability has been outmoded. Many of us have been primed by the conference keynote that took place two hours earlier, when the Science and Technology Studies researcher John Law spoke of the political implications of 'mistranslations' between actor groups.

Jonathan, the roundtable initiator, makes a brief introductory remark, and the panelists follow with five-minute opening comments. Then the next one and a half hours go by swiftly in almost a blink of an eye. As the session moves along, there is a very engaged but polite atmosphere. I realize I forgot to turn on the GenderTimer, a tool that allows me to measure the share of speaking, as it would have been interesting to document the proportion of talking time between men and women. The discussions revolve around criss-crossing issues related to the overarching concern on how to research contemporary urban sustainability, such as application and bid-writing tactics (of course, my ears are particularly sensitive to these things!), to reflections on the academic practice of sustainability. As an aside, I also note that there is less talk framed around urban specifics, which may indicate that the planetary concerns with current urbanization have reached the point whereby most societies are considered as almost synonymous to urban life. Reflections are also articulated on topics such as planning studies' sense of what planners actually do when they do 'sustainability,' on the more radical and less utilized parts of the Brundtland Report, on the impasse of ecological modernization as the operationalization of Brundtland, and the whereabouts of Agenda 21 nowadays. To my ears, however, two main positions develop out of the statements and comments made by the pannelists and participants (I will leave these for now and return to them later). The session ends less by conclusion than by calls for continued reflection and networking on these matters.

The Typical Settings Slightly Reflected

The three settings described above are important to understand in terms of how very differently their dialogues and debates are cultivated. That is, they are important for programming in the field of urban research and innovation, since they also refract what is one of the main difficulties in doing urban programming today—at least in the European context. It is difficult because of the fragmentation of sectors, issues, and policy lines, which at times are driven by almost incongruent urban imaginaries, logics, and knowledge practices.

The first two types of settings—i.e., the policy-oriented ones—usually generate quite incoherent discussions. Diverse kinds of details and aspects are proposed to the overall line or concern under discussion. Generally, the practice revolves around testing what can be added to and integrated into a document or action line in a policy, and what can be deduced, its congruency to existing policy, how to move it along, or what can be inserted to make it go in a new direction. When urban matters are handled in these two kinds of spaces, they come with different urban concepts, and different entry points to this imbroglio are represented or articulated. Some actors search for the larger and more comprehensive view, others seemingly assume they already have it. All of course are in favor of sustainable urbanization—somehow.

What we also often see or indeed experience in both these settings is the archipelagic sense of urban development. It is archipelagic since both in transnational and most national policy, as well as in research and innovation, fields and frontline issues are clustered in a non-symmetrical way that looks a lot like smaller and bigger islands clumped together with varying distances between them.[3] It is asymmetrical in that the fragmentation is not even, and clusters have more or less connectivity in between them. The policy lines discussed concerning or relating at times more or less to urban sustainability are rarely shaped or articulated by urban studies scholars. Even if integration and systemic approaches may be an explicit desire, there are still strong gravitational wells that seem to generate sectoral outlooks and issue clusters. In other words, it seems that the actors here talk a lot more about transitions in various fields or sectors, and struggle with the (perhaps) knee-jerk reaction to want to see 'the urban' as a more clear-cut sector, which it typically overflows.

A main complication here, to quote Rancière, lies in the un- or semi-recognized 'disagreement':

> Disagreement is not the conflict between one who says white and another who says black. It is the conflict between one who says white and another who also says white but does not understand the same thing by it or does not understand that the other is saying the same thing in the name of whiteness.
>
> (Rancière, 1999, p. x)

Because of the urge to avoid friction, someone may talk about 'urban planning' and why it needs this or that support or this or that deregulation, and not realize the multitude of understandings of what urban planners actually do. I have heard high-level policy actors in plenary panels characterize urban planners as the ones simply 'drawing stuff on maps,' others are depicted as managing urban development projects, and still more as the strategic economic growth mediators. Some conceive them as simply a (national and EU) policy implementation function. And so on. Of course, these different senses of 'whiteness' matter when policies and funding in different sectors and along different urban logics are crafted.

The academic situation also deals with the urban archipelago of imaginaries, but (not surprisingly) in a more reflexive manner. However, a main difference is the manner in which it welcomes and seeks friction between positions. This means that it typically revolves around debates on differing ontological strategies. Although the academic roundtable session described in the vignette above gathered participants more or less from planning studies and urban studies, hence somewhat aligned on certain baseline issues such as 'what is the "urban"?' or 'what do planners actually do?,' the more open contestation also highlighted different ontologies in how these baseline issues are understood. A kind of assemblage of standpoint theories emerges, that in some cases tries to assimilate and conquer others, in efforts to test ideas and offer possible ways to refurbish them, etcetera. Various academic sessions and conferences do show different balances between these practices.

As mentioned above, a case in point was the two positions that emerged in the roundtable between what I quickly labeled 'centralization' and, somewhat hastily, 'emergings-in-practice.' Centralization revolves around a 'scientific' way to go about shaping strong leaders, or even *a* strong leader, to drive sustainable urbanization. What seems to be needed, according to this position, is a new master narrative and charismatic person who can be used to align us all to realize urban sustainability. Emergings-in-practice, a more networked approach and one that is open to variations on the sense of sustainability as a platform, seems to argue for the need and practice of urban sustainability as a plastic notion that connects, but does not cover. It is more of taking at face value how urban sustainable development has developed both in practice and in academic fields.

Now, in terms of the role of dilemma-driven approaches in programming, the latter seems important to me, since I draw upon the practices experienced in the first two vignettes, the policy settings. Because of the archipelagic character of issues and approaches in sustainable urbanization, there seems less use for, let alone resources to, recentralize and shape a new unitary urban paradigm.

Programming Dilemmas

> We are like sailors who on the open sea must reconstruct their ship but are never able to start afresh from the bottom. Where a beam is taken away a new one must at once be put there, and for this the rest of the ship is used as support. In this way, by using the old beams and driftwood the ship can be shaped entirely anew, but only by gradual reconstruction.
>
> (Otto Neurath quoted in Cartwright et al., 2008, p. 191)

The main challenge for a practitioner in this landscape of fragmented urban imaginaries seems to be programming for urban research and innovation with the aim of promoting sustainable urbanization. That is, how to shape and move forward support and enabling activities for sustainable urbanization or the United Nations Agenda 2030 Sustainable Development Goal (SDG) 11.

But to achieve these goals—i.e. how to program urban research and innovation in a challenge-driven way—it makes less sense to simply restate them in a call and program environment, since they are typically manifested differently in different places. An interface is required to translate the particular challenge characteristics for urban stakeholders into e.g. a call. That is, challenge-driven is more than the opposite of 'blue skies' or curiosity-driven approaches. Working with challenge-driven research and innovation does not exclude curiosity—quite the contrary. But it has to do with power issues in terms of who is invited to actually take part in and frame the challenge. Ideally, it is the so-called problem owners, those directly affected by the issue, concern, or problem, who should be given sufficient room to articulate what the challenge looks like.

For sustainable urbanization, this is frequently translated into a call for city authorities (usually simply 'cities' in policy jargon) to explicate what they need and what obstacles they face in realizing sustainable urban areas, the logic presumably being that the territorial administrative authority also enables them to represent a city in its operative urbanity, so to speak. In practice, city authorities usually deliver cogent problems and issues as priorities, at times with the help of research or consultancy, but seldom in contradiction of national research and innovation or other societal policy (such as those concerning e.g. migration) or in divergence with urban research fields' focus.

Urban sustainability as a *societal* or grand challenge, then, to elaborate the EU line on challenge-driven programming, was a call for policy and research and innovation systems to understand the challenges that European societies face. These challenges were to be understood less in rigid thematic categories, and more along how these challenges actually criss-cross sectors, thematics, disciplines, silos, and so on, in various ways, and for European national programming and EU programming to align so as to better tackle them together. An important part here, to boost this inter- and transdisciplinary approach, was the call for affected actors, problem owners as well as potential 'solution providers,' to mutually engage through coming together and co-creating challenge specifications, as well as suggestions for how to tackle them. Thus, the Lund Declaration called upon EU member states to move beyond the rigid thematic focus in research and innovation cooperation and to "focus on the grand challenges of our time ... Identifying and responding to Grand Challenges should involve stakeholders from both public and private sectors in transparent processes taking into account the global dimension" (Lund Declaration, 2009, p. 1)

Ten years after the Lund Declaration, JPI Urban Europe, a transnational programming collaboration which is borne out of this line as well as the societal challenges pillar in Horizon 2020, drafted its second agenda—SRIA 2.0. The dynamics in urban research and innovation and policy debate settings by this time, roughly outlined above, made us realize that integrated urban thematic priorities (as in the SRIA 2015 and in line with the Leipzig Charter) still made it difficult to connect or 'invite' a broader, more inclusive set of actors, stakeholders, and publics into the programming. Extensive public and open consultations, national consultations, held when drafting the SRIA 2.0 was pointing to different types of friction, disagreement, and conflict between academic communities, between innovation genres, between city representatives and policy-makers, between civil society representatives and industry, and between thematic islands in the urban archipelago of issues, sectors, and disciplines. What to do?

My colleague asked the daring question, "what if we treat the thematic areas as dilemmas instead of thematic priorities?" The idea was that it would be very difficult for us to synthesize the both divergent and 'mixed-up' issue understandings that were articulated in the consultations. Rarely was there a clearly formulated 'mobility issue,' 'energy issue' or 'social issue.' More importantly, such a synthesis would just be yet another standpoint and position among many others. Furthermore, what many of the consultations showed was a lack of trust among actors—and in particular argued that other types of actors had got it wrong or were on the wrong track. It was also, in different manners, suggested that the main reason why issues are not tackled was that other actors refuse to proceed in the correct 'white' —to use Rancière's example—fashion.

The reason I thought that the dilemma-driven approach was daring was not because phrasing these challenges as dilemmas is a particularly new thing. It actually builds upon classic planning craft in terms of understanding complexities and conflicts in urban development. (I am still a bit confounded as to "why didn't I think of this before?"; instead, it was my colleague with no background in planning or urban studies who thought of it.) The idea also resonates quite well with what in science and technology studies and political philosophy has been explored as issue-oriented approaches and agonistic democracy (see e.g., Marres, 2010).

If we now revisit the vignettes, they showcase at least two very different but connected ways of handling dilemmas in urban sustainable development. Both tend to keep them at arm's length. The first, the policy setting, does so with some difficulties around the conflicts and frictions involved. Why? It is centralized and usually riddled with power games, but has a fear of conflict. The other, academic research, may perhaps revel or even wallow in dilemmas and complexities. But to some extent it also cops out by tending to quickly take sides. In planning studies and urban studies at least, there are better and worse sides, and dilemmas are not necessarily seen as trade-offs. Apart from this, the more important aspect that differentiates the two types of knowledge practices is perhaps the approach to conflict. And this difference is not necessarily a bad thing, since it shapes an affordance for agony on the policy side instead of antagonizing too much; and it still enables research to put pressure on and test relations, explore complexities, and fulfil the commission to reflect upon issues, provide suggestions on ways forward as well as potential challenges along the suggested pathways. It is a division of labor at times perhaps forgotten on both sides, when researchers expect the policy side to follow the researcher logic of practice and vice versa. Of course, for *both* sides, bringing in other stakeholder expectations in this makes it quite cumbersome.

In the SRIA 2.0 drafting, the dilemma-driven approach was developed to reshuffle conventional lines and issues a bit:

> In its simple definition, a dilemma means having to decide between two or more alternatives that seem equally desirable or undesirable. However, dilemmas may also mean difficult situations where the path taken is not clearly beneficent and the need to compromise continuously appears. In other words, typical implementation, transition, and innovation situations.
> ...
> [U]rban transitions and sustainable urban development usually involve many different (sub)targets, which often result in a set of strategies or actions pursued in parallel or disconnected from each other. While some targets support each other, others conflict across administrative departments, sectors, or societal groups.

> In an interconnected and hyper-complex urban environment in constant motion—practitioners and strategists oftentimes encounter dilemmas rather than simple problems with an easy fix readily available off the shelves.
>
> (Wrangsten & Bylund, 2018)

What the dilemma-driven approach is intended to inspire is to take seriously and to dare fragmentation, nudge interfaces, and invite connectivity through grounded and warranted assemblage layers in order to be congruent with a post-foundationalist view and ontology and the urban setting and its subjects as multi-epistemological and plural knowledge practices. It is a bit like an inquiry into 21st-century urbanism—what urban studies does *during* transitions, to support rebuilding the ship at sea.

Interestingly, not all—and researchers in particular—harbor the intuition we use to suss out the frictions and connectivities: some actually hand back or propose typical research questions that run along sectoral lines, do not really pick up the wickedness, or they simply 'revolt' against why two (or more) 'incongruent areas' are pitted together by the JPI Urban Europe staff.

The dilemma-driven approach is important from a methodological point of view as well in that it serves to unsettle any given (or taken) distinction between 'resources' and 'subject matter.' Looking at urban transition issues from a dilemma point of view therefore means that your instruments and tools to survey, and perhaps remedy, are not necessarily innocent. In this respect, the dilemma-driven approach is even closer to standpoint theory, in the sense that it is an effort to support open approaches and dissuade arrogant 'God's eye views' on urban challenges, and moves away even more from technocratic responses to challenges (a type of response that even a challenge-driven approach may succumb to).

IV: A New Hope

The challenge of programming in the field of urban research and innovation for sustainable urbanization is fraught with hype and superficial victories, while many of the 'heavy' issues remain untackled to a large extent. Hence, the dilemma-driven approach was developed also with the hope that we can now pursue and programme more of the issues that are 'hard to reach,' a way to 'step up the game' (cf. de Jong et al., 2018). In order to do this more inclusive and fewer scapegoating approaches are required. So, one of the reasons for us to develop the dilemma-driven approach is to increase the stakeholder or simply actor connectivity.

This connectivity has been made conscious over the last decades, more and more in policy, in science and technology studies, in urban transitions/studies, in urban and regional planning, at least partly thanks to the broad adaptation of the idea of the Anthropocene. Stakeholder engagement has made a general impact, if not on urban development craft and everyday practices then at least in its discourse and visions. Some of the main reasons for this are that (a) it is relatively well accepted that technocracy did not get us very far; and that (b) the types of societal challenges we are facing are too complex for a single-set solution. And currently we are not just witnessing the proliferation of the typical highly scripted 'citizen dialogues' of planning, but also ambitions to find ways to allow a more diverse set of actors to present their points of view and perspectives on challenges. This is what then shapes a substantial challenge-driven innovation, one that may be well suited to tackle the UN Agenda 2030 Sustainable Development Goals (Kabisch et al., 2019).

From a programming point of view, a challenge-driven approach means that public actors take a lead to support co-creation among a diverse set of actors as well as transnational collaboration to tackle and shape innovative ways to deal with the complex and frequently wicked issues in today's societies. In order for these issues to be categorized as a challenge, they need to show a critical need or problem in society at large and to be defined by the problem owners themselves by drawing on their everyday practices. New business opportunities and markets are expected in the wake of this convergence of resources and innovativeness. In other words, the 'tradition' of the challenge-driven approach underpins what the forthcoming EU research and innovation framework programme Horizon Europe calls 'missions' (cf. Mazzucato, 2018).

In terms of programming, these missions are somehow 1950s-style innovation management recycled. It still means that commercial entrepreneurs are not the heroes of the myth that dominated many contemporary Western societies since the 1980s. Mazzucato makes a very good point: an overwhelming part of the risk in innovation has always been on the public side. The commercial side does not really have any business models for radical innovation or systemic transitions.

If we take into account the current experimental ethos in local urban policy and planning, development, etc., for various aspects of sustainable urbanization, then at least I could reimagine my job as part of an urban transitions mission. Hence, there is a good argument why we should let the public money and research and innovation do the cutting-edge stuff—the risky stuff—again.

So, that is a kind of conceptual European transnational policy setting where urban sustainability and the challenges faced in programming for sustainable urbanization are to be found.

What Is Required for Transdisciplinary Settings to Work?

This programming environment hence points to the need for transdisciplinary ways of working, in the sense that 'the system' is not a linear conveyor belt between so-called basic research over applied to 'uptake' at the end of the line, but rather a landscape of concurrent knowledge practices processing and ecologizing—whereby science is but one type of family in the biome, so to speak. This leads us to the second occasion and actually the main reason for this chapter, as a reflection on some aspects of the difficult doing of programming sustainable urbanization research and innovation. This is the 'Difficult Doings: Investigating the Challenging Practice of Sustainable Urban Development' research workshop held in Cambridge, UK, in April 2018. It was organized mainly in the context of the Organizing Sustainable Cities project, which was a transnational research project to gauge how sustainability is actually used or practiced in contemporary urban planning and development work. However, there were also trace elements of the Decode project which was a transdisciplinary project with the objective to develop knowledge practices suited to sustainable urbanization. The workshop mingled the two projects as well as external guests from both practice (such as myself) and research. Papers were presented by project participants and practitioners were invited to give talks about their challenges in and around urban sustainability. In other words, it was a transdisciplinary setting.

Vignette 4: A Transdisciplinary Workshop

The point of the Cambridge workshop was, in my understanding, to enable a dialogue between academic researchers and practitioners in urban policy and planning, with a specific emphasis on how dilemmas in urban sustainable development are actually handled in everyday settings. As the invitation phrased it:

> There are innumerable academic studies of sustainable urban development. However, surprisingly few of these actually take a 'view from practice,' based upon the concrete and practical challenges of the everyday work experience of those who are tasked with realizing such ambitions.

In terms of transdisciplinarity, there was an ambition to at least open the gates. The Cambridge workshop was set up with a less explicit intention by the organizers, i.e., to find a tentative answer to the question of what is required for transdisciplinary settings to work. As noted below, it was not very clear to what degree any of the papers were actually generated in a transdisciplinary mode; however, the point was for the workshop itself to be such a setting. Nonetheless, there was some kind of chiasm between two types of reflections on an area which was more of one of the types of actors' 'backyard,' so to speak, that was built into the workshop from the beginning.

The workshop was a seminar in the sense of a space set up to test propositions on the world (the urban planners' practical worlds). Participating in the role of practitioner, I was asked to put the academic papers to trial with a view to determining what relevance they might have to my practical world. That is, it was not quite transdisciplinarity in the sense of 'generating and creating together' but rather something like kneading and processing prototypes that had already been designed, even if the materials in some of the papers were generated through the bona fide transdisciplinary circumstance of the Decode project.

Furthermore, it is certainly possible that the researchers and the practitioners gained some kind of transdisciplinary added value out of each other during their encounter. The more troubling issue may rather be around how the academic researchers work with their materials to shape academic currency. That is, their orientation towards having a bearing on debates and research frontiers that are not necessarily familiar ground for urban planning practitioners, and hence does not indicate relevance to the latter. From this point of view, one requirement for making transdisciplinarity work and for researchers to produce more 'relevant' knowledges does not really hinge on the setting of collaboration per se but rather in the steering of academic thinking and writing towards the community's established output channels and validation practices, and the settings where academic debates are both fueled, nourished, and turned over, in particular in academic journal publishing.

One example of such publishing is the *Urban Transformations Journal*, which was created with the objective to provide transdisciplinary researchers (and practitioners) who work on sustainable urbanization with an outlet to translate these knowledges into 'academic currency' in the system. The project is to secure the journal as a high impact academic outlet, with the aim of increasing the workability and, over time, the critical mass of transdisciplinary approaches and hence support the competitiveness of this community of practice in academic evaluation procedures (for funding and positions, etc.).

Second, and this has more to do with the setting in question, another requirement may be simply not to write papers but rather to find other ways to formalize collaborative knowledge-making across the borders, so to speak. Academic writing can be very effective at conveying a precise meaning, just like electric cars are very effective today so long as you have the infrastructure set up to support it. Without the infrastructure, outside the road system way out in the woods or deep in some jungle, it is not moving very well. Academic text certainly has that infrastructure in the academic system and to some degree in higher-level policy making. But in many other no less knowledge-intense areas, text is not always the best way to move and explore with, as it simply cannot avoid the reductionism and absolutism of fixed wordings.

So, one difference here in the fourth vignette is between an interactive transdisciplinary setting that works among a diverse group of actors, seen in comparison with how academic research later debriefs, reports, and writes up the results. Perhaps the knowledge practice(s) around a specific type of text are in this case a more central problem than any deeper differences between how academics and practitioners otherwise think. Maybe this is too speculative. But this is a way of thinking that commonly pops up in my line of work and the settings this work takes me through. Having not been active as a university researcher for the last few years, a self-reflection related to this—when *writing* this chapter—is how slightly estranged this type of writing is for me now. Moreover, that the kind of text is most of the time very different in and around the practitioners, business, and civil society actors. Of course, text in a very general sense is in heavy use among practitioners to manipulate and shape the bits and pieces they need to keep on 'worlding' the way they do—a policy is usually a bit of text and maybe some tables and figures. Nevertheless, it is rarely a long read and usually it is in bullet list composition (even when there are no bullets, the same near-telegramese rhythm is usually present).

Transdisciplinary Settings Require New Protocols?

Hence, and remember that this reflection comes from the programming point of view, maybe the requirements to make transdisciplinary settings work (well) have to do with protocols. What my reflexive hang-up on text (as shown above) perhaps points to is the role of protocols to work well with framings in transdisciplinary practices. Academic papers come with a protocol. Knowledge practices for the Anthropocene may, however, simply require different protocols to optimize knowledge sharing, learning, and impact. For instance, look at Bruno Latour's work with exhibitions to jointly explore intersections in current knowledge practices and how the AIME project was set up as a platform with capacity (in some respects developed during the course of the project) to deal with more varied types of materials—visual, audio, theatrical, etc.—in a co-creative exploration of Modernity. These still need handles and anchoring points, but is it possible that the academic text is not necessarily the most suitable tool for this?

I used to take a position that it is not the researchers who should have to 'dumb down' their communication, it is the receivers—public administration and civil servants mainly—who have to step up. I kind of still agree, but also have had to recognize elements as to why this competence upgrade seems so difficult. So, here are a couple of requirements for the new protocols as a departure point—to which we may add more later on.

First, civil servants rarely use single research project 'findings.' Rather, I suspect, they make use of a critical mass of statements, claims, and findings (academic as well as other types) regarding an issue and may at times highlight one or two references to make a proposition 'evidence-based.' Second, at the same time, in many parts of Europe, there is a blatant under-capacity in public administrations. They are generally severely under-resourced. There are many competent staff who are skilled in their areas of expertise. They simply do not have the resources of time or staffing, and further lack the mandate to move across silos or domains to actually act transversally on issues in the manner that urban research and innovation proposes (and many civil servants see with their own eyes) as critical. This goes for high-level policy making and implementation as well as for local urban governance and planning practice. What we see are burnouts by those that try to engage beyond the typical checkbox-bureaucracy forms in public organizations. This situation is further exacerbated by an increasing projectification, that is, processes and actions are increasingly circumscribed in time as one-off actions rather than being integrated into everyday bureaucratic practices among public administrations. In particular, when it comes to how they are allowed to join transdisciplinary explorations and actions to tackle sustainable urbanization, this not very helpful.

Many of the papers presented at the Cambridge workshop seemed not to have observed this, been touched by it, or even noticed this condition, one that it is not always politically favorable to talk about in contemporary Europe. Although in the practical settings, the policy conferences, the meeting rooms, policy debates and workshops with stakeholders, and not least very much commented upon in the JPI Urban Europe consultations for SRIA 2.0, this public sector capacity issue runs like a red thread. And when we raise the issue cautiously, the response is generally a massive support for this concern.

So for the programming work with JPI Urban Europe and the practice settings and exchanges I traverse, much of the Cambridge papers' view on 'practice' is as if they are watching a house and try to talk about what's going on inside by merely looking at what is on the outside, maybe talking to the stray inhabitant that ventures outside. For transdisciplinarity to really work, instead they will probably have to try to muster the courage to walk up to the house, knock on the door and ask, 'how do you really do? Can I have a look inside?'

Endnote on Swarm Intelligence in the Programming Environment

> Yet the city is still set within a world of ruptures between the world and humans that cannot be gainsaid and especially an assumption that resources will continue to be forthcoming on a planet that is being drained of its goodness.
>
> (Amin & Thrift, 2016, p. 70)

It could have been worse. But still: policy-makers want a recipe, a best practice, a map. Academics want to be clever. And at times it seems everybody wants someone else—the programmers?—to do the job.

How to tackle this daunting task? In this regard, perhaps the cultivation of 'swarm intelligence,' as Anders Bergmark at Färgfabriken in Stockholm used to call it and to hopefully steal it away from the current military usage, may be fruitful. Swarm intelligence is when there is a vision but none of the concerned actors fall in line, so to speak. All have their own agendas, sometimes overlapping, sometimes with friction between each other, yet they collectively work towards realizing the vision. In this sense, it is not the place to ask whether the vision is realistic. And yes, there has to be reflexivity and non-linear movement involved—that is part of the collective exploratory work. Still, what may be crucial is to support communication lines in between actors or issues. Could swarm intelligence, a distributed cognition that includes not-always-congruent agendas and with some friction between desires, help us to shape this common world? The together-go, the common trajectory of urban sustainable transformations? With directionality and without succumbing to romanticized pipedreams of 'self-organization' touted as excuses for de-capacitating our organizations, settings and people? Could the programming and funding of a collective thinking and working-through of dilemmas help us to focus on rebuilding the ship at sea?

Notes

1 "The European Research Area (ERA) is a unified research area open to the world and based on the internal market. The ERA enables free circulation of researchers, scientific knowledge and technology." See https://ec.europa.eu/info/research-and-innovation/strategy/era_en.
2 A DG is a policy area department in the European Commission.
3 I borrow this metaphor from Michel Serres, who used it to characterize science and research, and the interrelationship between its disciplines and fields. The metaphor is a useful contrast to the sciences' rational and reductionist self-image of a hierarchical tree as well as the metaphor commonly used to critique knowledge-intense practices as working in silos. The archipelago does not necessarily evoke such well-balanced images and hence may enable better-gauged understandings of the power games involved in policy-science exchanges.

References

Amin, A., & Thrift, N. (2016). *Seeing Like a City*. Cambridge: Polity Press.
Bornemark, J. (2019). Intervention/presentation at ArkDes book launch: Stadsutveckling & design för motstridiga önskemål. 17 May. Retrieved March 23, 2020, from https://arkdes.se/en/arkdes_kalender/bokslapp-stadsutveckling-design-for-motstridiga-onskemal/.
Cartwright, N., Cat, J., Leck, L., & Uebel, T.E. (2008). *Otto Neurath: Philosophy between Science and Politics*. Cambridge: Cambridge University Press.
De Jong, M., Joss, S. & Schraven, D. (2018). Review of Research Findings generated under JPI Urban Europe's Strategic Research and Innovation Agenda 2013–2018. Portfolio review commissioned by JPI Urban Europe. Retrieved 15 March 2020, from https://jpi-urbaneurope.eu/app/uploads/2019/02/De-Jong-et-al-1.pdf .
JPI Urban Europe (2019). *Strategic Research and Innovation Agenda 2.0*. Retrieved March 23, 2020, from https://jpi-urbaneurope.eu/app/uploads/2019/02/SRIA2.0.pdf.
Kabisch, S., Finnveden, G., Kratochvil, P., Sendi, R., Smagacz-Poziemska, M., Matos, R., & Bylund, J. (2019). New urban transitions towards sustainability: Addressing the SDG challenges (research and implementation tasks and topics from the perspective of the Scienctific Advisory Board (SAB) of the Joint Programming Initiative (JPI) Urban Europe). *Sustainability*, 11(2242), 1–10.
Lund Declaration (2009). *The Lund Declaration: Europe Must Focus on the Grand Challenges of Our Time*. Lund: Government of Sweden.
Marres, N. (2010). Front-staging nonhumans: Publicity as a constraint on the political activity of things. In B. Braun & S.J. Whatmore (Eds.), *Political Matter: Technoscience, Democracy, and Public Life*. Minneapolis: University of Minnesota Press, pp. 177–210.
Mazzucato, M. (2018). Mission oriented research and innovation in Europe: A problem-solving approach to fuel innovation-led growth. Retrieved March 23, 2020, from https://ec.europa.eu/info/sites/info/files/mazzucato_report_2018.pdf.

Rancière, J. (1999). *Disagreement: Politics and Philosophy*. Minneapolis: University of Minnesota Press.

Wrangsten, C., & Bylund, J. (2018). A dilemma-driven approach to urban innovation. Retrieved March 23, 2020, from https://jpi-urbaneurope.eu/news/a-dilemma-driven-approach-to-urban-innovation/.

Chapter 10

Evidence

Evidence-Based Urban Development:
Beyond the Urban Anecdotes?

Magnus Johansson and Joakim Forsemalm

At the beginning of the 21st century, an evidence-based turn in planning slowly emerged, mainly in the United Kingdom (cf., Davoudi, 2006). This turn can be understood as a response to the communicative turn in urban planning that dominated much of the debate from the 1990s onwards (Faludi & Waterhout, 2006). The communicative, or argumentative, turn in planning theory and research was a discussion of the political nature of planning as well as a critique of the domains of experts in planning who, during the 1960s and 1970s, based their work on scientific knowledge (Krizek et al., 2009). The current literature on evidence-based practice highlights how systematic use of research can improve and inform public services and decision-making (Nutley et al., 2007), decision-making in management (Barends & Rousseau, 2018), and the professional field of planning (Davoudi, 2006; Krizek et al., 2009; Brown & Corry, 2011).

Brown and Corry (2011) use the medical profession as a role model when they call for an architectural practice based more on facts than on personal or collective anecdotes. Characterizing medicine as a professional field emphasizes the close connection between research and practice. Doing research is a natural part of a professional medical career and new forms of treatment and ways of working are not initiated without research and clinical tests. Of course, even physicians from time to time rely on the rule of thumb and tacit knowledge. Nevertheless, there is a strong norm among medical practitioners and within medical research to work in an evidence-based manner and to produce knowledge with the potential to improve medical practice. The norm in urban planning is rather the opposite. Professional planners seldom use research in a systematic way. When asked, urban planners state that they often find research literature too abstract and theoretical or too narrow, as it focuses on specific cases or issues and thus has little relevance for professional practice (Krizek et al., 2009).

Contrary to medicine, it is hard to conduct 'clinical tests' on an urban plan or development vision before it materializes into streets, parks, and neighborhoods. The argument here is not to suggest a return to modernistic and reductionist ways of urban planning and development that, by default, put scientific facts before professional experience and community knowledge. We do, however, think that there is a need for a more systematic approach to planning that is based on the methodological use of a broad range of knowledges. Urban planning may be a "wicked problem" (Rittel & Webber, 1973), implying that it is difficult for professional planners to learn from previous experiences (Schön, 1983). A carpenter or a bricklayer can develop a broad range of knowledge based on previous experiences and successively make decisions based on routines. In the end, a house must be built on basic rules when it comes to construction and production.

The design and construction of a city district is a jigsaw puzzle of almost endless pieces—public transportation structures, the location of new schools, public amenities, various forms of housing, places for consumption, etc. In his study of urban planners, Donald Schön (1983, p. 207) described planning problems as dilemmas comprising conflicts of values and interests, which were unresolvable by resources or facts. The professional planner serves more as a mediator. Still, plans seem to be the general outcome, and cities slowly grow through new combinations of houses, roads, drainage and water pipes, tram stops, and an increasing number of people moving into urban geographies.

Without neglecting the complexity of urban planning, we would like to challenge the idea of professional planning as a mainly communicative act of mediation between conflicting interests, where facts have little or uncertain relevance. The communicative turn in planning puts people in the center of the planning process. In contrast, an evidence-based turn, which we develop in this chapter, puts *knowledge*, in its widest possible meaning, in the center. We want to call attention to how professional training and organizational learning emerge as key factors for sustainable urban development (Cooper & Symes, 2008). In this chapter, we introduce an approach to evidence-based urban planning that we contributed to develop iteratively and in close collaboration with the public housing company Bostadsbolaget in Gothenburg, Sweden, during a process of city district development. We participated in this process as support for the company's steering group regarding strategic development of two exposed suburbs. We also conducted two larger urban dialogues as part of our assignment. In this process, different forms of evidence were collected in order to ground professional learning with the ambition to make requisite actions in two challenging environments a little bit less difficult.

The Initiative: A New Approach to an Old Problem

Bostadsbolaget owns the majority of the 2,800 apartments located in Hammarkullen, a city district that is home to approximately 8,000 inhabitants in Gothenburg's north-eastern outskirts. This district is one of 23 categorized by the national police as 'particularly vulnerable.' Seven of these districts are located in Gothenburg, Sweden's second largest city. The category suggests a living environment marked by high crime rates, high unemployment, poor school results, low general trust, and low average income.

For Hammarkullen and the other 22 districts, the situation is not new. Almost since they were first inhabited at the end of the 1960s, social problems have characterized the outer suburbs in several of the larger cities in Sweden (*miljonprogramsområden* i.e., the national program in the 1960s charged with building one million new homes over the course of a decade). Several national ventures have since been conducted to overcome these problems. The three-year program *Blommanpengarna* conducted in the mid-1990s (named after the Minister of Immigration) was followed by *Storstadssatsningen* a couple of years into the new millennium at the time. Limited to three- to four-year periods, many projects funded by these national ventures saw their financial support terminated. The time, energy, and hope invested became just another disappointment.

Learning from these failed attempts, the public housing company in question concluded that for Hammarkullen (along with Norra Biskopsgården, a district in another part of the city with very similar problems and preconditions), they needed to be leading the long-term presence and support. No longer would there be additional projects, but instead an 'initiative.' The chief executive officer of Bostadsbolaget and her closest members of staff invited other public sector administrations such as the Parks and Recreation Administration and the City District Administration in addition to the company managing shop floor facilities in publicly owned real estate in Gothenburg. Everyone signed a letter of intent for long-term responsibility. But what was the initiative really? Did the engaged stakeholders share a view of how to be a part of this long-term engagement? Did they have the right competencies for the job?

When Bostadsbolaget started the process, it faced not one but several challenges: how to renovate older apartments in a way that did not result in higher rents forcing tenants to move; how to increase the energy efficiency of older apartment buildings; how to increase the feeling of safety and belonging among the inhabitants in a socioeconomically vulnerable neighborhood; and how to make room for new buildings and more privately owned condominiums without gentrifying. In short, Bostadsbolaget needed to address how to support sustainable development in its widest sense. Dialogue workshops were not enough—there was a need for a more evidence-based approach.

Turning to Evidence for an Un-doing of Urban Difficulties?

Inspired by a model developed by Eric Barends and Denise Rosseau (2018) labelled *evidence-based management*, the project sought to build a knowledge base that would support very important decisions. Here, 'evidence' is understood as all kinds of information that could help public managers and others to make more informed decisions by using it in a systematic way. In the model, there are four general kinds of evidence: evidence from professionals; evidence from stakeholders; evidence from scientific literature; and evidence from organizations. The insight that evidence has many forms is, of course, nothing new. Krizek et al. (2009) present a table with several forms of evidence, such as professional experience, case studies and benchmarks, empirical research studies, theoretical analysis, and systematic research reviews. These cover and condense a broader body of research as well as argue that planners need to learn to combine different forms of knowledge.

What Barends, Rosseau, and Brinner add to this is the insight that not only individuals (stakeholders and professionals) and research (evidence from scientific literature) are sources of evidence but that also organizations produce evidence. The focus on management (i.e., how evidence can be used for decisions that lead to actions) adds a more practical dimension to the previous discussion on what characterizes evidence-based planning.

In professional practice, problems must be sorted from situations that are messy, wicked, and ambiguous. Schön (1983) understood this to be a process of naming and framing, whereby professionals apply a frame to a field of experience. This frame enables professionals to highlight distinct features of the situation, including specific symptomatic challenges. At the same time, they must ignore, or single out, certain other features of the situation as noisy and irrelevant. In the end, professionals bind together the salient features of the situation, including the relevant worries, into a pattern that is coherent and graspable.

Such coherent patterns could end up in path dependency, whereby professionals increasingly act in a routine manner and within certain communities of practice. Sometimes, it is difficult to separate professional experiences from, put bluntly, bad habits (Wenger, 1998). In the end, this can result in actions that are unsustainable in the long run, regardless of how rewarding they seem to be in the short term for clients or customers. A key condition for sustainable urban transformation is to increase the problem-solving capacity among planners, real estate developers, and others involved with urban development to name and frame their work in new ways. Different forms of evidence can be used to challenge routines—but they also to make way for new forms of learning.

Per-Erik Ellström (2001) distinguishes adaptive learning learning from developmental learning, and creative learning. Adaptive learning occurs when we know our working tasks, how to complete them, and what kind of results are anticipated in relation to a specific community of practice such as an urban development project. In organizations, at least productive and stable ones, there is an established way to name and frame a problem. As a newcomer, one must adapt and learn the standards and procedures. Developmental learning can take place when there are possibilities to reflect upon working task as well as to solve them in different ways. Creative learning is only possible if there is flexibility in the process of naming and framing, or in other words, creativity around how to interpret working tasks, choose methods, and be more dynamic in relation to project goals. Creative learning could also be labelled 'innovative learning.' We see such a level of professional learning as crucial in every process of sustainable urban development.

We see evidence-based planning as a process of professional learning and problem-solving that uses different types of information to simultaneously open and close a planning process. The method contains four forms of knowledge, or evidences, to challenge (i.e., reflect upon) the everyday and formalized work practices and to make planning processes at the same time more and less wicked (Forsemalm & Johansson, 2019). It can also be understood as movement between different forms of naming and framing problems (Schön, 1983), adaptive and creative learning, or wicked versus structured problems (see Figure 10.1).

Hoppe (2010) developed a nuanced view of wicked problems. He defines three kinds of problems with different characteristics of wickedness: structured, moderately structured, and unstructured problems. Hoppe put these into a model of two dimensions—a knowledge dimension and a value dimension. Structured problems are characterized by agreements concerning norms and values and have a high degree of certainty regarding required and available knowledge. Wicked problems, in contrast, are characterized by the opposite. In the figure below, our approach to evidence-based planning is illustrated. As a process that uses a more structured learning approach to urban planning, it can move projects from being unstructured wicked problems to more structured ones.

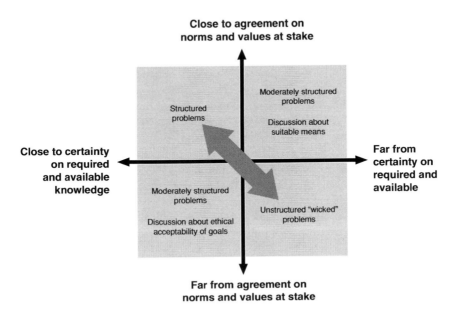

Figure 10.1 Four types of problem structures (Forsemalm et al. 2019, after Hoppe 2010). Source: The authors.

Traditionally, evidence has been seen as something that helps practitioners to structure problems. We will emphasize that evidence can actually make problems even more wicked. However, wicked problems are also an excellent source for creative learning. Evidence can be used to both structure and make problems more wicked while at the same time open up avenues for creative learning. This could be described with the truism "reflection can destroy knowledge" (Davoudi, 2006, p. 19), or as we like to say, 'evidence can confuse professionals.'

In the next part of our chapter, we will illustrate how we used different forms of evidence to open up and close the developmental process with Bostadsbolaget. Here, we bear in mind the core of evidence-based management—to help professionals make better decisions. In the end, we must finish in the upper left corner represented in the figure above, where there are problems that have been named and framed in a way that makes it possible to solve them regardless of how wicked they were at the beginning.

Opening Up the Wickedness: What Does an Organization Know?

In the process of supporting Bostadsbolaget, we started out by gathering evidence from the organizations that were involved and had signed the letter of intent. Initially, we conducted around 20 in-depth interviews with managing directors and arranged a two-day workshop in order to consolidate ideas and ambitions. The aim was to build organizational capacity. In an era when problems seem more and more wicked—and the case we present here surely is anything but 'lame' or easy for the stakeholders to manage—is a company like Bostadsbolaget adequately organized to meet the challenges that confront it? Is it prone to act on difficulties that are new and outside its core remit (i.e., to manage real estate)?

The interviews provided not only evidence from stakeholders but also from the organization. Organizations produce a lot of data and knowledge both from those who work in the organization and from its interactions with users or clients. This data can be quantitative and/or qualitative, or 'soft' data, such as a perception of organizational norms and cultures.

When we worked with evidence from the real estate company's organization, we systematically tried to translate practical issues and frustrations into answerable questions. One method used was 'walkshops,' meaning to walk around with representatives from all organizations involved in the management of the area where the company's housing stock was located. This afforded the visualization of lots of interactions between the private company and the public partners including the management of public areas such as green space, bike lanes, and parking lots. The ownership of public areas was divided between the municipality and the real estate company and consequently the maintenance differed. Those who lived in the area could not see the administrative borders around different parts of the municipality. They noticed only how some public areas were managed in different ways when compared with others, which is a long-standing source of complaint from tenants.

As a first step in the developmental work, representatives from the real estate company and the other parts of the municipality walked around the area and developed a joint agreement about maintenance. At first, this seems like a very trivial thing. However, during the walkshop, the discussion revealed organizational evidence that could explain why things were as they were. Administrative borders were in fact knowledge borders between the private company and the municipality. The development of a joint agreement for the maintenance of public spaces triggered a process of collaborative learning. Through the walkshops, stakeholders from the area developed shared knowledge and shared norms about how the area *ought* to be managed. This resulted in new maintenance routines, namely learning at the organizational level. An unstructured problem became structured.

In the process of formulating the right questions, there is a need for evidence from stakeholders. Through dialogues, we can question and reflect upon basic assumptions for how *it is* in society or a city district and thus gain knowledge from stakeholders about everyday life. Since a dialogue is an encounter of different competencies regarding life in the urban cityscape, you need a contextual framework, or a linguistically common ground, as a point of departure.

Common knowledge emerged by helping the different participants to translate their own experiences and professional skills in a way that others could understand. In the model we discuss and argue for in this chapter, stakeholder evidence is just as important as any other evidence. Urban dialogues can be discussed from several different standpoints, methodological and political, but for us it is inevitable that working with evidence-based urban development always involves a dialogue, regardless of scope and style. Without the knowledge gleaned from local inhabitants, businesses, and associations, you simply cannot ask the right questions.

Opening Up the Process with Evidence from Practitioners

The importance of gathering information from stakeholders as well as from organizations is a well-known way to improve planning processes. It is, however, even more important to find ways for this information to be used by professionals in their everyday decision-making. Evidence from practitioners includes all kinds of tacit, embodied, practice-based, situated knowledge that is used more or less deliberately in order to carry out work. Evidence from practitioners might come into conflict with evidence from the organization, for example when personal and tacit knowledge are ignored by the organization. Yet, as Ellström (2001) illustrated through the concept of adaptive learning, professional habits and tacit knowledge can be a hindrance for learning. Evidence from practitioners, or the perception that 'we know what works,' can be either an asset or a hindrance in processes of urban development. Evidence from practitioners, as well as evidence from the organization, sometimes need to be challenged—mainly with evidence from external stakeholders and scientific literature.

In the work with the real estate company, evidence from practitioners emerged in discussions about what could or could not be done. Evidence from practitioners was often presented as anecdotes or stories. Sometimes, such evidence was used to challenge and debate how things were done and organized. Frequently, evidence from practitioners emerged accidentally in conversations. Because of its tacit character and because it is not considered significant knowledge, it is not regularly expressed and talked about. We tried to circumvent this through interviews with key personnel at the managerial level as well with local managers and service staff. Consequently, we gained rich material with different perspectives on what ought to be done. Based on previous professional experience of what works, we found a broad variety of ways of naming and framing how the real estate company should carry out work in this specific neighborhood.

Opening Up the Process with Evidence from Scientific Literature

Another important part of the work on the initiative was finding reasonable research evidence to support decisions that would alter the cityscape quite dramatically. According to the local police who were interviewed early in the process, the best remedy for the serious problems confronting Hammarkullen was 'more urban life.' Their suggestion was to "build a city out of the housing district!" What suitable scientific results would be useful for such a call? What evidence from scientific literature could be used to tame this wicked problem and open up for new learning? When it comes to planning, research has traditionally been used to 'open up,' which is definitely the case in the communicative or argumentative turn in planning research. Nutley et al. (2007) distinguish between conceptual and instrumental uses of research. Increasing awareness and understanding of a phenomenon is an example of conceptual use. Here, research is a way to increase knowledge. At the same time, an issue could be more wicked. When research is used in an instrumental way, the aim might be to change attitudes and polices or to change a practice. In that case, we apply science to a structured and well-framed problem.

In the work with the real estate company, we began to use scientific knowledge in a conceptual way. There is a broad and varied range of literature about socioeconomically deprived neighborhoods from which we could draw conclusions as well as some contemporary research about urban planning. However, we struggled to find research that was relevant to this specific task that could supply the group of actors involved with some concrete starting points for *action* and not only for reflection. In this case, we used UN-Habitat's five principles for sustainable neighborhood planning (UN-Habitat, 2014) (see Figure 10.2). This scientifically developed a way for doing both analysis *and* work with regard to an ideal ambition for key aspects of sustainable urban development: density, social mix, street land use, residential floor area, single function block area, and economic floor area.

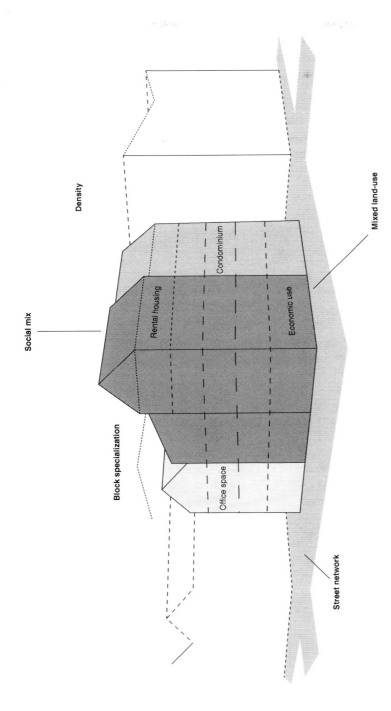

Figure 10.2 UN-Habitat's five principles as a city block
Source: Radar Architects.

Studies of the way in which professionals use scientific facts (Weiss, 1980) show that professionals prefer scientific evidence that is aligned with how they already name and frame different working tasks. In other words, scientific evidence that supports professional and organizational evidence seems easier to use and reference. Contrary to this, scientific evidence that comes into conflict with established ways of doing things—for example, with professional evidence—is seldom used. Therefore, scientific evidence must find ways to connect with professional as well as organizational evidence in order to become useful. Here, it is important to reflect upon why we bring scientific evidence into an urban development process. Are we striving for conceptual or instrumental uses of scientific evidence? Are we looking to support solutions of well-defined (tamed) problems? Or, would we like to open up new perspectives to make things more complicated with the intention to pave the way for more creative and innovative learning? In our process, the need was *chiefly* to close the process and tame the wicked problem that was a district in need of new order. The concrete scheme of the UN-Habitat model was well timed and well suited as a means to spark discussion among a motley group of actors.

Evidence from scientific literature can thus be used as a way to challenge other forms of evidence and make a structured problem more wicked, although the opposite can also occur. We argue here that planning problems must be closed down through processes of naming and framing. One way is to passively avoid hardships by ignoring aspects of wicked problems. If you're lucky, that might 'tame' them and make it possible for them to be handled in a professional situation (Cooper & Symes, 2008). We do not believe, however, that it is a long-term, sustainable way of attacking the serious problems that the inhabitants of Hammarkullen live through every day. Processes of opening and closing can be moments back and forth along the arrow in Figure 10.1 above.

According to Barends and Rousseau (2018), practical issues are translated into answerable questions through scientific evidence if they are used as a tool for translation between various parts of an organization. In the work with the real estate company, we used UN-Habitat's five principles for neighborhood planning in order to highlight which aspects the company should focus on if it wants to develop its housing stock into something more sustainable.

Concluding Discussion

In this chapter, we acknowledged that professionals have a key role in many ongoing processes of urban transformation. In the end, professionals must act in new ways if we want to see green utopias—or socially equal cities—materialize into new kinds of urban environments. The 'evidence-based turn in planning' could be part of an increased insight into how such approaches in planning can help professionals to act differently.

Evidence is an ambiguous concept. In this chapter, we introduced a model that relies on four kinds of evidence that arise from a wide variety of sources:

the experience of professionals; the deep knowledge of everyday life among stakeholders in districts; the vast and complex data and knowledge that emerge from organizations; and all information that dwells in scientific literature. We have argued for a learning approach to evidence-based practice, whereby different kinds of information should be used proactively for accomplishing the opening-up and closing-down of issues, ideas, projects, and processes. We describe this as a process during which unstructured, wicked problems become structured and revised—in other words, they become tamed. Using evidence such as knowledge in more structured and broad ways increases complexity (i.e., using research in a more conceptual way) and opens up more innovative and creative learning among professionals.

At the end of the day, professional planners need to close down and frame complex issues in order to fulfil an assignment such as the production of a plan or the development of an urban district. Much of contemporary planning research is good for conceptual usage, but it does not help practitioners with their daily struggle with difficult doings. Instead, it just makes things more difficult.

We believe that an evidence-based approach to planning, which acknowledges the complex and wicked character of urban planning, is a sustainable way to help professionals to close down planning processes through more accurate decisions. The case discussed in this chapter illustrates some ways to do this through a systematic use of the four forms of evidence. Bostadsbolaget had a

Figure 10.3 Evidence-based development model (Forsemalm et al. 2019)
Source: Radar Architects.

solid knowledge base for decisions that were both inside the box and outside of it. Of course, renovation of the properties was one important item on the agenda, as the houses had nearly 50 years of public service. However, through the initiative and the new and solid input from various stakeholders in the district, the company could also get to work on being the reliable and long-term actor that Hammarkullen so desperately needs in order to steer societal development away from social exclusion, child poverty, limited life expectancy, and high crime rates. As we describe in this chapter, the city's planning department has new housing in the pipeline in a location that has been decreed as fit for purpose by the local inhabitants. Various previously dubious sites have been transformed into offices for local branches of the International Committee of the Red Cross and Save The Children as well as into a district dialogue facility where inhabitants can report general societal problems and make suggestions on a regular basis.

Hammarkullen is on its way, albeit slowly but surely, to being something other than the perfunctory 'black poetry' so common in local media coverage. Beyond the urban anecdotes, through the use of readily available information, Bostadsbolaget has been able to complete a jigsaw puzzle of data that, although it takes a bit of time to access, has become a more solid way to make the necessary decisions.

References

Barends, E., & Rousseau, D.M. (2018). *Evidence-Based Management: How to Use Evidence to Make Better Organizational Decisions*. London: Kogan Page Publishers.

Brown, R.D., & Corry, R.C. (2011). Evidence-based landscape architecture: The maturing of a profession. *Landscape and Urban Planning*, 100(4), 327–329.

Cooper, I., & Symes, M. (Eds.) (2008). *Sustainable Urban Development: Changing Professional Practice*. Vol. 4. Abingdon: Routledge.

Davoudi, S. (2006). Evidence-based planning: Rhetoric and reality. *disP-The Planning Review*, 42(165), 14–24.

Ellström, P.E. (2001). Integrating learning and work: Problems and prospects. *Human Resource Development Quarterly*, 12(4), 421–435.

Faludi, A., & Waterhout, B. (2006). Introducing evidence-based plannning. *disP-The Planning Review*, 42(165), 4–13.

Forsemalm, J., Johansson, M., & Göransson, P. (2019). *Evidensbaserad stadsutveckling: Bortom urbana anekdoter*. Årsta: Dokument Press.

Hoppe, R. (2010). *The Governance of Problems: Puzzling, Powering and Participation*. Bristol: Policy Press.

Krizek, K., Forsyth, A., & Slotterback, C. (2009). Is there a role for evidence-based practice in urban planning and policy? *Planning Theory & Practice*, 10(4), 459–478.

Nutley, S.M., Walter, I., & Davies, H.T.O. (2007). *Using Evidence: How Research Can Inform Public Services*. Bristol: Bristol University Press.

Rittel, H.W., & Webber, M.M. (1973). Dilemmas in a general theory of planning. *Policy Sciences*, 4(2), 155–169.

Schön, D.A. (1983). *The Reflective Practitioner: How Professionals Think in Action.* New York: Basic Books.

UN-Habitat (2014). *A New Strategy of Sustainable Neighborhood Planning: Five Principles.* Nairobi: United Nations Human Settlements Programme.

Weiss, C. (1980). Knowledge creep and decision accretion. *Science Communication*, 1(3), 381–404.

Wenger, E. (1998). *Communities of Practice: Learning, Meaning, and Identity.* Cambridge: Cambridge University Press.

Chapter 11

Smart

Climate-Smart Cities: A Corporate Takeover of Urban Environmental Governance in Malmö?

Darcy Parks

In January 2016, a project group gathered for a meeting at the offices of the City of Malmö Environmental Department. The group consisted of representatives from the City Planning Office, the Property Department, the Transportation Department, and the Environmental Department—the latter being represented by three employees at this particular meeting. Also represented were two important infrastructure companies: VA Syd, the municipally owned water and waste company, and Eon, the multinational energy company that owns the city's electricity and district heating networks. What brought them together every month was a vision called the Climate Contract for Hyllie, signed five years earlier. Hyllie was a new city district that would become home to thousands of new apartments. The Climate Contract was supposed to cement Malmö's international reputation as a sustainable city by making Hyllie into a 'climate-smart' city district.

Oscar and Patricia both had updates about wind turbines, a matter that the project group had been discussing all fall. Oscar was Eon's project manager for all things related to Hyllie and the Climate Contract. Eon had promised to build wind turbines for Hyllie but the company was struggling to make these turbines a reality. The company had acquired a plot of land located near Hyllie around the Petersborg highway interchange, but the county government had recently overturned Eon's building permit. He explained that the company had submitted an appeal. Patricia, from the City Planning Office, went on to describe the city administration's response. The director of the City Planning Office would book a meeting with the county government to discuss the rules for building urban wind turbines. The city's comprehensive plan had identified similar sites along the highway as being suitable for wind turbines, but it seemed that the county government had a different opinion.

Wind turbines were central to the realization of the Climate Contract, whose proponents envisioned in 2011 that Hyllie would become "the most climate-smart city district" in the Malmö-Copenhagen region and that the district would "lead the way for Malmö's future development as sustainable city" (City of Malmö et al., 2011). The Climate Contract stated that 100% of the energy used in Hyllie should come from renewable or recycled sources by 2020. Without the promised wind turbines, there would be a lack of renewable electricity to match the increasing electricity consumption of the growing city district. For the project group, wind turbines were an important problem that lacked a credible solution.

Oscar had more news to bring up at the meeting. He first explained that January marked the formal split of Eon into two separate companies. While Eon remained the owner and operator of Malmö's electricity and district heating networks, it spun off most of its fossil fuel, nuclear, and hydroelectric power business into a company called Uniper. In relation to the Climate Contract, he explained that the corporate split meant that the project group would lose access to some members of the company's communications team.

The second item on his agenda also had to do with the split, albeit in more symbolic terms. He had good news about the smart grid demonstration project that Eon was operating in Hyllie. Smart grids were a collection of new technologies that Eon was testing. These technologies were definitely not being spun off into Uniper. They were part of Eon's new profile as a sustainable energy company. First, he pointed out that the project had recently paid out a record amount of funding to property developers, a sign that Eon had finally been able to get developers interested in smart grid technologies. Second, he described how the Swedish Energy Agency had extended the demonstration project so that Eon could test its new technologies in other parts of the city. Finally, he described the intensive work that was being done to prepare an application for a follow-up project, based on several workshops with city departments. All this stood in stark contrast to the project group's struggles with wind turbines and renewable electricity.

The Climate Contract was not the first ambitious sustainability vision for a new city district that had struggled to achieve its goals. And the City of Malmö was not unique in seeking the collaboration of the for-profit energy utility that owns the city's energy infrastructure. But in Malmö, as in other cities around the world, realizing such visions is a difficult endeavor. This chapter discusses the challenges of making good on the promise of creating a 'climate-smart' city district. The challenge arises not only through making a shift from sustainable to climate-*smart*, but also from doing so in collaboration with a for-profit energy utility. How can a city government go from sustainable to climate-smart without falling victim to a corporate takeover?

This chapter continues with a section that provides some background about the notion of smart cities, before tracing the history of the Climate Contract back to the City of Malmö's efforts to recover from an economic downturn. Thereafter, it follows the troubled pursuit of the Climate Contract's renewable energy goals and the parallel efforts to demonstrate smart grids in Hyllie. The chapter concludes with a discussion about the challenges facing cities that hope to become 'climate-smart.'

Why Is Sustainability Getting Smart?

The spread of smart city ideas within urban environmental governance reflects a broader societal trend. Along with the popularity of smart phones, smart watches, and even smart refrigerators, there is more and more interest in *smart cities*. But the spread of these ideas is not simply a matter of city government bureaucrats picking up the latest buzzword. While smart city ideas are certainly popular in policy circles at many levels, their introduction in urban environmental governance is encouraged in part by corporations in the business of urban infrastructure. So along with the introduction of new ideas, smart city ideas might be accompanied by a shift in responsibility that represents a dilemma for city governments.

There are two reasons for this corporate interest in smart urban infrastructure. One reason has to do with the business models of multinational technology companies. Companies such as IBM and Cisco introduced smart city ideas as they began to invest more heavily in technologies that could be used in urban governance and urban infrastructure (for examples of corporate interest in smart city technologies see Paroutis et al., 2014). But another reason is a situation in urban environmental governance that some researchers characterize as a paradox: city governments find themselves increasingly responsible for environmental issues but lack the authority and resources to make urban infrastructure more sustainable.[1] In many western countries, the liberalization and privatization of energy utilities has left this infrastructure in the hands of for-profit corporations. While these corporations are subject to regulations, the regulatory authority belongs to higher levels of government, so city governments that want to influence their local energy systems are forced to turn to other modes of governance. For example, city governments establish visions and negotiate with for-profit energy utilities, which requires a bit of give and take. In terms of smart cities, a pertinent question is: who benefits from this give and take? Does it result in good public policy or a corporate takeover?

Some reasons for concern have been discussed in a strand of social science research that has been critical of the increasing popularity of smart city ideas. Four reasons are relevant to keep in mind in the case of Hyllie. First, some researchers warn of increasing corporate influence over city governments, particularly in cases where city governments might become locked in to the services of a particular company (Viitanen & Kingston, 2014). Second, others ask whether the popularity of smart city ideas might unduly prioritize problems that can be solved by smart technologies, at the expense of matters such as poverty or basic infrastructure (Söderström et al., 2014). Third, many smart city technologies involve data collection that increases the amount of surveillance in society (Galdon-Clavell, 2013). Fourth, adding information technology to urban infrastructure might result in "buggy, brittle and hackable cities" (Kitchin, 2014, p. 10). It is worth nothing that the question of increasing corporate influence is implicated in the rest of the concerns. Should corporate influence increase, city governments might lose their ability to temper other risks. The challenge for city governments, and in particular planners and other practitioners, is to prevent these collaborations from slipping into the hands of their corporate partners.

The analysis below is based on empirical work done over several years as part of my PhD thesis.[2] It is based on a combination of interviews with employees involved in the Climate Contract, participant observation of meetings including the above-mentioned project group, and a variety of documents related to the Climate Contract. The interviews and participant observation took place between 2014 and 2016, which made it possible to follow many developments as they unfolded, although the story of how the Climate Contract originated is based on interviews and documents. (This chapter uses pseudonyms to refer to the interview respondents.) This research was based on a sociomaterial perspective, which gives attention not just to people and organizations but also to changes to the material world such as buildings and urban infrastructure. The research perspective also prioritizes how smart city ideas are used in practice and it attempts to be impartial about the positive or negative influence of companies and technologies.[3]

From Sustainable to Climate-Smart in Malmö

The Climate Contract's vision of a climate-smart city district was a progression of the city government's earlier sustainability ambitions. Malmö's reputation as a sustainable city dates back to a housing exhibition that the city government organized in 2001. The housing exhibition was one part of the city government's efforts to transform the city, which had suffered economically from the shutdown of a shipyard and the loss of manufacturing jobs in the 1980s and 1990s. Called Bo01, it was the first step towards transforming the old shipyards into a city district called the Western Harbour, which eventually became home to over 4,000 apartments and a new university. (See Figure 11.1 for a map of Malmö.) City planners and developers in the Bo01 neighborhood agreed to a quality program that, among other goals, would "ensure that the neighbourhood's environmental profile is of high quality so that it becomes an internationally leading example of how environmental accommodation of densely built areas can act as a motor in Malmö's transition to environmental sustainability" (City of Malmö 2002, p. 5). The research behind this chapter was undertaken in 2015, but the Western Harbour has continued to attract study visits from people and organizations interested in sustainable urban development.

The Bo01 housing exhibition was the first of several developments through which city planners developed new ways of encouraging sustainable buildings. With each neighborhood of the Western Harbour, planners tested different dialogue processes and planning programmes. In 2002, the city government approved its first policy focused on sustainable buildings, a voluntary program

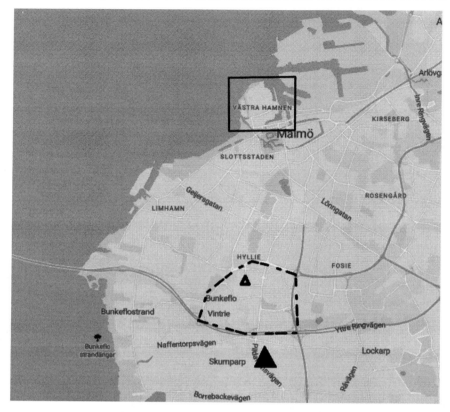

Figure 11.1 Map of Malmö with the Western Harbour (solid rectangle), Hyllie (dotted line), Hyllie station (unfilled triangle) and the proposed location of Eon's wind turbine (solid triangle). The west side of the map shows the Öresund Bridge towards Copenhagen.
Source: Map data © OpenStreetMap contributors, under ODbL. Tiles courtesy of jawgmaps.

called 'Ecologically Sustainable Construction in Malmö.' In the second phase of the Western Harbour development, a neighborhood called Flagghusen, planners followed the model of Bo01 by holding a dialogue with developers and negotiating an agreement that set sustainability targets beyond existing regulations. In 2009, the City of Malmö established a new model for sustainable construction that combined dialogue, targets, and local regulations. The 'Environmental Construction Programme for Southern Sweden' specified three levels of targets for various aspects of construction, including energy and urban biodiversity, and required that developers meet the lowest level, which still exceeded national regulations. The city administration applied this new programme in the Western Harbour's third neighborhood, called Fullriggaren, where construction started in 2010. The city's sustainability ambitions for this third neighborhood also received financial support from a national government program for sustainable cities.

Hyllie was the next city district to be developed after the Western Harbour. The city government's comprehensive plans had long pointed out Hyllie as the location for an urban center in the south of the city, but until the early 2000s the area was bare but for fields and a water tower. Following the construction of the Öresund Bridge, which opened in 2000 and connected Malmö and Copenhagen by road and rail, the Swedish government decided to construct a railway tunnel under Malmö that would shorten the journey between the two cities. Plans for the tunnel included a station in Hyllie, which spurred plans for the city district. The first part of Hyllie to be developed was a commercial center around the train station, which opened in 2010; an arena, a shopping mall, office buildings, and a conference center were completed between 2008 and 2012. Planning for the first residential neighborhood began in 2007 and the first building was completed in 2013. As of 2015, the city administration planned that Hyllie would be home to 9,000 apartments by 2040.

As plans for Hyllie progressed, city planners looked for ways to build on their experiences gained from the Western Harbour. They attempted to find funding from the European Union, discussing projects with other European cities but never succeeding in becoming more than an observer city. While these efforts were taking place, the city government also approved a new version of the Malmö Environmental Programme (MEP). The 2009 version outlined ambitions that Malmö would become "Sweden's most climate-smart city" and that 100% of the city's energy needs would be provided by renewable energy by 2030. It was in this context that city planners began discussions with Eon that led to the Climate Contract. According to Emil, a planner in the Environmental Department, the Climate Contract needed to show that the city government really meant to achieve the MEP's ambitions:

> The city government consolidated with the societal actor with responsibility for energy infrastructure and that's Eon. And the actor with responsibility for waste infrastructure and that's VA Syd. That's how I usually describe the reason for creating the Climate Contract. There are other perspectives, of course. But what was important with the Climate Contract was credibility. To create credibility for the Malmö Environmental Programme and the direction that the programme points out.
> (Interview, 2015)

Discussions between the City of Malmö, Eon, and a municipally owned infrastructure company called VA Syd resulted in the signing of the Climate Contract in February 2011. The importance of Malmö's climate goals is clear from the first page, which begins by referencing the MEP, and goes on to explain that reaching the MEP's goals "require that Hyllie takes important steps and leads the development toward a sustainable city" (City of Malmö et al., 2011, p. 2). From Eon's side, Oscar explained that the company had pushed for a holistic perspective on Hyllie's energy systems:

> There were a few aspects that we pushed for. One was to see the solutions in Hyllie from a holistic perspective. Not one solution for heating, one for electricity, and another for natural gas. We see the energy system as a whole. And we want to demonstrate how this energy system as a whole can be designed in the best way possible, with a link to other infrastructure too: waste, wastewater, transport, etc. That was very important to us.
> (Interview, 2015)

One effect of this perspective was that the Climate Contract included not only renewable energy, but also recycled energy from incineration and the production of biogas. The smart grid was another example of Eon's influence.

Once the Climate Contract was signed, work began to achieve its goals. The signatories constituted three inter-organizational groups tasked with its implementation. The project group, introduced at the beginning of the chapter, met monthly and comprised employees from Eon, VA Syd, and several city departments. There was also a steering group, comprising mid-level managers from each organization and department, as well as a commissioning group, made up of high-level bureaucrats and directors with the authority to make decisions about how to interpret the contract. The Climate Contract soon attracted funding from the Swedish Energy Agency for a project called Smart Grids for Hyllie (officially Smart Grids for a Sustainable Energy System in Hyllie). The project operated from 2011 to 2016 and demonstrated smart grid technologies, but it also provided resources to work on the Climate Contract's goal of making Hyllie climate neutral. The next section of the chapter looks at the challenges of finding renewable energy for Hyllie.

Renewable Energy in the Climate-Smart City

To provide Hyllie with renewable and recycled energy did not seem so complicated in the beginning. The Climate Contract was clear in its ambition—100% by 2020—and Eon made commitments soon after it signed the Climate Contract. However, Eon's plan to build wind turbines within city limits led to several challenges. After several years, as it became clear that Eon's commitment would not provide sufficient energy, the project group was forced to investigate alternatives.

The very first step of making Hyllie climate neutral was to calculate the scale of the commitment. The Climate Contract stated that 100% of Hyllie's energy would come from renewable or recycled sources by 2020, but Hyllie's energy consumption in 2020 would depend on the number and types of buildings that had been constructed by that time. The project group calculated an energy balance that matched the estimated energy consumption for 2020 with the estimated production of energy from renewable and recycled sources. In terms of consumption, the Climate Contract clearly delineated Hyllie on a map. This map drew the boundaries of Hyllie with broad strokes, without any special consideration of areas that had already been built before 2011; indeed, large facilities in the commercial center had already opened, and a small residential area had existed in the south of Hyllie for many years. The energy consumption of these areas, as well as all new construction in Hyllie, was included in the energy balance.

Eon took the lead when it came to the production side of the energy balance. The Climate Contract specified that the energy for Hyllie should be produced within the Öresund region, which was defined as southern Sweden and eastern Denmark. The energy balance started with the recycled energy generated by incinerating and creating biogas from waste produced in Hyllie. Eon then committed to converting one of its district heating plants to use biomass, thereby providing enough annual heating capacity to cover all district heating use in Hyllie. It also proposed a plan for renewable electricity based on wind turbines, as Oscar explained during an interview in 2015:

> When it came to wind power we stated our intention that we were prepared to build wind turbines. But we didn't own any land on which to build those turbines. There was a ... I think it was the city's comprehensive plan. Where they had located a bunch of potential locations for wind turbines within the city limits.

This plan would require the help of the city administration to bring it to fruition. The comprehensive plan showed potential locations for wind turbines, but the city would have to sell this land to Eon if the company was to build wind turbines.

Eon's attempt to build wind turbines within city limits was an arduous and unfruitful endeavour. Even finding sites to allocate to Eon proved challenging. Emil, one of the Environmental Department's representatives at the project group meetings, explained that there were conflicts between the Property Department, which had the authority to sell land, and other city departments:

> We discussed where in the city there could be wind turbines. One suggestion was along the outer ring road. ... One area that we looked at was by the shopping center and the industrial area in the south of the city. ... South of there is countryside, land that the city owns. But the Property Department absolutely doesn't want to build wind turbines there. Because they think the land could be sold for development some day. And according to the prevailing logic at the Property Department, wind turbines are a threat to development. They decrease the value of neighboring land. And because the city council has given them the responsibility to earn as much as possible when they sell land, they don't want wind turbines there.
>
> (Interview, 2015)

In the end, Eon was only allocated a single plot of land upon which it would be able build just one solitary wind turbine, but it ran into problems there too. Residents contested the company's plans and the County Administrative Board overturned the wind turbine's building permit because of the location's cultural significance. Eon appealed the decision but over time gave up its plans.

Eventually, Eon and Malmö decided to look at alternative ways to realize the energy balance for Hyllie. As they debated alternatives in the fall of 2015, the credibility of the Climate Contract remained important. For the city administration, it was something that could be used to motivate developers to build sustainable buildings; for the city administration and Eon together, it was part of the justification for their application to the Swedish Energy Agency for a follow-up project relating to smart city infrastructure. The project group debated whether it was reasonable to insist that Hyllie's renewable energy should come from within the Öresund region. If they could include production from other parts of Sweden, they could count wind power that the City of Malmö already purchased from northern Sweden; furthermore, they might be able to convince some of the large energy users in Hyllie to purchase wind power of their own. Eon also proposed to count two wind turbines that the company owned that were located in the Öresund region; the company had not built these turbines for Hyllie, but the turbines were constructed after the Climate Contract was signed. Notably, the project group did not place much attention on the consumption side of the energy balance. At one point, the steering group asked them to consider whether behavior change could decrease energy consumption enough to influence the energy balance, but the project group did not dedicate any meeting time to this suggestion. But neither did they consider excluding the facilities built prior to the signing of the Climate Contract in 2011, because they believed that such a change would damage the contract's credibility.

The result of the debate was a change of perspective. At its meeting in November 2015, the Climate Contract's commissioning group decided formally to stick to its commitments. It accepted Eon's wind turbines, since they fit the contract's temporal and geographical delimitations, but did not accept wind turbines from northern Sweden. The result was an imbalance in the energy balance—Hyllie would not be climate neutral by 2020. They justified this decision by stating that the Climate Contract was a pilot project for the rest of Malmö. Even if the Climate Contract's signatories did not meet their goals, the commissioning group claimed that the lessons learned would help in the pursuit of the long-term climate goals for the rest of the city.

This decision did not end all efforts to meet the climate neutrality goal. As described at the beginning of the chapter, the project group continued to look for opportunities, and the City of Malmö sought meetings with the County Administrative Board to discuss where it would be possible to build wind turbines. But while the promise of renewable energy lost momentum, urban smart grids remained an area of success for the Climate Contract. The next section describes how Hyllie's smart grids can be contrasted with its renewable energy ambitions.

Making Buildings Climate-Smart

While smart grids ultimately became a part of Hyllie's success story, the Smart Grids for Hyllie project was not a slam dunk. The project aimed to demonstrate many different types of smart grid technology and depended on buildings that had not yet been constructed at the time of the project application. Slow construction in Hyllie was a challenge. Still, by the end of the project, Eon had demonstrated new technologies, and the city administration had incorporated smart grids into a new planning programme for Hyllie.

The aim of the Smart Grids for Hyllie project was to demonstrate smart grid technologies in three contexts: in apartments, in buildings, and in energy distribution infrastructure. In apartments, the project tested displays to visualize energy use for tenants, technologies to automate the control of energy use, and other energy efficiency measures. In buildings, the focus was to develop a demand response controller: a small device that could be connected to the building management system and accept signals from Eon to curtail energy use. In energy distribution infrastructure, Eon developed a district energy management system that could monitor energy flows and send signals to buildings, as well as technology to accommodate more renewable energy production in a district's electricity and heating networks.

The project was complicated by the slow pace of construction in Hyllie Avenue, the first residential neighborhood in Hyllie. Eon had some initial success in influencing the Hyllie Avenue Sustainability Agreement. Signed by all the developers in the neighborhood, the agreement specified among other things that "the monitoring and control system [of each building] shall be able to communicate with Hyllie's common energy management system" (City of Malmö, 2012). However, the slow pace of construction and a lack of interest from developers meant a single building with 54 apartments was the focus of most tests in the neighborhood. Another residential building was included in the demand response tests, as were an office building and the arena.

Four years later, the project had recorded some successful results despite the lack of residential buildings in Hyllie. The results were not on the scale that the project originally intended; despite an initial project extension from three years to four, Eon did not manage to engage many developers. Still, the company had demonstrated that the demand response technology functioned as hoped. The manufacturers of building management systems cooperated in Eon's development efforts. Eon produced a demand response controller through which it could send signals to buildings. The company also reported to the Swedish Energy Agency that it could reduce a building's heat demand by 60% for five hours on any day in December; the building's indoor air temperature would decrease by less than half a degree Celsius, which was less than the natural temperature variation. These results were promising enough for the Swedish Energy Agency to grant another project extension, which not only gave Eon another year, but also expanded the project's scope to include tests of demand response technology in other parts of the city.

The city administration recognized the potential of smart grid technology in a new initiative called the Hyllie Environmental Programme (HEP). The HEP was a voluntary program that the city administration released in 2015 when the fourth year of the Smart Grids for Hyllie project was coming to an end. The program's stated purpose was to give developers an answer to the question of "How can my project become a part of Climate-Smart Hyllie?" (City of Malmö, 2015, p. 5). The HEP addressed this question by specifying 20 goals for each building in Hyllie, and for each goal it assigned tasks to the developer, to city departments, and to other stakeholders such as Eon. The city administration believed in smart grid technologies enough to propose a goal stating that "Hyllie's buildings and facilities are connected to Smart Grids" (City of Malmö, 2015, p. 11). This goal proposed that "The developer, together with Eon, identifies which installations (heating systems, cooling equipment, ventilation systems or other) are appropriate for connection to Smart Grids" (City of Malmö, 2015, p. 11). Should developers follow the HEP, they would involve Eon in the design of their buildings, potentially giving additional attention to energy issues. While the program was not mandatory for developers, the inclusion of smart grids provided Eon with more legitimacy for its smart grid technologies.

The fifth and final year of the Smart Grids for Hyllie project resulted in additional success for Eon. The extension allowed Eon to further test the demand response technology, which it had demonstrated in new buildings in Hyllie, in existing buildings in other parts of Malmö. It performed two tests. The company tested demand response in the district cooling network of the Western Harbour, where there were problems with providing the capacity to cool office buildings on warm days. It also tested demand response in the district heating network in the southwest of the city, where bottlenecks in the distribution network sometimes required Eon use two district heating plants that ran on natural gas and oil. Both of these tests were successful. In the final report for the Smart Grids for Hyllie project, Eon wrote that it could transfer the technology to other city districts and cities; the impact on the district cooling network was enough that the technology could be used in existing operations.

In the end, the demonstration of smart grids in Hyllie was more successful than the construction of wind turbines. Like the search for renewable electricity, the demonstration of smart grids also ran into challenges. The slow pace of construction prevented Eon from testing demand response technology on the scale that it had hoped. However, Eon managed to overcome these challenges and to produce some successful results within the scope of the Smart Grids for Hyllie project. The results were not only lessons learned for next time; there were new demand response technologies that the City of Malmö endorsed, and that Eon could spread to other cities. The Climate Contract gave Eon a chance to experiment in Hyllie and the company managed to get something out of it.

Conclusion

The Climate Contract was signed in 2011 and set goals for Hyllie in 2020. By 2016, as described at the beginning of the chapter, it was clear that Hyllie would not become climate neutral—a disappointment for the city government, whose ambition it was to power the entire city with renewable energy. In contrast, as the Smart Grids for Hyllie project ended in 2016, Eon had demonstrated new technologies that it could start to apply in other city districts and even other cities. In terms of achieving their respective goals, it would appear that Eon got more out of the Climate Contract than the City of Malmö. This chapter set out to ask how a city government can go from sustainable to climate-smart without falling victim to a corporate takeover. Did Eon's participation allow the smart city to push the sustainable city out of the way? Did practitioners in Malmö let control slip into Eon's hands?

The struggle to build wind turbines shows that there were more factors at play. The plan for renewable energy reflected the city government's underlying challenge, namely that it was dependent on the energy company to fulfil its objectives. But in the case of Hyllie, all signs show that Eon attempted to follow through on its promise to build wind turbines. The plan failed for other reasons, one of which was skepticism towards wind turbines within another city department. The difficulty in constructing wind turbines in a city stems from their physical properties: they are large; they require land that could be used for other purposes; they are imposing structures that are not always appreciated by local residents. The failure to build wind turbines near Hyllie occurred despite the combined resources of Eon and at least two departments within the city government. There was corporate influence, but it was in *support* of the Climate Contract, yet it was still not enough to achieve the Climate Contract's goal of making Hyllie climate neutral by 2020. Other factors made it too difficult to achieve this goal.

The Smart Grids for Hyllie project provides an opportunity to examine the other three concerns about smart cities that were raised in the second section of this chapter. The project's main success story was the demand response system that could control energy loads in buildings. First, did the project result in an undue prioritization of problems that could be solved by smart technologies? The demand response system does redefine energy efficiency in a sense, as it focuses on peak energy demand. In contrast, the City of Malmö's climate goals were defined in terms of total annual energy use. But it is hard to say whether such a redefinition is better or worse in terms of overall climate change mitigation. At any rate, Eon showed how the demand response system could reduce the need for fossil fuels in the district heating networks. Second, did the project result in increased surveillance? While the demand response system did involve monitoring of heating and cooling demand, the system monitored demand of the entire building rather than the individual apartment. This implementation avoids some of the 'big brother' concerns that accompany many smart city technologies, which often measure the behaviour of individuals in detail. Third, did the project result in buggy, brittle and hackable buildings? This question is more difficult to answer. The project did not report any problems relating to the security or reliability of the demand response system. But only time will tell whether the system is maintained sufficiently to avoid such problems in the future. Altogether, the demand response system neither unequivocally supports nor discounts these three concerns.

There are nevertheless some reasons for to hold out hope for a shift from sustainable cities to climate-smart ones. At the very least, the story of Hyllie is not as dystopian as the image portrayed by those most critical of smart city ideas. A rather common narrative for smart cities is as follows: smart cities are an invention of multinational corporations such as IBM and Cisco who want to expand their businesses into urban governance; these companies push unnecessary technological solutions, lock in city governments, and secure profits while leaving societal problems unsolved. In the case of the Climate Contract, this narrative would be an unfair characterization. The vision of a climate-smart city district in Hyllie was not simply forced on to the city government by a powerful corporation. When it came to the vision for Hyllie, Eon fit its ambitions for urban smart grids within the city government's pre-existing vision of a climate-smart city. The democratically approved vision for the city, to be powered by renewable energy by 2030, remains in place.

Another reason to hold out hope for the climate-smart city is the slow progress made in the name of sustainable cities. Reducing energy use in buildings and increasing the share of renewable energy production are long-standing ambitions that have proved difficult for practitioners of sustainable urban planning. Energy efficiency measures, including concepts such as passive houses, are often resisted by property developers who consider them to be too expensive, or they are ignored by practitioners in the construction industry who are unwilling to deviate from established routines. Similarly, the physical design of wind turbines makes them contentious in almost any setting and constructing them in cities seems particularly challenging. In contrast, the demand response system that Eon developed seems to be less expensive and invasive, which could facilitate widespread adoption thereof, especially if developers engage with Eon early in the design of their buildings, or if the technology is easy to integrate in existing buildings. While the demand response system might not have the same climate mitigation impact of passive houses or large-scale construction of wind turbines, it has the potential to make a difference.

One of the most difficult aspects of such initiatives is perhaps how to deal with expectations. Only time will tell whether the results from Hyllie will revolutionize urban energy systems—or make a small step in the right direction, if perhaps too slowly for the global climate. It might be unfair to expect a revolution, but one cannot be blamed for getting one's hopes up after reading an ambitious vision like the Climate Contract. City governments make big promises in the hope of building a coalition of energy utilities, developers, and residents, and perhaps they must make such promises if they are to receive funding from higher levels of government. But in doing so, they also set themselves up for disappointment. City governments establish visions and recruit coalitions precisely because they lack the resources and authority to act on their own; when the pursuit of such visions doesn't go as planned, city governments find themselves in a dilemma. They are left to hope that a coalition partner such as a multinational energy company will make up the difference. If not, the city government is left to explain how its failure is in fact a constructive learning experience.

Notes

1 For more on this topic, see Hodson et al. (2013).
2 More details about the study can be found in Parks (2018).
3 Two papers that are particularly inspiring from a theoretical perspective are Farías (2010) and Blok (2013).

References

Blok, A. (2013). Urban green assemblages: An ANT view on sustainable city building projects. *Science & Technology Studies*, 26(1), 5–24.
City of Malmö (2002). *Quality Programme for Spatial Plan 4537*. Malmö: City of Malmö.
City of Malmö (2012). *Hållbarhetsöverenskommelse för Hyllie allé*. Malmö: City of Malmö.
City of Malmö (2015). *Miljöprogram Hyllie: Mål och åtgärder för förverligandet av Öresundsregionens klimatsmartaste stadsdel*. Version 1. Malmö: City of Malmö.
City of Malmö, Eon, & VA Syd (2011). *Klimatkontraktet för Hyllie*. Retrieved March 23, 2020, from https://malmo.se/download/18.72bfc4c412fc1476e02800065623/1491303409157/hylliekontraktet_slutlig_signerad.pdf.
Farías, I. (2010). Decentering the object of urban studies. In T. Bender & I. Farías (Eds.), *Urban Assemblages: How Actor-Network Theory Changes Urban Studies*. London and New York: Routledge, pp. 1–24.
Galdon-Clavell, G. (2013). (Not so) smart cities?: The drivers, impact and risks of surveillance-enabled smart environments. *Science and Public Policy*, 40(6), 717–723.
Hodson, M., Marvin, S., & Bulkeley, H. (2013). The intermediary organisation of low carbon cities: A comparative analysis of transitions in Greater London and Greater Manchester. *Urban Studies*, 50(7), 1403–1422.
Kitchin, R. (2014). The real-time city? Big data and smart urbanism. *GeoJournal*, 79(1), 1–14.
Parks, D. (2018). *The Sustainable City Becomes Climate-Smart: How Smart City Ideas Reshape Urban Environmental Governance*. PhD thesis. Linköping University. Retrieved March 23, 2020, from https://doi.org/10.3384/diss.diva-147310.
Paroutis, S., Bennett, M., & Heracleous, L. (2014). A strategic view on smart city technology: The case of IBM smarter cities during a recession. *Technological Forecasting and Social Change*, 89, 262–272.

Söderström, O., Paasche, T., & Klauser, F. (2014). Smart cities as corporate storytelling. *City*, 18(3), 307–320.

Viitanen, J., & Kingston, R. (2014). Smart cities and green growth: Outsourcing democratic and environmental resilience to the global technology sector. *Environment and Planning A*, 46(4), 803–819.

Chapter 12

Ownership

Delivering Sustainable Development: Landownership and Accountability in Cambridge

Sophia Peacock and Phil Allmendinger

"Sorry, I didn't quite catch that—what did you say?"

The Hot Numbers café off Mill Road, Cambridge, UK, was a noisy location for the first interview. Only a few minutes in, against the never-ending drum of the espresso machines, I (Sophia) found myself learning about the German town of Freiburg. Our interviewee—someone who had worked in both central and local government—recollected a study tour they had attended 10 years previously along with councillors, officers, and other professionals from Cambridge. However, rather than linger on the city's development projects or the sustainable planning solutions that inspired them and the group in their work in Cambridge, Freiburg inspired a discussion about the balance of power between central and local government in England.

"Sorry, could you repeat that again?"
"Wulf Daseking," they answered, spelling out the letters.

Our interviewee clarified how Wulf, the head of urban planning in Freiburg, had been in the role for almost 30 years. This longevity was a recurring theme. As our interviewee went on to explain, "the lead politician had been in post for 20 years, the investments they were making were 30-year investments" (1). Our interviewee explored the implications in relation to large urban development projects with a mix of disbelief and envy: "And they didn't need to go cap in hand to their treasury—they just did it, and they had local taxation they could rely on, and they could borrow against future income streams. All those things that we can't do, they were doing to create great places" (1).

Afterwards, feeling curious, I searched 'Freiburg study tour' online, and came to the realization that Freiburg is a fairly common destination for professionals and politicians in search for inspiration on urban sustainable development solutions—it was even cited as a case study in the 2010 Conservative Party election manifesto. However, it was frustratingly clear to the Cambridge-based attendees of the study tour that best practice was not a matter of simply absorbing and adopting (URBED, 2006). Successful policies and best practices are context-dependent, and the differences in governance between England and Germany meant that the Cambridge planners on the tour could do little more than nod enviously at the planners in Freiburg, who were working with 25-year strategies and durable financing structures. This difference in governance, and the powers gained from local government landownership, as our interviewee indicated, created the means, and the culture, for a more long-term and intergenerational view of urban development in Freiburg.

Understanding the Role of 'Ownership'

This chapter will consider a particular dilemma facing the implementation of sustainable urban development: land ownership. It will discuss the current policy context and governance arrangements in England. It will then turn the discussion to the key issue, which is local government discretion (or rather the lack thereof) in its quest for sustainable development. A softening of regulatory tools in planning over the past few years has made Cambridge dependent upon those private actors with long-term financial interests, such as the University of Cambridge, to implement sustainable development in the built environment. Overall, we question the extent to which such a process is accountable, or replicable, for the country at large, despite the generally positive outcomes in Cambridge. Therefore, our research question is as follows: *regardless of whether private landowners and developers have demonstrated commitment to sustainable development through a particular planning application, to what extent does the planning system ensure this commitment, and are such actors accountable to the public for ensuring those outcomes?*

Land ownership, and the political context and patterns of such ownership, is an issue which lies at the heart of sustainable development in England, due to its particular governance arrangements and planning regulations (see Ryan-Collins et al., 2017). Ownership more generally is a concept that is gaining traction (see e.g., Common Wealth, 2019). This current debate is being shaped by three factors. The first of these is social and has to do with the climate of austerity in England and its impact on local public services, and the growth of inequality, including that of land ownership itself (see Monbiot et al., 2019; Ryan-Collins et al., 2017). The second factor is environmental: with news of mass extinction from unsustainable human land use (Díaz et al., 2019) and the continued threat of climate change (IPCC, 2018), we need to ask why sustainable development has done so little so challenge the current growth model. Third, and more positively, the debate is influenced by the growing experimentation of alternative ownership models, such as the co-operative movement and new municipalism gaining ground in towns such as Preston. This question of ownership can therefore explain current challenges but also provide solutions to imbalances between economic, social, and environmental factors. Furthermore, ownership offers a dual meaning. A common phrase is to 'take ownership' of issues. The question is if private landowners and developers take responsibility of the question of sustainable development, particularly given the political context whereby environmental and planning regulations have softened in favor of private-led housing development.

Land ownership in simple terms is divided between private and public actors. Publicly led and owned housing developments, particularly by local government, have been a widespread and common method of revenue raising, as well as a form of market intervention to ensure socially desirable outcomes in welfare states. These include increasing, both directly and indirectly, the affordability of housing by providing social housing or council housing at a subsidized rent, or more indirectly, by stimulating housing supply. More recently, this form of intervention has also been a way to achieve *sustainable* development, in terms of place-making, climate change mitigation and adaption, the protection of biodiversity, and improving connectivity, with a particular long-term and intergenerational view. However, while England saw a huge growth in public-led housing development from the 1950s to the 1970s, today change in the built environment and housing delivery is mainly driven by the private sector (Rydin, 2013). Therefore, while achieving sustainable development is necessarily a public concern, in England its implementation through the built environment has over the years increasingly fallen on private actors (developers and landowners), who are, for the most part, driven by profit motives and maximizing shareholder value (Monbiot et al., 2019, p. 45). This change has been associated with a longer-term shift in emphasis from government to governance in the policy sphere, and a rise in anti-regulation discourse over the past 30 years (Rydin, 2013). As a senior councillor we interviewed argued, "it's a market economy, and there's a limit to which councils can actually make the decisions or are in control" (6). In addition, this shift towards private sector ownership and power in land markets intensified from 2010, with the centre-right coalition (2010–2015), Conservative (2015–2017) and Conservative (2017–) governments which have overseen some consistent and overlapping policy agendas. Before and after the 2010 election, the positive rhetoric focused on localism and empowering local communities, as well as enhancing growth. The negative rhetoric labored on the ills of what was termed 'big government,' including swipes at too much bureaucracy and regulation. The solution to big government included cuts to public spending (austerity), abolition of regional governance structures, and the 'red tape challenge' which aimed to reduce 'unnecessary' regulation. This challenge was partly aimed at the planning system when the coalition government consolidated over 3,000 different planning regulations into one single 50-page document, which they named the National Planning Policy Framework (NPPF) (DCLG, 2012). This document was originally published in 2012 and was revised in July 2018.[1] The project to streamline national planning guidance faced an onslaught of criticism, particularly in its draft stages, from conservation charities which argued that it had a weak understanding of environmental sustainability.

This chapter complements recent research that highlights the role of private actors within the planning process (see Parker et al., 2018). These perspectives indicate how ubiquitous the private sector is with regards to implementing sustainable development. Private ownership and interests now strongly influence, if not dominate, both sides of English planning—on the one hand, planning policy formation and regulation (Parker et al., 2018), and on the other, project delivery in terms of release of land and the design and structure of development as specified in planning applications. This shift from public to private has implications on the delivery of longer-term policy objectives due to a clash of interests: while the private sector is more commonly associated with shorter-term profit objectives, public organizations have potentially greater ability—as well as incentive—to invest for the long term. This fragmented system currently in place is perceived as preventing strategic interventions as well as ensuring accountability. As one of our interviewees, previously a senior planner in Cambridge, argued: "there's so little power, by comparison with European cities—German cities, Dutch cities—the public sector could actually get on and do things, rather than going cap in hand to a lot of privatized fragmented industries" (2). Another interviewee, previously a local government official, similarly observed: "we have got an imperfect system. I must admit, one of my tests is that I come out of meetings and I always think to myself 'would the Germans do it like this?' and the answer is more or less 99% of the time 'of course they wouldn't'" (5).

The research for the chapter is based on 20 in-depth, semi-structured interviews with local councillors, planners, officials, university staff, and residents, conducted over the course of a year, from March 2016 to May 2017.[2] The chapter is structured as follows: first, in section one, to give context as to *why* land ownership is an increasingly important factor in the implementation of sustainable development, we explore how local government has lost powers and discretion in its own planning policy following national-level reform. In particular, local government has had to adopt a national-level definitions of sustainable development, and has lost many of the regulatory tools that allowed it to set minimum sustainability requirements in planning policy. In sections two and three, we explore the implications with regards to the implementation of sustainable development. Given this loss of local government planning regulatory powers, implementation is increasingly dependent upon individual landowners and developers submitting planning applications that reflect local values of sustainable development. Section two outlines how sustainable development emerges through a bargaining process between public and private actors. Section three then explores more specifically the role of the University of Cambridge as a major landowner (see Greenwood & Adams, 2018) and local developer with long-term interests. The power of the University to influence the direction and character of development in the city at large, while generally positive, is unique. This chapter will conclude that this uniqueness exposes the importance, and the positive outcomes, from a greater emphasis on publicly-led housing development as a way to achieve *accountable* and *replicable* sustainable development across the country.

Local Government Discretion in the Quest for Sustainable Development

Growing Disconnect between Local and National

Our research suggests a growing disconnect between national and local interpretations of sustainable development. Cambridge[3] has adopted a particular stance on sustainability and sustainable development, one that is underpinned by significant growth pressures and planned development, with the city's population estimated to grow by around 50% in the next 15 years. Having overseen for several decades a plan to restrict growth in the city and to disperse development into satellite towns, in the 1990s Cambridge faced growing problems relating to the lack of affordable housing in the city, as well as car-based commuting and congestion. Attitudes surrounding growth and green belt release around the periphery of the city began to change in the early 2000s as a consequence of a shift in public opinion from a broad position of resistance to acceptance of certain development. Consequently, Cambridge has now seen high housing stock growth as measured against other cities (Centre for Cities, 2017, p. 57). Despite this growth, there is interest in balancing this need for development with respecting the environmental limits of the city.

Indeed, many interviewees in Cambridge took issue with the wording of the change in national policy contained in the NPPF and the implications the shift had in terms of local discretion in planning policy. The most common feeling was that the NPPF lacked commitment to sustainable development. The NPPF stipulates that local planning policy and decisions must have "a presumption in favour of sustainable development", which it defines as "positive growth—making economic, environmental and social progress for this and future generations." (DCLG, 2012, p. i). Several interviewees expressed the opinion that the NPPF's definition is problematic, mainly because it inhabited a bias towards *growth*—indeed, most interviewees found its policies overall to favor economic metrics, rather than striking a genuine balance between economic, environmental, and social concerns (1, 3, 11). A former councillor argued that this bias did not reflect local conditions, given that the economy in Cambridge had been booming and therefore required minimal government support: "It was felt that the economy would look after itself" (3). Instead, the councillor argued that local government efforts in Cambridge have been, and should remain, focused on social and environmental issues. However, since the election of the coalition government (2010–2015) and subsequent Conservative national governments, the city council felt that it was under greater pressure to pursue economic development.

The implication of all this is a growing chasm between local and national interpretations of sustainability. A local planning lawyer described Cambridge Council's definition of sustainable development simply as "definitely not the government's definition at the moment" (16). As national policy has become increasingly discredited locally, Cambridge-specific interpretations, such as the 'four Cs' (Community, Connectivity, Climate, and Character), as set out in the Quality Charter for Growth in Cambridgeshire (Cambridgeshire Horizons, 2007), have proved resilient. Although somewhat dated, the Charter remains an important document and blueprint for sustainable development in Cambridge. For example, the four Cs have been used to structure the 'Cambridge Sustainable Housing Design Guide,' the design specification document for Council-led development (Cambridge City Council & HDA, 2017). The following section will consider how loss of discretion in defining sustainable development has impacted the implementation of sustainable development.

Implementing Sustainable Development

For reasons partly relating to governance and land ownership as discussed earlier, the implementation of locally led planning policy in accordance with local values has been limited in England. However, this has been a long-standing problem—long before the change in planning policy with the NPPF. As a senior councillor in the city council argued, "the planning system has always, even since the Town and Country Planning Act in 1947, always favoured development over the 'no' answer from councillors or councils" (6). However, the councillor does concede that recent policy has served to exacerbate this tension, arguing how the government "keeps moving the goalposts in favour of developers," and appears to allow any development to proceed unless significant harm can be demonstrated in relation to sustainability indicators (6).

This bias in favor of developers and the growth of centralized decision-making in planning as embodied by the NPPF set out a change in the logic of the implementation of sustainable development. Rather than setting out the benchmark for *minimum* requirements of sustainable development, instead it ordered the *maximum* regulation permissable in local government. This is a reflection of the national-level anti-regulatory agenda of the coalition government, which entailed limiting local government discretion on setting planning requirements that went above and beyond the stipulations of the NPPF. This observation goes to the heart of a cultural phenomenon in England of highly centralized decision-making combined with neoliberal ideology (Gamble, 1988), a phenomenon that is crystallized in the NPPF through its prioritization of housing development over (a) autonomous local government policy-making, and (b) achieving sustainable development. As one of our interviewees, a former senior local government official, surmised, "we are very centralized in the UK, almost the most centralized of any Western democracy" (1). This centralized approach to governance can explain much of the challenges relating to the implementation of sustainable development.

The implication of this loss of local discretion is that the city council has struggled to implement what it considers to be a higher standard of environmental sustainability. This is exemplified by the abolition in 2015 of the locally popular Code for Sustainable Homes on the basis of removing red tape and encouraging faster development. This move reflected a general shift in policy emphasis towards preventing local authorities from using planning policies to demand higher standards of development. The Code for Sustainable Homes was a widely used government environmental assessment and rating method that was created in 2006, which rated the sustainability of the construction and design of new homes from Levels 1 to 5 (5 being the highest level of sustainability) (see DCLG, 2010). The Code was introduced in 2007 by the Labour government, and during that period many local planning authorities, including Cambridge City Council, required minimum environmental standards for housing development with reference to the Code. An interviewee, a planner in the council, admitted that "it was not a perfect standard by any means" (11), but it offered a tangible and practical measuring tool for local authorities to use, either through planning conditions on planning applications, or through local planning policy. At the time the Code was abolished, Cambridge was proposing a new planning requirement that all new housing developments would have to be built to meet at least Level 4 of the Code.

With the abolition of the Code it became more difficult for the Council to require, measure, and evaluate sustainability on development projects. Our key informant emphasized how it was an increasingly challenging environment within which to work, with new planning reforms reducing the discretion afforded to local planning authorities. This has included the ability of local planning authorities to set minimum carbon reduction requirements for new homes, as well as standards for rainwater and grey water harvesting (11). The result of these national policy restrictions and promotion of development is that the Council has been forced to settle for less ambitious levels of sustainable development. Given this context, interviewees based in Cambridge local government expressed a sense of frustration for not being able to pursue locally determined policies, requirements, and goals. Therefore, fewer restrictions on the private sector entailed greater restrictions on local government. As one local resident and activist argued, "[the concept of sustainability is] being modified. It's being modified to suit the desires of developers rather than the other way around" (18). Therefore, loss of regulation entailed a greater centralization of power. As a local planner argued, "Localism in these sorts of issues doesn't seem to really be a priority. I think government's priority is house building, it's increasing the amount of house building ... [however], we need to make sure that these homes are sustainable in the long term" (11). The following section will explore how local government in Cambridge has sought to achieve sustainable development through other means, primarily by working with the private sector.

Sustainable Development as a Negotiation

To overcome these differences and contentions, the Council has pursued its own housing development on council-owned land, through a local development agency called the Greater Cambridge Housing Development Agency (HDA), recently set up in 2017 between Cambridge City Council, South Cambridgeshire District Council (SCDC), and Cambridgeshire County Council, funded by the Greater Cambridge City Deal. The HDA has so far completed three housing projects (Virido, Chalk Hill, and Scholar's Court), and aims to (a) tackle the affordability issue hands on by building on infill sites that are less desirable to developers, and (b) build to its own environmental and design specifications in order to circumvent restrictions imposed by national policy, in accordance with the *Cambridge Sustainable Housing Design Guide*, which sets the minimum energy and water requirements for council-led/HDA developments as Level 4 of the Code for Sustainable Homes (Cambridge City Council & HDA, 2017, p. 5). This is in the context of an increase in council-led housing developments across the country (Morphet & Clifford, 2017), a trend that the government has recently encouraged by scrapping the borrowing cap on councils that was introduced in 2012, as announced at the Conservative Party Conference in October 2018.

This change in policy might see councils re-establishing their role in housing development and land ownership. Until this time, however, a major method of achieving sustainable development is negotiation and bargaining with the private sector and using different forms of organizations and personal relationships to appeal to developers to go above and beyond what is required in national planning policy. According to one of our interviewees, a former senior planner, "development control of all things is not a technical tick-box exercise—I mean, it can be in some areas—but, generally speaking, it's a mediation, it's a negotiation" (2). Therefore, the soft regulatory climate with regards to environmental requirements emphasizes the importance of the Council having a good working relationship with developers to achieve sustainability objectives. In this context, the Council has worked on developing a good relationship with those developers that are committed to sustainability as part of their business model and values. The Council, in return, promises a better future relationship, and that greater consideration will be given to those developers that can demonstrate commitment to local values in this area. As a local planner explains:

> there are developers, private sector developers out there who are actually quite committed to sustainability, so some of them have their own standards as well. They tend to be some of the smaller scale developers, but there are developers out there, and we're a member of the Good Homes Alliance as well, and they've got developer members who are committed to

developing good homes that are sustainable. So, there are still people in the industry out there who don't want ... us to take a step backwards.

(11)

Furthermore, in the design specification produced for the Council-led development through the Greater Cambridge Housing Development Agency, the Council seems to be encouraging developers to go above and beyond planning legislation and to take note of the document, showing that, beyond its initial purpose of guiding council development, it aims to inspire and encourage private development coming forward in the Cambridge area:

> The principles set out in this guide are applicable to all housing developments not just those delivered by the HDA. As such, this guidance is freely available for anyone seeking to deliver high quality sustainable new homes to use, be that in Cambridge or more widely.
> (Cambridge City Council & HDA, 2017, p. 5)

This sort of co-production, bargaining, and negotiation can also be exemplified by a combination of different kinds of structures, organizations, institutions, and networks in the city. It seems that sustainable development needs—or at least strongly benefits from—a local culture and community that is interested in and committed to protecting the environment. In this context, determining the character of development, and its level of sustainability, has increasingly become a bargaining process, involving a number of stakeholders, including local government and citizens, appealing to developers' 'better nature.' This is manifest in the form of institutionalized structures such as local enterprise partnerships, delivery bodies, local industry and lobbying groups, expert advisory panels, residents' associations, and neighborhood planning forums, as well as softer structures such as personal networks: "[Cambridge is] a small place and it's a sort of very well-networked place" (2). From this perspective, there appears to be a fairly complex local network of people and organizations influencing, interpreting, and implementing sustainability. This highlights the proactive co-production of interpreting and implementing a concept of sustainability that is appropriate to the local context. According to a senior councillor in the city council,

> If I was to write ... two to four pages on sustainability, at least half of what I would write would be about process, because it's all about linking people together and simply issues on organizational leadership and behaviour change.

(6)

The same councillor attributed much of the city's ambition to sustainable development to a local culture of 'analysis and progressive thinking':

We're just fortunate that we've got organizations that largely 'get it' when it comes to climate change ... They're not just doing their corporate social responsibility to tick boxes; they know that their future opportunities lie in being ahead of the game of sustainability.

(6)

This culture, according to a couple of interviewees, may be partly due to influence from the University of Cambridge, a major stakeholder and landowner in the city. The following section will explore the role of the University, in particular its own housing development in northwest Cambridge and the process of implementing sustainable development there.

The University of Cambridge and the Eddington Development

We have outlined an institutional environment where councils are reliant on the private sector, in an inevitably ad hoc and uncertain manner, to appeal to developers' better nature to go above and beyond national planning policy. Given this state of affairs, we argue that achieving sustainable development requires *locally invested* developers and landowners, who take ownership and responsibility for achieving sustainable development in their local areas. Landowners who are in a position to prioritize high-quality developments over maximizing short-term gains are known as 'legacy landowners' (Ryan-Collins et al., 2017, p. 197–198). Several interviewees have emphasized the role of the University in ensuring more sustainable outcomes in the city as a whole. These motivations and complex networks of relationships and actors have already had an impact on the shape, character, and 'sustainability' of the city through existing and emerging developments, where the University has, both historically and in the present day, taken on a custodial role with regards to the development of the city. As a member of the environmental team in the University stated, "considering we own most of the city, I think it would be hard not [to be a leader] ... Cambridge City Council owns 85 buildings, the University owns 350, plus the 400 in this commercial portfolio" (15). As a major landowner, the University may therefore be better placed to deliver sustainable development than the average developer.

Drawing comparisons with the 19th-century model villages of Bournville and Saltaire, which were both developed by industrialists for their workers, one of our interviewees observed that the large landowners are best placed to deliver sustainable development, since they are not necessarily looking to make immediate profits from their land. While such philanthropic approaches to planning has almost disappeared, our interviewee argued that the University had produced some of the best settlements (16). The University's achievements with regard to sustainable development on its northwest site in Eddington was a reflection of its long-term strategic interests, as well as a wish to 'set an example' by overseeing both an environmentally and socially sustainable development. The long-term strategic element of the development was crucial: as the University's Green Paper from 2010, which outlined the plans for the site, stated:

Provision of space into which the University can expand has long been regarded as critical to the long-term future of the University ... The University's mission is to contribute to society through the pursuit of education, learning, and research at the highest levels of international excellence. It is this strategic purpose that is the motivating force behind the current proposals.

(Cambridge University Reporter, 2010)

According to the Green Paper, a lack of good quality, affordable accommodation in Cambridge meant reduced ability for the University to compete for, and attract, "the world's best staff and students" (Cambridge University Reporter, 2010). These strategic interests also included environmental considerations as a way of complying with the wider environmental aims of the University as well as reducing costs. The University institutionalized this commitment by setting up an expert advisory panel for the site—the so-called Sustainability Panel—with the remit to "challenge the evolving designs," to push the scheme towards wider questions of place-making, and the creation of community and sustainable infrastructure to encourage residents to live sustainably (*Cambridge University Reporter*, 2010, para. 83). The entire site, as outlined in the North West Cambridge Area Action Plan, has been—and will be—built to Code 5 specification of the Code for Sustainable Homes. One might therefore suggest that the work towards realizing this particular translation, and vision, of sustainability in Eddington has depended on the position of the University as an actor with interests that are by default intergenerational. As the University's efforts have contrasted with those of regular developers, the tangible presence of the Eddington development has forced a general increase in ambition. As a local planner explains, "I think the scheme has caused some developers big headaches because they tend to compare everything to that site" (11).

However, following completion of the first phase of a three-stage development of the site, a couple of interviewees admitted that the University had not quite reached the standards it had set itself, mainly due to cost overruns which came to the fore in July 2015. As an article in *Financial Times* reported; "An independent assessment found forecast construction costs for phase 1 of the project had ballooned by more than £100m—from £259m in July 2013, to £378m in July 2015" (Hale, 2018). The outcome of cost cutting, and changes in priorities, resulted in a senior member of the sustainability panel resigning due to disagreements, indicating the imperfect processes of implementation, and the complexities of putting an idea into practice. As a (different) senior member of the University explained:

[They] have not always liked what we ended up doing, because the quality panel is only interested in what's the best we could possibly do by way of environmental sustainability. And what we've had to do in the project is build something that is affordable and practical, and we can't afford to take risks with fancy engineering that might go wrong. So, there's quite a big tension there.

(9)

Furthermore, the narrative of the University singlehandedly pursuing forward-thinking development for the 'greater good' ignores the fact that the Code 5 specification was a planning requirement set by the city council. According to a senior councillor, the University, as represented by the North West Development Project Team, "didn't want to go to Code Level 5" (13). This dispute was settled during planning inspection when the requirement in the local development framework (the North West Cambridge Area Action Plan 2009) was upheld. One interviewee, a councillor from the Cambridge City Council (Cambridge local government), likened the planning inspection to the story of David and Goliath:

> [There were] 12 men in suits kind of saying how they couldn't do Code Level 5. And we had recruited really good officers, who had sort of fire in their bellies, and knowledge. And they felt they had community backing ... the University's much bigger than us, far more resources, things like that. And we won. And we were sort of like 'huh!', you know, we were the first Code Level 5 development to get through inspection in the whole country ... what was important, I think we had some politicians who were keen on it, the times were right, we had huge support from various different people around the city, including academics in the University, and we had some really good officers with the right sort of skills and capability.
>
> (13)

Achieving social sustainability for the site has also been a challenge due to viability of the proposed rental scheme. While rent has been set as a proportion of an inhabitant's income to ensure affordability, concerns have been voiced over how the University will cover its debts without eventually needing to raise rents in the future. A further contention has arisen with regard to how the University prioritizes its spending, with the unions seeing the 'university developer' as a problematic phenomenon, arguing how universities "were choosing to prioritise capital expenditure over staff. Spending on staff has fallen since 2009/10 to just 52.9% of income in 2016/17, while capital expenditure increased by 35% over the same period" (UCU, 2018). Given these difficulties and tensions, while one of our interviewees made comparisons to Bournville and Saltire, a journalist at the *Financial Times* made a similar, but less flattering comparison:

> George Pullman, who made a fortune in railroad carriages, built his own town on the south side of Chicago in the late 19th century. For more than a decade it was lauded as a shining example of industrial paternalism, but when the financial crisis of the 1890s struck, wages fell. Rents, set by the business, did not. Tensions culminated in strikes so violent 30 people died and the events are now memorialised in Labor Day, a US national holiday.
>
> (Hale, 2018)

While there are clear successes in the University's involvement in developing the City of Cambridge and realizing a shared vision of sustainable development, questions remain over whether some of its promises with regard to the environmental sustainability and affordability of the Eddington development will be ultimately delivered. Therefore, the question of accountability—as well as replicability—inevitably follows. This question will be considered in the following concluding discussion.

Accountability and Replicability?

This chapter began with an anecdote about Freiburg. While the picture of Freiburg as a model for sustainable development is not without its faults (Mössner, 2015), its institutional and governing structure was seen by the interviewees as one that could begin to tackle the question of sustainable development. This was because local government in Germany had more land ownership, finance, and power in the development of their cities, and this power was better able to achieve the longer-term public good (for further comparison and discussion, see Bulkeley & Kern, 2006). The implication of this is that any governance arrangement that is less stable, and controls less land, is also less able to achieve long-term policies. In such circumstances sustainable development becomes more of a guide, a policy add-on, a planning requirement, or a form of measurement, rather than a way of fundamentally building a city.

We have discussed two major losses in local government planning powers in England. First, over a longer period of time, public delivery of housing has been undermined through successive policy reform. More recently, planning regulations have softened, as manifested by the NPPF. Both these long-term and short-term reforms have placed greater power in the hands of private landowners and developers in determining the character, design, and sustainability of developments coming forward. Despite this, the connection between land ownership and sustainable development is under-researched. While a discussion on 'ownership' essentially questions the difference between public and private delivery of housing, urban change, and sustainable development, it also highlights the issue of implementation and accountability. Although planning scholars have begun to investigate the role of the private sector in planning, there appears to be insufficient acknowledgement from within the planning profession as to the scale and significance of this shift, its possible implications, and the ways in which the cycle of reform affects ongoing practice. We hypothesize that such trends may be undermining the oversight and integrity of the planning system—a system which requires synoptic thinking and understandings in order to produce coordinated spatial plans across topics and boundaries (Parker et al., 2018, p. 745).

Sustainable development is an interesting political idea. At its heart it is radical: a call to balance—and even rein in—economic growth in order to protect the future livelihoods and right to life of voiceless future generations. However, similarly to other originally 'radical' and inclusive ideas of planning, such as Ebenezer Howard's garden city movement, or Henri Lefebvre's right to the city, sustainable development has inevitably become reinterpreted and co-opted in policy. As commented by Haughton et al. (2013, p. 231),

> there appears to have been a narrowing of [planning's] intellectual horizons, to the extent that planners rarely seem to offer an alternative to the mainstream paradigm and potentially disruptive ideas if they are seen as little more than 'extreme' or fanciful ideas.

It is for this reason why there is extensive critical research and debate on sustainable development as a concept. However, few of these critiques discuss *how* to maintain and reinvigorate the original radical purpose of sustainable development. Instead, the tendency is to replace the discussion with new concepts—such as resilience—which are at no lesser risk of being similarly co-opted and reinterpreted to suit the status quo.

We have described how local actors in Cambridge increasingly viewed sustainable development as having been co-opted, particularly since the publication of the National Planning Policy Framework in 2012. The general understanding among planners was that the NPPF had a development bias which was at odds with the local values. Local councillors, planners, and residents seem to be constantly bargaining and campaigning for minimum standards for sustainable development. However, if developers and landowners hold too much power, then the achievement of sustainable development hinges mainly on internal business models, and profit motives as well as perhaps marketing and/or public relations strategies.

Therefore, this chapter has sought to explore the dilemmas of implementing sustainable development. In particular, it identifies those actors who are motivated to achieve and deliver sustainable development in Cambridge. The example of the North West Cambridge Development scheme, and the role of the University, demonstrates the importance of local developers and landowners who have long-term interests in investing in their local area, as internalized in their business model and culture. This finding is significant, given the growing weight on the private sector to deliver sustainable development, and the loss of powers held by local planning authorities in demanding certain standards through the planning application process. One might therefore ask how local government and central government can respond to this.

Problematically, this reliance on locally invested institutions, landowners, and developers does not necessarily guarantee sustainable development, nor does it ensure accountability in process or outcome. The Eddington development met problems along the way that affected the University's ability to deliver on its original planning application. As the *Financial Times* article points out, "as the commercial activities of the University continue to grow in importance, it is becoming increasingly clear that the governance which is appropriate for the academic activities of the University is not necessarily appropriate for its commercial activities" (Hale, 2018). Events in 2018 such as the union strike, and student campaigning for fossil fuel divestments, show that the University is neither obliged to, nor necessarily has an interest in, providing accountability or transparency in its internal decision-making processes. While the public can trust that the University has long-term strategic interests which largely fall in line with the interests of the Council and the city at large, it is not the same as relying on political and democratic representation to achieve sustainable development.

The *least* attractive option, which is the option facing arguably most cities and towns in England that do not have a legacy landowner and institution like the University, is the reliance on private developers and smaller-scale landowners to deliver sustainable development. This was a point was made by a previous senior planning official who observed,

> So, you've got a major landowner, namely the University, with a specific need for its future, which is benefiting the whole of that place. So, if you compare that with [an anonymized market town], there isn't an equivalent, there isn't an institution that is thinking about things in that way.
>
> (7)

Private actors offer neither long-term interests nor accountability, yet, with the undermining of local government planning powers, they have extraordinary power to shape the implementation of sustainable—or unsustainable—development locally.

This leads us to the question of replicability. Whether the successes of the University's Eddington development are replicable is questionable. As Pro-Vice Chancellor David Cardwell discovered, "I did try to look around the world for any university, anywhere in the world, that's doing anything comparable. I couldn't find anything" (quoted in Hale, 2018). The Eddington development, and the position of the University in influencing the direction and character of development in the city at large, is undeniably unique. However, this uniqueness emphasizes the importance, and the positive outcomes, from a greater emphasis on publicly led housing development, as a way to achieve accountable and replicable sustainable development across the country. Given this, England would benefit from moving closer to its European counterparts in relation to housing policy. This reflects the recent U-turn on the part of the Conservative government on council borrowing limits being lifted to allow more housing to come forward. However, if sustainable development demands long-term interests and investments, there are other types of public and collective development that can help to bring about sustainable development as a way of doing, rather than a box to be ticked. We therefore suggest that government should consider supporting more community-led housing development, such as community land trusts, as well as supporting a new generation of local development corporations and new town development corporations which can demonstrate accountable, and politicized, governance structures. As was recently suggested in a policy paper, "Development should be led by democratically accountable public bodies and communities, not private developers operating according to the need to maximise shareholder returns" (Monbiot et al., 2019, p. 7). At the very minimum, local authorities should have their planning powers reinstated, and be given more, if not full, discretion in setting minimum environmental standards in planning policy, if governments are interested in seeing sustainable development implemented through the built environment (for further discussion on policy reform options, see Ryan-Collins et al., 2017, Chapter 7; Monbiot et al., 2019).

In conclusion, greater land ownership as well as policy ownership for local public actors and community organizations could make all the difference in promoting more appropriate governance structures for the delivery and implementation of sustainable development. While private developers will remain vital players in the English economy and housing industry, introducing institutional changes that encourage public development or reintroduce minimum requirements in planning policy can even the playing field and balance the negotiation process between the public (both current and future citizens) and the private sector, and hopefully can serve to move English planning and development away from short-termism to something that more closely resembles sustainable development.

Notes

1 Due to the timing of this research, any references to the NPPF is referring to the 2012—and original—version.
2 The interviews were between 30 minutes and 90 minutes long, and were recorded and transcribed. One key informant, a planner in Cambridge City Council (11), was interviewed twice. While all interviewees have been anonymized as part of our research design, we include Table 12.1 below to give an overview of the proportions of certain professions and stakeholders. This table can be used to cross-reference quotations included in the text.
3 Cambridge is used as shorthand for the three local authorities—Cambridge City Council, Cambridgeshire County Council, and Cambridgeshire South District Council—that comprise the wider Cambridge city region and other stakeholders such as the University, businesses, and community groups.

Table 12.1 Interviewees

No.	Date	Description	Organization
1	March 2016	Former senior local government official	Cambridgeshire Horizons, Cambridgeshire County Council
2		Former senior planner	Cambridgeshire Horizons, Cambridge City Council
3	April 2016	Local politician	Cambridge City Council, Cambridgeshire County Council
4		Senior planner	Cambridgeshire County Council
5		Former senior local government official	Greater Cambridge Greater Peterborough Local Enterprise Partnership
6		Local politician/Councillor	Cambridge City Council, Cambridgeshire County Council
7		Former senior planner	Cambridge City Council
8		Private sector, NGO	Cambridge Cleantech, Greater Cambridge Partnership
9	May 2016	Senior administrator/academic	University of Cambridge
10	June 2016	Local government official	Cambridge City Council
11	September and November 2017	Planning officer	Cambridge City Council
12	November 2016	Planning officer	Cambridgeshire County Council
13	December 2016	Former senior local politician	Cambridge City Council
14		Environmental Manager	University of Cambridge
15	January 2017	Environmental Manager, Former local government official	University of Cambridge, Cambridge City Council
16	February 2017	Planning lawyer, academic	Local law firm
17	March 2017	National politician, Liberal Democrats	House of Lords
18	April 2017	Local resident and activist	South Newnham Neighbourhood Forum
19	May 2017	Local activist and resident	N/A

Source: Table compiled by the authors.

References

Allmendinger, P. (2016). *Neoliberal Spatial Governance*. Abingdon: Routledge.
Bulkeley, H., & Kern, K. (2006). Local government and the governing of climate change in Germany and the UK. *Urban Studies*, 43(12), 2237–2259.
Cambridge City Council & Housing Development Agency (HAD) (2017). *The Cambridge Sustainable Housing Guide*. February. Retrieved 23 March, 2020, from www.cambridge.gov.uk/media/1503/cambridgeshire-sustainable-housing-design-guide.pdf.
Cambridge University Reporter (2010). North West Cambridge Project: A Green Paper. *Cambridge University Reporter*, 35(6194), 25 June, 1010–1028. Retrieved 23 March, 2020, from www.admin.cam.ac.uk/reporter/2009-10/weekly/6194/section1.shtml#heading4-1.
Cambridgeshire Horizons (2007). *Cambridgeshire Quality Charter for Growth*. Retrieved from www.cambridge.gov.uk/media/2950/cambridgeshire_quality_charter_2010.pdf.
Centre for Cities (2017). *Cities Outlook 2017 Report*. London: Centre for Cities. Retrieved 23 March, 2020, from www.centreforcities.org/wp-content/uploads/2017/01/Cities-Outlook-2017-Web.pdf.
Common Wealth (2019). *About*. Retrieved 23 March, 2020, from www.common-wealth.co.uk/about.html.
Department for Communities and Local Government (DCLG) (2010). *Code for Sustainable Homes: Technical Guide*. Department for Communities and Local Government. Retrieved 23 March, 2020, from https://assets.publishing.service.gov.uk/government/uploads/system/uploads/attachment_data/file/5976/code_for_sustainable_homes_techguide.pdf.
Department for Communities and Local Government (DCLG) (2012). *National Planning Policy Framework*. Department for Communities and Local Government, March 2012. Retrieved 23 March, 2020, from http://webarchive.nationalarchives.gov.uk/20180608095821/https://www.gov.uk/government/publications/national-planning-policy-framework–2.
Deas, I., & Hincks, S. (2017). *Territorial Policy and Governance*. London: Routledge.
Díaz, S., Settele, J., & Brondízio, E. (2019). *Summary for Policymakers of the Global Assessment Report on Biodiversity and Ecosystem Services* (unedited advance version). Bonn: IPBES. Retrieved 23 March, 2020, from www.ipbes.net/sites/default/files/downloads/summary_for_policymakers_ipbes_global_assessment.pdf.
Gamble, A. (1988). *The Free Economy and the Strong State: The Politics of Thatcherism*. Basingstoke: Palgrave Macmillan.
Greenwood, X., & Adams, R. (2018). Oxford and Cambridge university colleges own property worth £3.5bn. *Guardian Online*, 29 May. Retrieved 23 March, 2020, from www.theguardian.com/education/2018/may/29/oxford-and-cambridge-university-colleges-own-property-worth-35bn.
Hale, T. (2018) Cambridge University's £1bn bet on housing. *Financial Times*. 27 September. Retrieved 23 March, 2020, from https://ftalphaville.ft.com/2018/09/27/1538028000000/Cambridge-University-s–1bn-experiment-with-debt-and-housing/.
Haughton, G., Allmendinger, P., & Oosterlynck, S. (2013). Spaces of neoliberal experimentation: Soft spaces, postpolitics, and neoliberal governmentality. *Environment and Planning A: Economy and Space*, 45(1), 217–234.

IPCC (2018). *Global Warming of 1.5°C: Summary for Policymakers*. Geneva: Intergovernmental Panel on Climate Change. Retrieved 23 March, 2020, from www.ipcc.ch/site/assets/uploads/sites/2/2018/07/SR15_SPM_version_stand_alone_LR.pdf.

Lord, A., & Tewdwr-Jones, M. (2014). Is planning "under attack"? Chronicling the deregulation of urban and environmental planning in England, *European Planning Studies*, 22(2), 345–361.

Mance, H. & Evans, J. (2018). Theresa May lifts council borrowing cap to boost housebuilding. *Financial Times*. 3 October. Retrieved 23 March, 2020, from www.ft.com/content/246d425e-c703-11e8-ba8f-ee390057b8c9.

Monbiot, G., Grey, R., Kenny, T., Macfarlane, L., Powell-Smith, A., Shrubsole, G., & Stratford, B. (2019). *Land for the Many: Changing the Way Our Fundamental Asset Is Used, Owned and Governed*. London: Labour Party. Retrieved 23 March, 2020, from https://landforthemany.uk/wp-content/uploads/2019/06/land-for-the-many.pdf.

Morphet, J., & Clifford, B. (2017). *Local Authority Direct Provision of Housing*. Research report, December. Retrieved 23 March, 2020, from www.rtpi.org.uk/media/2619006/Local-authority-direct-provision-of-housing.pdf.

Mössner, S. (2015). Urban development in Freiburg, Germany: Sustainable and neoliberal? *Die Erde*, 146(2–3), 189–193.

Owens, S., & Cowell, R. (2011). *Land and Limits: Interpreting Sustainability in the Planning Process* (2nd edn.). Abingdon: Routledge.

Parker, G., Street, E., & Wargent, M. (2018). The rise of the private sector in fragmentary planning in England, *Planning Theory & Practice*, 19(5), 734–750.

Ryan-Collins, J., Lloyd, T., & Macfarlane, L. (2017). *Rethinking the Economics of Land and Housing*. London: Zed Books.

Rydin, Y. (2013). *The Future of Planning: Beyond Growth Dependence*. Bristol: Policy Press.

University and College Union (UCU) (2018). UCU to ballot higher education staff for industrial action over pay. University and College Union. 29 June. Retrieved 23 March, 2020, from www.ucu.org.uk/article/9562/UCU-to-ballot-higher-education-staff-for-industrial-action-over-pay.

URBED (2006). *Towards a Quality Charter for Growth in the Cambridge Area: Freiburg Study Tour Report*. London: URBED. Retrieved 23 March, 2020, from http://urbed.coop/sites/default/files/Freiburg%20Study%20Tour%20report.pdf.

World Commission on Environment and Development (1987). *Our Common Future* (Brundtland Report). Retrieved 23 March, 2020, from www.un-documents.net/our-common-future.pdf.

Chapter 13

Tools

Realizing the Vision of a Socially Inclusive RiverCity

Jacob Lindkvist, Kristian Käll and Anders Svensson

RiverCity Gothenburg (known as Älvstaden in Sweden) is the most extensive urban development project in all of Northern Europe. Here, room is currently being made for 5 million square meters of new floor space. Vision Älvstaden, that was adopted by Gothenburg City Council in 2012, is the result of an ambitious citizen dialogue process, and stakes out the path for an expansion of the inner city through the conversion of centrally located but defunct harbor and industrial areas into dense, mixed-use urban neighborhoods. The overall area consists of a number of sub-areas in which city-employed project managers, a consortia of stakeholders, and groups of property owners are working together towards developing the area in accordance with the overall vision, which is the result of a process of planning and coordination previously unseen in the history of the city.

The explicit aim of the vision is to ensure that RiverCity will provide space for a multitude of residents and activities. The public space has been purposely designed to function as an arena for meetings that is open to all. There is, however, a need to find ways to secure a varied supply of dwellings and workplaces that can be made available to different income brackets and accommodate diverse lifestyles. Furthermore, the new city center needs to adapt to a changing climate and to a global economy that is in rapid transformation. Overall, the project constitutes a unique opportunity to 'connect the city,' 'embrace the water,' and 'reinforce the core' as the vision puts it, while at the same time producing enormous economic and social value.

In the realization of the vision, the city will make historically large investments in new streets, parks, and social infrastructure. The project is also designed to be a testbed for sustainable urban development in which novel solutions, methods, and business models are applied. This ranges from models for co-localization and communal use, socially mixed living and vibrant ground-floor zones to solutions for climate adaptation, sustainable mobility, and smart communication. The development work is therefore being carried out in close cooperation with universities, research institutes, and the business community, and functions as a test case for a number of development projects in the realm of sustainable urban development.

The authors of this chapter all work as urban planning and development professionals on the RiverCity project, and in this chapter we will discuss some of the main challenges that we have encountered while working on it. We will begin by presenting some of the underlying challenges peculiar to this particular project. We will then show how these challenges articulate with the strategy for the early phases of the RiverCity development process, and this leads naturally to the more concrete planning stage. Finally, we exemplify how the project today works towards tackling the identified challenges on the social side, while at the same time ensuring that the qualities of the emerging urban environment are not compromised. A central dilemma in this is working to achieve a socially sustainable urban future within the context of a national system that does not provide strong policy tools for facilitating this. Consequently, any such development becomes dependent upon the solid commitment of local politicians, the facilitation and advocacy skills of local public servants and committed urban professionals, as well as the ability of property developers to commit to a holistic and long-term perspective on urban value-creation.

Understanding the Problem: Persistent Segregation and Polarization in a Booming Housing Market

The critical challenge for facilitating a sustainable future for Gothenburg is to combat socioeconomic polarization and ethnic segregation. Over the last decade the basic trend has been that people taking up residence in Gothenburg are youth (students) and foreign migrants, while well-established households with good incomes tend to move out of the city to the nearby municipalities when thinking about starting a family.

This migration pattern drives a socioeconomic and ethnic segregation process whereby middle-class people are drawn towards settling with their peers while economically disadvantaged migrants invariably find themselves living in areas already dominated by fellow migrants and other low-income groups. Accordingly, segregation must be understood not only as a problem of socio-economically challenged households being concentrated in deprived areas, but rather as the relational process whereby well-established groups congregate in certain areas, while low-income are pushed into other areas where they become the majority.

In areas where income and educational levels are lower than the national average, the inhabitants are in greater need of stronger societal support compared to those living in more affluent areas. It is more common that children living in areas where there is a large proportion of children with a foreign background do not qualify for upper secondary school compared to children living in other neighborhoods. The drivers behind these facts need to be further explored, but statistics show that the different parts of Gothenburg present huge inequalities in terms of income, education, health, well-being, and life expectancy. People are estimated to have a life expectancy that is nine years shorter if they grow up in Bergsjön than if they live in Askim, even though these two areas are only 20 kilometers apart.

This social segregation and its consequent effects is hampering equal opportunities for children growing up in Gothenburg. Furthermore, middle-class households moving out to adjacent municipalities means less tax income for Gothenburg, leaving the city with a diminishing tax base to finance the much-needed municipal services.

Taking the above factors into consideration, a central challenge for the RiverCity project was to construct housing that was accessible to households of lower economic means, while at the same time creating an urban environment that would also be attractive to higher-income groups. If this could be achieved, the RiverCity could truly live up to its vision of 'connecting the city' and becoming a harmonious living and meeting place for all Gothenburgers. However, in order to understand the magnitude of the challenges in bringing about such a development it is also necessary to explain some of the background concerning the development of the Swedish housing market in recent decades.

Since the mid-1990s, the Swedish housing sector has been one of the most market-oriented in Europe. At that point the national government cancelled all subsidies to the housing sector and left the field all but completely open for the market to provide housing. Coupled with a strong urbanization trend over the last decade, this development has led to a housing shortage in urban areas. The shortage is reflected in high prices for people buying a home and difficulties in finding a permanent home at all for those who are unable to purchase their own dwelling.

In many countries, the provision of state-subsidized social housing is regarded as the self-evident solution to creating a social mix in new development areas. Social housing is a means of providing housing for those who cannot afford what the market provides. However, Sweden is one of three countries in Europe that has not applied for an exemption from the EU legislation on 'services of general economic interest.' Therefore, subsidies for social housing are not possible today. The concept of social housing has also been rejected for decades by the governing political majorities. Furthermore, in 2011, a Swedish law was adopted that demands that the public housing sector must operate according to the models of the private sector, and must strive for a margin of profitability that is equal to its commercial competitors. Thus, municipalities were no longer able to indirectly subsidize a socially desired housing mix by providing low-rent public housing in attractive locations. Due to the scarcity and resultant high market prices for housing, social inclusion and social mix in new development areas is often deemed to be an ambition that is dead in the water.

In a Swedish context, given the existing conditions, the strategy for achieving any degree of inclusion and mix has been to promote mixed tenure within neighborhoods by fostering the development of both rental and owner-occupied dwellings. The idea is that by facilitating a higher share of rental apartments, residents who are unable to take out a mortgage will have a chance to move into the area. Unfortunately, due to increasing costs in new developments and a relaxation of the national rent control system, mixed tenure is no longer enough to create inclusive living for low-income groups. This means that in any given new urban development, it can be assumed that the lion's share of the constructed homes will be occupied by households from the middle- and upper-middle class segments, who have the means to afford the high rents or mortgage costs that consequently are associated with any new build properties. When low-income groups and immigrants cannot afford to buy or rent in new central areas such as the RiverCity, the risk is that such new developments drive rather than mitigate socioeconomic polarization and ethnic segregation.

The Concretization of the Social and Urban Design Challenges in the RiverCity Project

The realization of the RiverCity vision faces three planning challenges which together generate a demand for strong long-term leadership and a broad understanding of municipal and welfare economics. Given the existing institutional framework at the state level, the central dilemma is to provide a socially inclusive neighborhood with a good residential mix, which can support itself financially and provide the qualities that nowadays are the hallmarks of an attractive urban area. These include as a mixed-use development, a continuous street grid, and a careful balance between dense development and abundant well-designed public spaces. In the guiding vision document, the three main challenges are presented as being concerned with social exclusion, climate change, and a changed economy. With regard to social exclusion, the vision recognizes that "the Gothenburg of today is a socioeconomically excluded city" where "economic and social deprivation is clustered in specific parts of the city" that are characterized by high unemployment, low levels of educational attainment and skills, poor health and low levels of civic participation. The proposed solution to this is to 'connect the city,' particularly by ensuring that the RiverCity becomes a socially mixed neighborhood that can function as a physical and social bridge between the cluster of less affluent neighborhoods on the island of Hisingen, right across the river from the area, and the existing core of the city, with its economically well-off population.

The design qualities of the public urban environment require three overarching aspects to be attended to if the goal of a high-quality urban environment is to be achieved: land use, the traffic system, and urban density. Land use is to a large extent conditioned by the economy/market. The locational attractiveness for different land uses is to a large extent decided by the structure of the main thoroughfares and the frontage that is provided along these, while urban density is predicated upon the level of the housing offer and the associated need for open spaces and infrastructure. Together, these three factors also constitute the main terms of the municipal-financial calculus regarding the development of the inner city. Land use, transport provision, and urban density need to be planned in relation to each other, so that they also function as means to tackle the challenge of providing a robust and sustainable city, ready to confront future challenges, but simultaneously continuing to provide a good living environment for inhabitants.

Currently, the overall strategies presented in the RiverCity vision are being concretized and translated into manifest impact goals. This work proceeds from the work packages and programs that have already been formulated, or are in the process of being so, in the planning of different subprojects within the RiverCity project. The overarching purpose of this work is to clarify the current situation and challenges while pointing towards the choices that have to be made regarding quality and sustainability in the planning of the concrete physical environment. All the major decisions of political significance regarding the content, design, and structure of the RiverCity will be made as part of the process for a new comprehensive plan for the city, and will also be worked into the supplementary detailed plan for the inner city. An additional aim of this work is to formulate measurable goals—indicators for urban quality—that can be tested in the RiverCity. Every sub-area in the project will also develop goal frames and programs for land use as well as for the design of buildings and public spaces. This is tool is necessary to achieve quality and cost efficiency in the ongoing planning work.

Tackling the Identified Challenges in Practice

Given that it is dependent on land revenue to finance investments in an appealing urban environment, and incentives at the national level to produce affordable housing for future inhabitants, Gothenburg has an urgent problem to solve if it is to succeed in ensuring that the RiverCity is both an attractive environment for businesses and socially established households, while also ensuring a residential social mix that can contribute to mitigating the social segregation within the city. The city and the publicly owned development corporation, Älvstranden, are therefore currently actively exploring what can be done at the local level to provide affordable housing in lieu of new state support.

There are two unique tools that Gothenburg can benefit from:

1   A strong political leadership with a clear social agenda for the development of the city, namely the RiverCity vision.
2   A huge plot of undeveloped land in central parts of the city, owned and controlled by the city, which could be used for the development of the RiverCity.

With these two instruments, Älvstranden is currently working in collaboration with construction companies to encourage the market to develop affordable housing in Frihamnen, one of the main sub-areas of the project. The combination of attractive land (when developed Frihamnen will form part of the inner city) and a clear objective to create a social mix has led to an initial success in the land allocation of Frihamnen.

The property developers chosen by the city to carry out the development of the area have agreed to earmark a fair share of the planned rental apartments to be priced in accordance with the average rent level within the existing public housing segment of the city. Rents in Frihamnen will thus be affordable for the average resident of the low-income areas of the city.

By formulating clear conditions and specific targets for rents early in the development process the city has pushed the market actors to come up with different business models to meet its political ambitions. Some developers will reinvest the profits from owner-occupied apartments (in Sweden generally in the form of housing cooperatives) in order to finance affordable rental apartments. Some will use a private rent allowance system. Others work with more efficient production lines and economies of scale. As one developer stated, "we will accept reduced profit margins if we can contribute to making a difference for Gothenburg." This model of action and the outcome defines the RiverCity project as a crucial link between the broader political ambitions of the city and the creative and executive drive of the market forces in city development.

The negotiated lower rents in Frihamnen have made it possible for low-income groups to settle in the area. But connecting back to the question of urban qualities, and specifically high-quality public space, inclusive living for lower-income groups also demands an inclusive urban space. Frihamnen therefore needs to be planned to provide attractions that are inviting and accessible to different residents from different socioeconomic background, with varied lifestyles, backgrounds, and needs. A variety of non-commercial attractions is in this context particularly important. Affordable business premises are vital in creating low-cost establishments that meet the daily consumption needs of low-income groups. For instance, this can be done by conserving older buildings which attract lower rents. In Frihamnen, the city has already started creating an inclusive identity by working with temporary activities in the project of place-making. Residents from different parts of Gothenburg are taking ownership in the process by carrying out temporary activities such as urban gardening, social painting, building a sauna, or using the area for sports activities such as the roller derby. The strategy is to brand Frihamnen with an image of diversity and as melting pot for the whole city. This can create a sense of openness, curiosity, and warmth in the public perception of Frihamnen and Gothenburg.

Conclusion

Naturally, a lot of different stakeholders, such as civil society, business, and the different branches of the municipal services need to cooperate to reach a sustainable and fair development of Gothenburg. The public authorities' governance of urban development has a pivotal role in facilitating the construction of socially mixed areas, but other stakeholders also need to examine what can be done more extensively at the local level in order to combat segregation and create social inclusion. The experimental business models for affordable housing in Frihamnen are only at a pilot stage and are being used as a means to test what can be done at the local level given the existing institutional conditions provided by the central government. It is not the only solution—other models are also needed, and more should be done at the national level in order to resolve the issues of social mix and inclusive living.

At present, in the RiverCity, a pressing concern with regard to social sustainability is the need to generate criteria for the fair distribution of the affordable rental apartments under construction in Frihamnen, and how to ensure that they facilitate a variegated social mix. Furthermore, the city's processes to identify and concretize goals that will ensure a sustainable urban development need to be continually refined, and demand a balancing of collaborative planning based on a shared vision, a clearly governed statutory planning process based on the existing legislative framework, and the close involvement of property developers and other concerned parties in an iterative design and innovation process. We have seen that such a dynamic work model, in which the roles of planners are somewhat floating and variegated, often leads to frustration and a sense of opaqueness in the decision-making process. Therefore, work is being carried out at to more clearly specify the overall goal of the project both in qualitative and quantitative terms. There is also a need to develop more solid monitoring tools and models to describe the welfare-economic ramifications of this type of complex urban development project. These new work models are being tested and evaluated in a step-wise process throughout the project from comprehensive planning to concrete construction and maintenance, which in itself is a work-demanding process. At the same time, this has provided the planning and development professionals involved in the project with a unique opportunity to test and learn from the experiences of applying the models in different parts of the organization. This allows for learning from challenges and successes at the smaller scale while at the same time exploring more systematic solutions.

An important final point is to highlight the challenge of the very long-term perspective of the Älvstaden project. It is almost a decade since work formally began on the Älvstaden vision. For most of this period a stable political majority was in office that supported the project and its focus on multidimensional and social sustainability. However, following the national elections in 2018, the political landscape has shifted, and the overall policy agenda and priorities are therefore consequently in need of renegotiation. Without a clear majority in the city council, decision-making concerning urban development has substantially slowed down. How this may come to affect the realization of the existing plans for the RiverCity Gothenburg and the strategy that underpins its development, remains to be seen.

Chapter 14

Commons

Producing Collaborative Sustainable Urban Development: Experiences of Water Management in Bangalore, India

Hita Unnikrishnan, Vanesa Castán Broto and Harini Nagendra

Every year, in Kaikondrahalli, Bangalore, people gather together to celebrate the 'Kere Habba'—a festival of the tank. This festival, held to celebrate one of the city's rejuvenated lakes, brings together a great diversity of people—children, academics, school teachers, bird enthusiasts, local residents, all of whom participate in activities aimed at increasing knowledge of the lake, while promoting a sense of togetherness. It is an opportunity to showcase the incredible efforts of a citizen's collective in coming together and catalyzing urban change. As a successful example of coproduction, this is one citizen-led effort that has strived for inclusivity as well as ecological sustainability within the process of coproducing efforts around the restoration of urban commons.

Despite these efforts, every year, during the 'Kere Habba,' a number of people watch the festivities from the sidelines. There are people who are newly arrived, such as migrant labor who used to live in temporary hutments near the lake, and there are people who have seen their landscape change, such as herdsmen, farmers, and fishermen who live on the banks of the lake and once used its waters. While these people are very much part of the same landscape, they hold back from participating in the festival or being part of the social and ecological system represented by these urban commons. This could be for several reasons. First, they are not socially part of the festivity owing to its sheer urban character (constituted as they are by the dominant presence of middle- to upper-middle class residents from nearby gated communities). Second, they may be unsure about the results of such participation, their ability to communicate across social groups, and are wary about how change may affect them. Perhaps it is also the fact that despite intense lobbying by the collective, the state (responsible for the eventual fate of the lake) refuses to consider the needs of such marginalized groups from the lake area as being important or deserving of attention. They may thus feel unprotected because state institutions are not responsive to their needs.

The example demonstrates the ambiguity that is inherent to coproduction: on the one hand, coproduction efforts emerge from a deliberate attempt to be

inclusive, to celebrate the creative relationship between humans and nature; on the other, coproduction may in itself be used as a boundary-making device, whereby some people feel part of it and some do not. How coproduction occurs—within a particular institutional setting and a situated history of environmental change—is central to understanding the results and contradictions embedded in the coproduction effort.

The management of water tanks (or lakes as they are described in contemporary times) in Bangalore is particularly interesting in terms of the study of commons because of the variety of systems involved and the contradictions that continually emerge in the process. Coproduction has been central to the management of the water tanks in Bangalore. Historically, tanks were, arguably, commons (Nagendra & Ostrom, 2014). As urban development dynamics have led to tank encroachment, activists have turned to strategies for the coproduction of water services in order to advance sustainability. Our main question thus emerges from a deliberate engagement with the contradiction illustrated above: what are the conditions that contextualize and motivate collective action and thus coproduced landscapes? And how do the dynamics of power play out in these situations, particularly with respect to the production of a sustainable urban landscape? We attempt to answer this question using examples from empirical research we have conducted on the subject of the urban commons of Bangalore using a mixed methods approach that combines field ecological studies with detailed archival and oral histories that cover a period of over two centuries.

Commitment to water coproduction in the context of Bangalore, where lakes represent a layered political struggle, entails personal and social risks that activists take head on. There have been shifts in the management of these resources from community-based everyday management of commons, to state-led management and experiments with neoliberalization, layered in parallel with interest-based activist-led coproduction. Thus, we depart from the point of admiration: being an activist or community actor in Bangalore is complex and fraught with political challenges. We recognize, however, that these initiatives are far from perfect, and that while they constitute alternatives for the management of urban water commons, they also act as boundary-making activities whose eventual outcomes are not always entirely progressive.

Our aim therefore is to emphasize the difficulties of sustainable management of water commons in this complex context. In order to do so, we draw on notions of coproduction and alternative means of commons governance. The notion of coproduction has emerged from a concern towards understanding institutions that manage commons beyond regulatory and private approaches. Coproduction in this instance refers to the process by which individuals who are not involved in the service delivery process actively contribute their inputs in order to provide a good or a service (Ostrom, 1996). It builds on the idea that citizens can actively participate in creating goods or services that may be beneficial and important to their lifestyles (Ostrom, 1996).

Changing Waterscapes and Changing Regimes

Before engaging with the coproduction efforts of the tank system in Bangalore, it is important to become familiar with changes in the urban water commons of Bangalore as well as its multiple management regimes over time.

The Shifting Waterscape of Bangalore

Bangalore, the Garden City of India, is known for its benign climate, verdant landscape, and sophisticated network of water reservoirs operating along an elevation gradient—lakes or tanks—which stand testimony to an age-old culture of coproduced water management (Annaswamy, 2003). While the king (Bangalore was once a feudal country governed by kings and their vassals) held sway over the ownership of these resources, rules governing their access, appropriation, and management were designed and enforced by the communities who were entrusted with the resource (Nagendra, 2016a). The significance of the water tanks in the history of Bangalore cannot be underestimated. Built centuries ago to support a largely semi-arid landscape lying in the rain shadow of the Deccan Hills, these tanks served as the primary water infrastructure to the city until the late 19th century (Sudhira et al., 2007). Over time, the story of Bangalore's water tanks has shifted to one of land use change and the deterioration of public resources, particularly since the city shifted its entire water infrastructure to revolve around a system of centralized service delivery obtained through long-distance transfer from the river Cauvery, over 100 kilometres away (Nagendra, 2016a). In 1973, a survey of tanks made an inventory of the condition of 159 of the remaining tanks within the city. This report highlighted the dramatic disappearance of the tanks following the rapid growth of the city's population and infrastructure long before India's independence. Several decades later, the situation has worsened. As of 2007, there were only 93 tanks and these remain in varying states of pollution, degradation, and encroachment (Ramachandra & Kumar, 2008). In addition, Bangaloreans continue to rely on the same and increasingly unsustainable system of long-distance water transfers (Sudhira et al., 2007). However, the surviving tanks that even today hold immense potential to serve as secondary sources of water and provide a measure of water security to the city mostly stand neglected.

Traditionally and in the city's precolonial past, tanks were localized to the villages they connected and were managed through community institutions composed of members from within these villages. The village headman and accountant (*Patel*) was responsible for ensuring the compliance of rules relating to the everyday management of the tank. He was assisted in this task by the village tax collector (*Shanabhog*) who was responsible for collecting the revenue derived from the lands irrigated by the lake. Another villager—the *Neeruganti*—was responsible for monitoring the levels of water within the reservoir as well as operating the manual sluice gates (*thoobu*) to release the required amounts of water into fields irrigated by the tank. Changes in the levels of water or the condition of the tank were communicated to the villagers through the efforts of the *thotti*—the village crier. These people were then compensated for their efforts through a share in the produce from those lands (Dikshit et al, 1993).

However, since the mid-19th century there has been a loss of tanks and an erosion of such community-led structures of water governance. The reasons behind the loss of tanks are varied. On the one hand, there was a dramatic shift in the mode of service delivery (from localized supply through tanks in the pre-colonial to the early colonial history of the city, to a networked centralized infrastructure of piped water drawn from a distant river initiated by the colonial city in the mid-18th century). On the other hand, there was an equally substantial increase in population and concomitant demand for water owing to the rapid growth and industrialization of the city in the early 20th century (Unnikrishnan et al., 2017). The advent of colonialism heralded a drastic transformation of infrastructure management whereby resources began to be governed through centralized command and control mechanisms as opposed to the more decentralized and coproduced systems that had prevailed previously (Unnikrishnan et al., 2016). This mode of service delivery also meant that the state had to centrally meet the demands of ever-increasing populations through a still localized and dispersed form of infrastructure (i.e., the lakes). Increased modernization as well as industrial demands meant an increased demand for land both to create liveable settlements and to develop infrastructure and buildings.

The solution to this problem came in the form of creating new infrastructure for water services that were equipped for long-distance transfers from a few pre-identified sources. This system immediately rendered the former decentralized service delivery systems obsolete, and brought the service closer to homes in the form of piped water supply. Lakes now began to be neglected, polluted, reclaimed, and built over (Unnikrishnan et al., 2016). The threat of water-borne diseases such as cholera and malaria emanating from neglected and polluted water bodies paved the way to reclaim the lakes in order to meet the aforementioned demands for land (Unnikrishnan et al., 2016). The result was an almost complete decline in urban water bodies. The surviving ones saw a sharp increase of pollution levels.

Following Indian independence in 1947, the growth of the public sector (immediately following independence) and the demands placed by neoliberalism (beginning in the 1990s) accelerated this process of landscape change. The same period also witnessed the appropriation of lakes by government agencies to form residential layouts, bus stations, and stadiums. Section 14A of the Karnataka Town and Country Planning Act of 1961 (that has provisions for changing land use categories), the Regularization Act of 2007 (also known as the Akrama Sakrama legislation) allowing the regularization of encroachments on government-owned land (including lakes), and the flexible approach towards land use zoning in designing the city's Master Plan in 2015, are all examples of such appropriation (Sundaresan, 2017). This issue was brought to the public eye by the Laxman Rau Committee Report in 1987 and in subsequent years through increasing trends of water shortages and seasonal flash flooding especially in those areas that were once occupied by the tanks. Over time, multiple social groups from experts to local dwellers have called for urgent action to halt and reverse this trend and find alternatives for water management. Starting from the broader concerns about the contradictions of coproduction, this chapter discusses the conditions (historical, institutional, infrastructural, and cultural) as well the motivations for collaborative management of urban commons using the case of urban water commons in Bangalore. We critically explore the implications of these conditions and motivations along associated dynamics of power in the sustainable production of urban landscapes and for social-ecological justice. Understanding these dynamics is very important to capture the range and diversity in agencies of technologies and resources, and the extent to which the cycle of water degradation can be reversed within this landscape. It can also provide important insights into the practice of coproduction itself—into what makes it viable in certain environments and what are the considerations that need to go into designing and coproducing landscapes revolving around urban commons in the global south.

Shifting Grounds: The Management of Bangalore's Water Infrastructure

One key factor shaping the fate of water tanks in Bangalore has been the transference of management competences to state institutions. With the onset of colonialism in Bangalore (*c.* 1799), the management of lakes in the city became centralized with the colonial state assuming responsibility for their upkeep. Finding this a herculean task (given the sheer number of tanks within the region), efforts to decentralize management were made under the larger umbrella of the state. An example of this approach was the creation of the Tank Panchayet system in 1911, that placed responsibility for the maintenance and upkeep of tanks (of a certain size) onto villagers (the headman being held responsible), while still possessing absolute control over both the revenue generated from irrigation as well as the tank itself. Logistical issues such as delineating tank sizes coupled with a general reluctance on the part of villagers to assume responsibility for the maintenance of this infrastructure meant that this system fell into sharp decline and was eventually abolished.

However, ownership of the lakes and responsibility for their maintenance and upkeep continued to rest with the state and was inherited by independent India. Post-independence, several approaches to manage these tanks have been explored at different levels of influence, albeit with varying degrees of success. Today, the management of lakes in Bangalore chiefly rests upon the shoulders of six nodal agencies: the Bruhat Bengaluru Mahanagara Palike, the Bangalore Development Authority, the Forest Department, the Bengaluru Metropolitan Regional Development Authority, the Indian Army, and the Department of Minor Irrigations (Unnikrishnan et al., 2016). Furthermore, even though these institutions have different mandates, their competences in managing water bodies continue to overlap. In the early 1990s, in a regime that encouraged neoliberalization within the country, the Karnataka State, where Bangalore is, experimented with schemes such as public-private partnerships (PPPs) for infrastructure management. In 2004, the city of Bangalore, under the now defunct Lake Development Authority, began to experiment with PPP models for the management of lakes. Criticized both by ecologists for their largely unscientific methods and by citizens for their modes of enclosure and gentrification, these schemes have proved to be unsuccessful (D'Souza & Nagendra, 2011) This was largely due to the efforts of a public charitable trust, the Environment Support Group, in employing legal instruments to halt privatization on grounds of ecological and social justice. Private companies have also enclosed lakes within their campuses in some cases (such as those in the Bagmane Technology Park), by using the legitimization of 'beautification' as an excuse. In contrast, water activists across the city have sought to find alternatives through the efforts of residential welfare committees, lake protection groups, or community collectives. Among these we find initiatives for collaborative management such as those around the Kaikondrahalli lake in southern Bangalore and the Jakkur lake in the north, but these are too few and far in between (Nagendra, 2016b). What is interesting to note here is that these are all different groups, staking their claim upon the same resource, yet with very different objectives and interests.

It is this last effort by activists to promote means to coproduce urban water services in order to protect the lakes that called out for attention. Promising initiatives such as these have been loaded with a number of challenges related to the context within which water infrastructure management is conducted.

Coproducing Bangalore's Waterscapes

Coproduction was a radical idea when it was proposed and that continues to gain traction as evidence has emerged that coproduction of service delivery may entail significant benefits to both communities and landscapes. Citizens' involvement in decision-making processes tends to guarantee a better quality service delivery (Calzada et al, 2017). Coproduction also means an increased engagement with users especially with respect to decisions over governance of infrastructure and the delivery of services or goods (Brandsen and Helderman, 2012). Increased user engagement has the potential to provide services that are context-specific and tailored to meet the needs of the community, and thereby lead to greater user satisfaction (Percy, 1984). Coproducing landscapes implies an increased moral ownership of the service or good with greater accountability and replicability (Rosentraub & Sharp, 1981). Efforts of coproduction also mean a decreased burden on central delivery mechanisms in terms of costs, logistics, and labor. However, many coproduction scholars would argue that while coproduction is, in essence, linked to better governance, the most compelling reason to engage in coproduction efforts is the belief that a commitment to justice must underpin any efforts to govern the commons, and justice implies both the recognition of disadvantaged perspectives on the commons and the emphasis on deliberative styles of decision-making.

In a world that is rapidly urbanizing, there is a constant challenge to ensure development that is sustainable, equitable, and just. Urban commons occupy an especially challenging niche in this paradigm. By commons, we refer to common property regimes—with goods that are non-excludable and subtractible (the more you withdraw from them, the less there is for other commons users) (Ostrom, 1990). Lakes, forests, parks, and several other resources are all examples of urban commons. As urban natures have now taken center stage in the management of commons, sustainable coproduction of resources in urban settings has become a very important consideration. This is because in many developing countries such as India, urban commons provide a range of important ecosystem services that are important not just for the urban elites, but are also essential to sustaining the lives and livelihoods of the urban poor. Coproduction of these resources therefore necessitates consideration of community complexities, justice, and equity (Platteau, 2004), while balancing the demands of urbanization and development with those of ecological sustainability and social justice (Mansuri & Rao, 2004).

Contextualizing the Process of Coproduction

One key emerging lesson from the work on coproduction is that coproduction practices and motivations need to be contextualized within historical trajectories and ecological contexts. The sense of disenchantment that has motivated an engagement in coproduction practices in Bangalore relates directly to localized histories of water governance and their outcomes, and their interaction with ecological and biophysical factors, embedding them within a particular water culture. In this section, we thus describe the contexts in which coproduction efforts in Bangalore have emerged.

Historical Context

Bangalore has had a rich precolonial tradition of coproduction with respect to its lakes—communities actively participated in the processes of decision-making, the creation of rules, regulations and the enforcement thereof as well as monitoring resource quality and utility. This rich tradition of coproduction finds resonance in evoked nostalgia among today's lake user groups, creating a remembered narrative of pride in and moral ownership of the resource. It is, however, pertinent to note that while there has been a rich history of coproduction in the context of the urban commons, it was not by any means egalitarian with power imbalances and socioeconomic inequalities being highly prevalent among participating communities. For instance, while the *neerganti* was an important member of the lake management system, he was surprisingly far below the social hierarchy in terms of the caste to which he belonged. As such, he thus had reduced privileges over use and appropriation of these resources as opposed to other members of the village who were placed above him in this hierarchy. Indeed, during field-based interviews, our respondents would often recollect the presence of two separate open wells—one from which the upper castes could draw water while the other was for the use of the lower castes. In other cases, while the upper castes drew water from the lake, a well dug on the outskirts of a village would serve to meet the domestic water needs of the people who were lower on the social hierarchy.

The imposition of centralized command and control mechanisms heralding the onset of a colonial regime in the city was thus a major disruption in this landscape. In one stroke, it put paid to the idea of place-specific landscape management, instead shifting the focus onto technocratic and engineering-based visions that sought to tame urban nature through generalized practices borne out of lessons learnt from other places across the globe.

Geophysical Contexts

The success of coproduction efforts is also influenced by complexities induced through geophysical and ecological conditions. One of the largest lakes in Bangalore is the Bellandur lake with a catchment area of 148 square kilometres. Once a majestic and highly important reservoir for the city, today this lake is heavily polluted with both point and non-point sources, rendering its waters unusable and highly toxic. This ecological change is manifested through a toxic white foam that covers the surface of the water body and extends vertically several meters above it (especially during monsoons). Carried by winds, the foam disperses and settles on neighboring roads, vehicles, households, and people causing a great deal of trouble and concern in the area surrounding the lake. As if to emphasize the problem further, the lake also spectacularly and periodically sets itself ablaze, thus grabbing international headlines, media coverage, political attention, and citizen concern.[1] Community-led collectives have also rallied around this water body but have largely been ineffectual in dealing with the issues surrounding it. The reasons are manifold with the most pertinent being the sheer size of the water body and therefore the logistics of cleaning, monitoring, and managing the lake. It also does not help that the bulk of sewage generated in south Bangalore flows into this lake through the sewerage infrastructure of the city. Furthermore, generally attention has focused on isolated lakes such as Bellandur Lake. Given that the lakes are built along an elevation gradient, events that occur upstream in the network are likely to exert an influence on and even amplify effects that are observed downstream in the chain.

This, then, is a classic example of how coproduction has been rendered largely ineffectual due to the geophysical considerations associated with the landscape. These considerations could take the form of size, blurred boundaries, existing infrastructure, and environmental conditions associated with the resource. This complexity necessitates that coproduction efforts are place-specific, and that due consideration is afforded to the scale of planned activities and the logistics of the attempt being considered.

Cultural Contexts

Water bodies in many cities are also cultural spaces, and these cultural dependencies reflect the many ways in which people benefit from the resource. Success of coproduction in such terrain can also be influenced by how many of these dependencies are represented in these efforts. In Bangalore, where the lakes served to meet the water requirements of the city for several centuries, there is great diversity in the cultural traditions associated with its waterscape. Communal commons associated with the lake, for instance temples, village forests (*gunda thope*), cemeteries, pasture lands (*gomala*), and livestock tethering commons (*gokatte*), all carry significant cultural weight for communities living around lakes. Furthermore, several rituals and traditions have been found to be associated with water bodies.

These traditions are collective (in that they require participation in groups) as well as individual, and several of them are still practiced. As these lakes are interconnected by means of channels, an overflowing tank represented bountiful rains, and therefore more water for the entire city. Hence, a procession (known locally as the *theppotsava*—festival of the boats) was conducted by villagers every time a lake overflowed out of its channels. This festival involved an animal sacrifice (delivered by a boat—or *theppa*—into the center of a lake), along with lighting numerous lamps and setting them afloat on the water body. A similar procession around some lakes (though without the animal sacrifice) called the *Gange Pooje* was held to celebrate the perceived sacredness of water (Unnikrishnan et al., 2016).

Various occupational groups have their own traditions and rituals associated with lakes. Farmers and livestock owners conduct a yearly procession around some lakes of Bangalore in order to pray for bountiful harvests, adequate rainfall, and for protection from pests and disease. Commercial washermen (*dhobhies*), communities of whom are often found around lakes, worship the water bodies in their own way through offerings made to their patron deity (known locally as *uppudyaavaru*). These offerings are made to seek blessings in the form of adequate water for their trade, safety for unattended children on the banks of lakes, as well as for the safety of clothes entrusted to their care. Also, fishermen have particular traditions associated with their trade—that of showing respect to the water body by not wearing footwear while fishing (an Indian tradition that is often practiced in temples denoting respect to the deity), or not fishing during particular seasons. Individuals have traditions associated with water bodies—offerings are made for protection against disease, during significant life events such as marriage, attaining puberty, the birth of a child, or a death (Unnikrishnan et al., 2017).

All these traditions reflect the various provisioning dependencies people have associated with the lakes for several centuries—that of water for farming, commercial laundering, and household activities, of forage for livestock, and of fish. However, several coproduction efforts undertaken to rejuvenate these water bodies are composed only of urban elite communities for whom these provisioning and cultural dependencies are quite alien, and often contradictory to their perceived vision of what a rejuvenated lake should look like. This leads to the exclusion of several community groups from the planning process, which has profound implications for the longevity and sustainability of such efforts.

Motivating the Coproduction of Sustainable Urban Environments

What moves different urban actors to adopt coproduction strategies? Research into the theory of coproduction and its motivations has suggested that the reasons are many and varied. A classical paper within the circle of debates of Ostrom's Workshop on Political Theory and Policy Analysis explored the multiple reasons why coproduction was a key strategy for resource management (Percy, 1984). Since then, citizens' participation in service coproduction has been a key academic question. In Bangalore, there are two key motivations. First, there is a practical motivation that follows the spread of the discourse of privatization in which many citizens have seen themselves as private actors who would like to get engaged in partnerships for lake management. Second, there is a reactive motivation emerging from within a sense of disenchantment with the formal structures of governance that relates directly to people's past experiences and memories of Bangalore as a garden city.

Motivations Evoking Nostalgia for the City's Past

As has been described previously, post-colonial governments consolidated a model of water management in which water was seen as a resource that necessitated mechanized transfer across longer distances rather than an ecological system that permeated nearer spaces. Mysore (later Karnataka) State took away power vested in decentralized community-led hierarchies associated with the management of urban commons, and concentrated it within new bureaucratic roles (such as that of the Water Inspector in the late 1880s) (Unnikrishnan et al., 2017). At the same time, this new regime stripped away from communities the sense of ownership and pride that was central to community-based coproduction strategies, leaving behind memories that have today given rise to a nostalgic narrative of lakes lost.

This nostalgia is extensively evoked in contemporary discourses that seek to motivate citizens to engage collectively towards the management of the resource. The ideas of reviving traditional knowledge relating to water infrastructure, activists soliciting the involvement of communities traditionally associated with creation and maintenance of water infrastructure, photographers capturing social-ecological relationships with water infrastructure—these are all examples of how this historical tradition has informed and motivated present-day imaginations of coproduced landscapes.

Practical Motivations

Coproduction as a practice can emerge out of logistical concerns that seek to cut down on infrastructural costs of service delivery or to provide services to largely inaccessible regions. In these cases, the practice involves a partnership of sorts between bureaucratic nodal agencies and citizens (in the form of private enterprises, or corporate entities) formalized towards infrastructure maintenance. In Bangalore, the creation of PPP regimes and the management of lakes by corporate entities are both examples of such practices. PPPs arose out of the challenges induced by plural nodal agencies responsible for lake management in Bangalore and through an inability of these nodal agencies (particularly the Lake Development Authority which has since been dissolved) to exert control over the management of lakes within its jurisdiction (Center for Science and Environment, India, 2013). In the PPP model, coproduction encouraged commercialization in order to obtain returns from the labor and capital invested in private rejuvenation and management of the urban commons (D'Souza, 2006). This commercialization resulted in the enclosure of the commons and its transformation from a utilitarian resource into one that was seen as predominantly recreational—hence the emergence of parks, boulevards, boating and water sports, fountains, and food courts in the landscape—all entities for which access was paid for by those who could afford to do so (Unnikrishnan et al, 2016). Missing in this narrative, however, were other uses of a commons—foraging, agriculture, livestock maintenance, spiritual services, building community relationships—all of which were seen to be against the dominant ethic of recreation and were often practiced by the more vulnerable and marginalized members of the society (Unnikrishnan et al, 2016). Coproduction in this case was neither egalitarian nor viable with respect to the sustainable management of urban commons.

Motivations Borne Out of Frustrations with Existing Governance Mechanisms

Bangalore has had an intimate, complex, and constantly changing relationship with its water commons. As lakes were formed along an elevation gradient, the widespread change into a built urban landscape impacted natural flows of water, particularly during the monsoon season. The resulting annually occurring flash floods and associated hardships helped to draw attention to the complexities of the landscape. Pressure was then placed (by the media, activists, academicians, and political parties) on nodal agencies to respond to these crises. These voices have become more pronounced over the last decade, when in addition to flooding and inundation, heavily polluted lakes such as Bellandur lake (in south Bangalore) made international headlines by foaming, frothing, and catching fire.

Fed up with what was largely perceived as government inaction, apathy, and corruption, several citizen-led collectives (formed mostly of upper- to middle-class urban residents) have been formed over the past decade with the intention of coproducing neighborhood lakes in Bangalore. Some such as those along the Jakkur and Kaikondrahalli lakes have been largely encouraging initiatives, whereas others have been less promising or well known. Several factors contributed to dismantle some of these collectives—a sense of being forced into taking responsibility, negotiating with individual aspirations, insufficient support from local bureaucracy, and faltering long-term sustenance of the collective being some of the difficulties they encountered.

On the other hand, successful initiatives show a common factor in their approaches to dealing with the challenges of coproduction: their ability to connect with different members of the community in a way that cuts through individual aspirations and fosters a sense of pride and moral ownership over the resource. These identities are reflected in the various initiatives they have taken to showcase the project—through academic writing, citizen-led resource monitoring groups on social media, or through the organizing of recurring festivals celebrating their efforts (an annual lake festival as in the case of Kaikondrahalli lake, and weekly musical gatherings on the banks of Jakkur lake) (Nagendra, 2016b).

These stories show that coproduction of infrastructure governance can therefore also emerge out of a desire to create independent mechanisms for urban service delivery most commonly due to frustration with government inaction or ineffectuality in dealing with the service (Das, 2016). They can take the form of formal as well as informal structures (as formal and informal institutions are often indistinguishable) and can play out in different ways depending upon whether the action was induced through a sense of forced engagement and whether the communities involved have a sense of pride in their ability to handle the challenge.

Furthermore, coproduction can take the form of violations that act against resource sustainability. Official sanctions and conversions of lakes into built-up structures acting in conjunction with encroachments and illegal land use conversions served to produce a drastically different landscape (Sundaresan, 2017). Planning of water infrastructure for the city of Bangalore has been in effect coproduced by actors both within and outside the bureaucracy and largely serves private interests. This in turn created responses that challenged such private interests through citizen-led networks aimed at monitoring resources, encouraging bureaucratic patronage, and using legal instruments to act against what was perceived to be harming urban commons. Coproduction moved beyond the simple notions of participative processes of service delivery into one that was shaped and molded by differing motivations, actions, and responses towards dealing with the challenge that was itself framed in multiple ways (such as scarcity of land, ecological sustainability, differing priorities, to name but a few).

Coproduction and the Dynamics of Power in Bangalore

Looking into coproduction practices in context enables a critical analysis of the forces that shape outcomes in the governance of water commons. To what extent does coproduction challenge or simply reproduce existing dynamics of power? Does coproduction in contemporary landscapes produce more equitable and just delivery of services from urban commons or does is serve to foster greater inequality? Our experiences in Bangalore seem to indicate that coproduction—while holding immense potential to achieve egalitarian societies—still falls short of actually realizing it. Lake communities are not homogenous entities that share a common and sustained interest towards the resource. Rather, what is termed 'community' is actually a collection of heterogeneous individuals each of whom have different priorities with respect to the utility of the urban commons. For instance, a fisherman concerns himself with the availability of fish within deep waters of the lake, while a washerman seeks to benefit from the shallow waters of the outflow from the lake. A bungalow owner benefits from the prime views afforded by the lake and perhaps would use its banks for recreation and exercise. These groups of actors would also differ in the political bargaining power they hold over decision-making with respect to the resource. Yet 'community' would encompass all of these actors, and in most discourses it is assumed that they would share common interests in the sustainability of the resource. What is then seen today in many coproduction efforts is the creation of interest-based communities that are politically shaped, in which dynamics of power can exclude other interests.

The narrative created by the experiment with PPP models described earlier has shaped the visions of coproduction and distorted their implementation. PPP experiments created a powerful ethic of aesthetics and recreation within these urban commons which also excluded the more marginalized and vulnerable sections of communities who had access to them in the past (D'Souza & Nagendra, 2011; Unnikrishnan & Nagendra, 2015). In these instances, it is clear that coproduction has acted as a tool for the enclosure of urban commons and has helped to exclude those for whom the lake was not representative of the dominant ethic. Such forms of coproduction have coexisted with more progressive attempts to rejuvenate the lakes for public use. The reactive character of activists' initiatives has constituted the coproduction movement as a protest tool, but has not delivered fully inclusive responses to Bangalore's water dilemma. In the context of a failing process of decentralization, in which the decentralized management of urban commons has not really resulted in a devolution of power hierarchies, some forms of coproduction have inevitably further fostered inequity, exclusion, and marginalization.

Coproduction as a Tool to Achieve Egalitarian Societies?

Coproduction rests upon the foundational idea that citizens can actively participate in service delivery for issues that are of importance to them (Ostrom, 1996). The case of Bangalore emphasizes the need to unpack complexities within this statement in order to effectively understand and design through coproduction sustainable, just, and equitable urban landscapes. Similar trends have also been observed in other cities in India and around the globe such as Hyderabad and Maputo (Boyd et al., 2014; Das, 2016).

In order to unpack this complexity, it is important to reflect upon the motives that have enabled coproduction and its implications for social ecological systems at large. The case described here supports our assertion that consideration should be paid to motives that underline efforts of coproduction—whether these efforts are brought about through logistical or governance-related concerns. This is important because these motivations can play an important role in community perceptions about the nature of the activity they are undertaking. It can help us to understand whether an initiative has emerged as a flip side of neoliberal outsourcing to resolve issues—or whether the activity fosters a sense of pride in the community, or a sense of being forced into taking the burden of service delivery due to a lack of other options of provision. At the same time, these motivations are influenced by historical and geophysical contexts surrounding the landscape. A history of coproduction can help to build new narratives that encourage civic participation in contemporary processes of coproducing landscapes. Coproduction efforts in Bangalore rely on the ability of activists to foster new initiatives that reenergize the relationship with the water commons and build a sense of pride and justice around water governance. Successful initiatives have been able to do so with a deliberate strategy for the wider inclusion of vulnerable groups. However, coproduction efforts remain provisional and under revision, with a reflexive attention to the thin line whereby acting for the commons becomes an enclosure strategy.

Water landscapes can be coproduced as a result of complex interactions between state machinery and citizen networks that both operate towards enabling and curbing violations (Sundaresan, 2017). Narratives built around these interactions can be important indications of the direction taken by a coproduction effort. These complex interactions are also influenced by the diversity of actors around a landscape, their plurality of visions for the landscape, and the political bargaining power that they possess within a given historical, socio-ecological, and cultural context (Unnikrishnan et al., 2016).

Different combinations of context, motivation, and power can act to bring out different outcomes, not all of which may be beneficial to the sustainable or egalitarian management of urban commons. Coproduction in its simplest definition fails to account for this dynamic and very often is limited in its ability to bring about the devolution of power. It is these difficult doings that need to be addressed by practitioners looking to engage with coproduction efforts—reflecting on who are the actors involved, and why they are motivated to engage in the effort; what contexts have enabled these efforts; and who is likely to raise the stakes politically? Furthermore, what do these multiple dimensions and complexities mean in terms of defining urban sustainability and the direction that coproduction efforts can take? In engaging with these difficult doings, coproduction holds considerable potential as a powerful tool to create change, foster institutional innovation, and deliver services in unorthodox ways. Through reflections on the complexities associated with coproduction, it could potentially be used as a tool to engage with notions of urban sustainability and social justice.

Note

1 See www.thehindu.com/news/cities/bangalore/bellandur-lake-catches-fire-again/article 22471775.ece; https://news.nationalgeographic.com/2018/02/bangalore-india-lake-bella ndur-catches-fire-pollution; www.thenewsminute.com/article/fiery-friday-bengalurus-bellandur-lake-catches-fire-first-time-2018-74989.

References

Agarwal, A., & Narain, S. (Eds.) (1997). *Dying Wisdom: Rise, Fall and Potential of India's Traditional Water Harvesting Systems*. New Delhi: Centre for Science and Environment.

Annaswamy, T.V. (2003). *Bengaluru to Bangalore: Urban History of Bangalore from the Prehistoric Period to the End of the 18th Century*. Bangalore: Vengadam Publications.

Boyd, E., Ensor, J., Castán-Broto, V., & Juhola, S. (2014). Environmentalities of urban climate governance in Maputo, Mozambique. *Global Environmental Change* 26, 140–151.

Brandsen, T., & Helderman, J.K. (2012). The trade-off between capital and community: The conditions for successful co-production in housing. *Voluntas* 23(4), 1139–1155.

Calzada, J., Iranzo, S., & Sanz, A. (2017). Community managed water services: The case of Peru. *Journal of Environment and Development* 26(4), 400–428.

Centre for Science and Environment (2013). *Protection and Management of Urban Lakes in India*. New Delhi: Centre for Science and Environment.

Das, P. (2016). Uncharted waters: Navigating new configurations for urban service delivery in India. *Environment and Planning* 48(7), 1354–1373.

Dikshit, G.S., Kuppuswamy, G.R., & Mohan, S.K. (1993). *Tank Irrigation in Karnataka*. Bangalore: Gandhi Sahitya Sangha.

D'Souza, R. (2006). *Impact of Privatisation of Lakes in Bangalore*. Bangalore: Centre for Education and Documentation. Retrieved March 23, 2020, from www.doccentre.net/index.php/privatisation-of-lakes-in-bangalore.

D'Souza, R., & Nagendra, H. (2011). Changes in public commons as a consequence of urbanization: The Agara lake in Bangalore, India. *Environmental Management* 47(5), 840–850.

Mansuri, G., & Rao, V. (2004). Community-based and -driven development: A critical review. *World Bank Research Observer* 19(1), 1–39.

Nagendra, H. (2016a). *Nature in the City: Bengaluru in the Past, Present and Future.* New Delhi: Oxford University Press.

Nagendra, H. (2016b). *Restoration of the Kaikondrahalli Lake in Bangalore: Forging a New Urban Commons.* Pune: Kalpavriksh.

Nagendra, H., & Ostrom, E. (2014). Applying the social-ecological system framework to the diagnosis of urban lake commons in Bangalore, India. *Ecology and Society* 19(2), 67.

Nair, J. (2005). *Bangalore: The Promise of a Metropolis.* New Delhi: Oxford University Press.

Ostrom, E. (1990). *Governing the Commons.* Cambridge: Cambridge University Press.

Ostrom, E. (1996). Crossing the great divide: Coproduction, synergy, and development. *World Development* 24(6), 1073–1086.

Percy, S.L. (1984). Citizen participation in the coproduction of urban services. *Urban Affairs Review* 19(4), 431–446.

Platteau, J.P. (2004). Monitoring elite capture in community-driven development. *Development and Change* 35(2), 223–246.

Ramachandra, T.V., and Kumar, U. (2008). Wetlands of greater Bangalore, India: Automatic delineation through pattern classifiers. *Electronic Green Journal* 1(26): 1–22.

Rice, B.L. (1897). *Mysore: A Gazetteer Compiled for Government*, rev. edn, vol. 2, *Mysore, by Districts.* Westminster: Archibald Constable.

Rosentraub, M.S., & Sharp, E.B. (1981). Consumers as producers of social services: Coproduction and the level of social services. *Southern Review of Public Administration* 4, 502–539.

Sudhira, H.S., Ramachandra, T.V., & Balasubrahmanya, M.H. (2007). City profile: Bangalore. *Cities*, 24(5), 379–390.

Sundaresan, J. (2017). Urban planning in vernacular governance: Land use planning and violations in Bangalore, India. *Progress in Planning* 127: 1–23.

Unnikrishnan, H., & Nagendra, H. (2015). Privatizing the commons: Impacts on ecosystem services in Bangalore's lakes. *Urban Ecosystems* 18(2), 613–632.

Unnikrishnan, H., Manjunatha, B., & Nagendra, H. (2016). Contested urban commons mapping the transition of a lake to a sports stadium in Bangalore. *International Journal of Commons* 10(1), 265–293.

Unnikrishnan, H., Sen, S., & Nagendra, H. (2017). Traditional water bodies and urban resilience: A historical perspective from Bengaluru, India. *Water History* 9(4), 453–477.

Chapter 15

Expectations

Hope and Despair: Professionals' Struggle to Navigate Multiple Planning Ideas in a Public–Private Collaboration in Gothenburg

Mari Kågström

It is a crisp, sunny morning in early 2017. I have just taken the small commuter ferry across the strait that separates central Gothenburg and the city district of Lindholmen, where the offices of Älvstranden are situated. Älvstranden is a property development company owned and operated by the municipality of Gothenburg and I am now standing in their reception area looking curiously at the centerpiece, which is a white cardboard model of a planned city development. I wonder how the planners reached this result. What does the process of developing a sustainable city look like? A cheerful "good morning" soon interrupts my thoughts. As I turn around, I am greeted by Anna[1] who is hurrying towards me a bag and cycle helmet in her left hand. We are both part of a research project[2] and are meeting today so that I can find out more about her work as a sustainability process manager for one of the city's development projects.

We take the stairs up to a conference room with large windows and decorated in the same color palette as the reception area. Before we sit down at the table, Anna points in the direction of the city district to be developed across the water, close to where I started the ferry trip this morning. She tells me that currently she and her colleagues and collaborating partners are busy compiling the draft of a project-specific sustainability program. It seems to be going well. Anna is enthusiastic and tells me about the work that has been done and what there is still left to do. The situation seems to be characterized by many things going on at the same time. Sorting this out involves collaborating with several actors, both external and internal, of her organization. She tells me about a planning process that has included several reorganizations, and in some cases restarts. Nevertheless, Anna emphasizes the benefits of the collaboration process. She believes that these processes have led to a good working environment and more complete, or higher, sustainability goals. "I get energy from the group. We have raised the ambition level by working together," she says. Over the coming months, I meet Anna and her process management colleagues during interviews. I also participate in different work meetings and workshops,[3] which are part of their work for leading the process forward towards the implementation phase of the city development project.

When I set up my computer for a meeting another day, it is late autumn and the sun has already started to set. This time I am going to chat with process managers Daniel, Maria, and Erik via video link. They are in an office at Älvstranden sharing one computer, which means that they shift the web camera back and forth. I can only see two of them at a time. I am sitting at home, in Uppsala, a city approximately 400 km away. It becomes a reflective and personal conversation. Mainly I listen while they talk to each other about their collaborative practices. They reflect on the process thus far, put questions to each other, and try out different perspectives and solutions on how to proceed. Their belief in the collaboration process seems to be not as strong as it was earlier in the year, and Maria is now less hopeful that they will be able to achieve the sustainability goals. Daniel, Maria, and Erik have different experiences of the process, but they all talk about moments of uncertainty. Today they share a concern about whether this way of collaboration is the right way forward. Erik says, "We are going through a tough period now. It makes me wonder, what is the added value of collaboration? It is extremely resource-intensive, what could we achieve with those resources if we instead put them into something else?" The question raises a mixture of feelings, from a sense of failure and fatigue to curiosity and a fighting spirit.

The short vignette above recounts the experiences of a certain group of municipal civil professionals, namely sustainability process managers. In 2017, they struggled to work within a private-public collaborative framework, and were concerned about losing control of the process. This is a story in which things are good, bad, and then good again, and the professionals oscillate between pride, happiness, fatigue, and doubt. Thus, collaboration can be both rewarding and difficult. The aim of this chapter is to provide an insight into the practical challenges of collaboration in sustainable city development. The collaborative challenges are explained from the perspective of the multitude of parallel ideas or models for how planning should be managed and what collaboration should comprise. These ideas emphasize different, sometimes conflicting, values and offer guidance as to what should be prioritized, how power and responsibilities should be distributed, and which roles and actions are relevant. This, then, is a situation that puts excessive pressure on individual professionals to work out how to proceed, and at the same time leaves them quite ill-prepared for doing so.

The chapter is structured in two main parts, one descriptive and one analytical. The first part includes a narrative describing the work of four process managers leading a collaboration process for developing and implementing a sustainability program for a city development project in Gothenburg. This is followed by an analysis which begins with a short introduction to different planning ideals that are present in the context of Swedish city planning and development. The chapter concludes with a summary of the lessons learned.

Towards Sustainable City Development through Collaboration

Gothenburg is situated on the west coast of Sweden, by the mouth of the Göta river. It is the second largest city in Sweden with a population just over 560,000. In 2012, the Gothenburg City Council adopted a vision that was intended to guide future planning and development of sustainable city districts in the inner parts of the city (City of Gothenburg, 2012). The following three strategies were developed to realize the vision: 'Connecting the City,' 'Embracing the Water,' and 'Reinforcing the Center.' Not only does the vision have high ambitions for sustainable outcomes, it also emphasizes *how* these should be achieved. The planning should be carried out through collaboration across municipal administrative boarders, and with a broad range of actors such as citizens and the private sector. The process should also support continuous learning processes. Keys for realizing the vision are stated to be test-beds for trying out new models and technologies, in particular for developing working models for how to plan and collaborate together:

> We need clear roles and a working model that can change and adapt over time. We need working forms where we test, measure, follow up, and learn from what we have done. We need to improve the way we communicate and continue to discuss the type of city we want. All this requires openness, a capacity to see beyond the established norms and practice and a sense of curiosity and courage to test new ideas and innovations.
> (City of Gothenburg, 2012, p. 36)

To realize the intentions of the vision, a collaborative platform organization was created. The platform includes a steering group comprising chief executive officers, directors, and senior managers from different departments and municipal companies, such as Älvstranden, and a project management group which looks after seven urban development projects. The organization is to function as a platform for collaboration where information is exchanged and decisions are discussed. The process managers, who are the focus of this chapter, are engaged in the city development projects. One of their primary tasks is to drive processes and motivate others to make decisions within their respective areas that support sustainable city development. The process managers have different educational backgrounds, ranging from international relations and political science, environmental management and economics, to environmental engineering and human ecology. Their respective work experience within the public sector spans between three and 14 years. They all share a genuine concern for sustainability.

One of the city development projects is Södra Älvstranden, which includes two sub-districts, Skeppsbron and Masthuggskajen, the latter being the focus of this section. Masthuggskajen is situated just outside the historic city center of Gothenburg. Today, the area comprises various hard surfaces and older buildings. It is surrounded by major traffic barriers, resulting in high levels of noise and air pollution. However, there is also great value in terms of a strong cultural environment, proximity to the water, a mixture of functions for diverse communities, good public transportation, and a central location. The complexity and current character of Masthuggskajen is expressed as an important starting point for the planned development of the area, which envisages approximately 1,300 new homes and 6,000 jobs, new residential buildings, workplaces, schools and hotels as well as public spaces, green areas, and opportunities for sustainable mobility (Älvstranden Utveckling, 2017).

A core part of the planning process is the development of a sustainability program for Masthuggskajen. The program includes sustainability goals and ambition levels as well as action plans for how to achieve these goals. Work on the program is carried out in collaboration with administrations and companies within the municipality of Gothenburg, as well as with property development companies (private developers). This work is led by the sustainability process managers, which for this project are meant to function as a bridge between the private developers and the municipality. The aim of this specific collaboration is to

> manage planning and implementation to a high quality and at a rapid pace by forming a common organization, target image, budget, and work process for the project. Fundamentally, cooperation is governed by agreements between all the actors, but on a daily basis it consists of cooperation between people from the different organizations.
> (Älvstranden Utveckling, 2017, p. 14)

The agreement implies that if the private developers take an active role in the collaboration, they are entitled to buy and build on land earmarked for the project. Later, if they show that they can achieve the high sustainability goals that have been agreed, they earn the right to buy and develop more land within the project. Daniel later calls this a 'negotiating advantage' and says that this is one of Älvstranden's few incitements for forcing the private developers to act in accordance with the organization's agenda. He also emphasizes that from the moment they have distributed the land plots, this advantage will be lost. In the sustainability program, the process is described as an "intensive, patient, and challenging collaboration process" (Älvstranden Utveckling, 2017, p. 2).

Agreement of Common Goals

By early 2017, the collaboration had been going on for several years. The organization for the sustainability work had been rearranged several times in order to achieve smoother collaborations and to enhance the possibility for the sustainability issues to influence the project and further decision-making. The process was characterized by testing new ways of working together and searching for innovative solutions, both in terms of what should be achieved and the process of how to get there. A key challenge expressed by Anna is that the group has been, and still is, quite diverse when it comes to experience of sustainability work. She continues by explaining that some of the private developers have considerable experience of working on sustainability issues and strive for improvements, while others are quite inexperienced and need a lot of support. She and her team thus need to find ways to adapt in terms of the type and level of support they give to different developers. This also means that the developers do not proceed at the same speed, which creates some tension within the group. Nevertheless, Anna chooses to emphasize the benefits of gaining early access to all the private companies' knowledge and experience concerning the implementation phase. This access is mentioned as a key argument for this kind of collaboration, along with securing implementation.

During this period of collaboration, there have been ups and downs. However, at this point in the process, Anna and Daniel emphasize that overall there is a positive atmosphere within the group, and a feeling that although the process has been challenging it has continued to function well, meaning that they have reached greater heights—together. It has taken time to get to know each other and to build trust, but now there is a good foundation for the future. There is a feeling of having reached a milestone by managing to formulate and agree upon goals and ambition levels. The work and agreements are featured in a sustainability program, which outlines the agreed objectives. The ambition level is high and Anna is hopeful for the continuation of the project. Maria emphasizes that having a common goal is crucial for a smooth collaboration and the next phase of the project.

Action Plans for Realizing Goals

In early 2017 the group sought to take the sustainability program one step closer to implementation. One of the main tasks for each private developer, supported by the group, was to develop an action plan in which they concretized their own activities and commitments in order to meet the agreed ambition level and sustainability goals. Daniel states that it was planned to successively relinquish responsibility to the private developers, recalling that before it was often the case that "even if they [private developers] feed in, it was us at Älvstranden that made it happen ... that we tell them what to do." It meant that the process managers did not really get the added value they had expected. He continues by adding that the idea was to turn this around so the private developers "take the lead in developing the best solutions."

The measures specified in the sustainability program that are to be implemented vary a great deal. They range from guaranteeing parking spaces for bicycles at specific locations, to ensuring an organization and project culture that promotes innovation in order to respond to what we do not know enough about today.

The work with the action plans proves to be a tough process, with time pressures and external realities, such as political decisions, placing even more pressure on the collaboration. A core concern for the process managers in trying to proceed with their work is that this phase requires a lot of feedback and coaching resources. Anna explains that they give many rounds of feedback and repeatedly ask the private developers for clarifications. She points out that the focus of the feedback is to ask the developers for more concrete solutions for how they are going to ensure that the goals, measures, and activities they are suggesting will be achieved. Erik emphasizes that this way of working turned out to be "very resource-intensive; more than we thought." The intense work in combination with slow improvements in the action plan becomes tiresome.

Furthermore, Daniel expresses concern about whether later in the process the private developers will try to avoid taking responsibility for parts of the sustainability program that have been previously agreed upon. This has apparently happened before. To overcome this, the process managers have adopted several quite different strategies, ranging from providing more support to exerting stronger control. For example, they continue to provide support by giving more feedback, coaching, and inspiration, and by offering examples of good practice. However, much of their time is also taken up by thoughts about the balance between facilitating and forcing action. Maria, for example, reflects on "how much Älvstranden should facilitate, and how much responsibility they [the private developers] should be forced to take on." Hence, the process managers speed up the process of exploring the incentives as well as their alternatives to force action. Questions that become central are what can we do that is legally acceptable? What can be put in written agreements? How can we exert better control and ensure that we follow up the process? Daniel opines that they need to be "able to confront" the private developers if they do not do what has been agreed upon.

During 2017, there are quite a lot of ad hoc activities. This reflects, and creates, an uncertainty as to how to proceed and what the relevant alternatives for collaboration are. Erik explains that they need to "gain more insight into the inherent incentives of the process," in other words, they need to be more knowledgeable about what controls a collaborative process. This is also seen in the ambiguity within the role distributions in the group. The process managers see themselves, and are recognized by their collaborating partners, as having a certain responsibility for the overall process. Beyond that, it remains unclear to the private developers who should take responsibility for what and when. The private developers are uncertain about what things they must be do and what is voluntary. This means that predictability is weak, which results in a difficult situation for everyone.

A core concern for the implementation of the project is that the process managers are uncertain about whether the private developers' actions plans are 'enough' for achieving the goals. The idea is that the process managers and their organization will sum up and aggregate the measures when the private developers have finalized their actions plans. But the action plans are delayed. Despite the feeling of having come a long way together, the process managers still feel uncertain about what is enough for achieving the goals. This also includes being uncertain whether the municipality shares their sense of what is enough. There is thus uncertainty about whether they will reach a satisfactory level of sustainability and how they can assess whether it is good enough.

This also leads to reflection among the process managers on what could be considered as valuable results from a collaboration process. Learning is a key issue; in particular, who should be responsible for and provide resources for teaching others. One of the key premises of the project is that the collaborating partners should learn from each other. However, when the competence and drive for sustainability differs so much between the partners, the process managers start to question if it still is reasonable to put many resources towards learning. Is it perhaps better to prioritize working with those who are more experienced in this field, thereby going further and faster, and leaving others behind? Or as Daniel says, should we "move the elephant or ride the cheetah?"

Towards Further Implementation

The collaborative process reveals moments of hope as well as despair. Frustrations arise when the actions of individual actors risk delaying, changing, or even closing down the process. For example, late in the process, a private developer refuses to do their share of the measurements. Another one wants out. Later, the municipality refuses to adopt the detailed plan, which serves as the main foundation for further work. These are events that take a lot of energy from the process managers and incite doubt about this way of working. Erik reflects that "we need to examine ourselves, how we use the tools we have today, and what it would be best to do."

Nevertheless, and despite being temporarily delayed, the collaboration proceeds and a few months later things seem to be back on track. All the private developers are back in the collaboration and the process managers once again speak with pride about how far they have come. Some of the private developers even claim that they have never achieved such high ambition when it comes to adopting a holistic view on sustainability. In early 2018, when the spirits of the process managers are once again high and their collaboration continues towards implementation and realisation, we leave them for a while and return to the task of providing explanations for what happened during the preceding year.

What Are the Difficulties About?

Here we have professionals struggling to proceed by shifting back and forth between different roles. This includes shifting the rhetoric that explains and justifies the collaboration as well as the focus for what kind of activities are needed. To understand why this is happening, the reasons behind what can be seen as quite contradicting actions, there is a need to zoom out and say something about the context in which this process is taking place. What you see depends on which analytical lenses you are using. In this section, I focus on the multitude of parallel ideas or models for how planning should be managed and what collaboration should comprise. This gives insights into the practical challenges that professionals face in their struggle to lead collaborative processes for sustainable city planning, and how they are dealt with.

Multiple Planning Models Create a Dilemma

Planning for ecologically, socially, and economically sustainable cities is difficult, not just in Gothenburg. These challenges intensify with the increasing expectation that city planning and development are central to the prospect of sustainable development (United Nations, 2015). Gothenburg, and Swedish cities in general, are nowadays characterized by rapid urbanization, demographic changes, and increasing socioeconomic disparities. There is also a shift in norms and ideals regarding housing types and forms of ownership, influenced by the pressure of market forces and the pluralization of society (IQ Samhällsbyggnad, 2017. To tackle this, many municipalities have significantly increased the planning of new housing areas and densification, which is also the case in Gothenburg. In this work innovation and collaboration become keywords that challenge the traditional ways of planning in Sweden and call for new relationships and partnerships with private actors.

However, Sweden has a long tradition of a municipal 'planning monopoly,' which includes a high degree of autonomy at the regional and national level, but also within the private sector (Kalbro and Rosnes, 2013; Smas et al., 2015). As a result, it is the municipalities that have the power to decide "where, when and how to plan" (Kalbro and Rosnes, 2013, p. 51) for future housing developments—at least on paper.

There is also, however, a long tradition of different forms of collaboration in Sweden (Smedby and Neil, 2013). This is influenced by planning ideas that emerged in the 1980s under the label 'collaborative planning,' which is an umbrella concept encompassing numerous approaches (Healey, 2007). A common approach emphasizes the idea of building consensus through conversation and sees planers as facilitators. Important values in this approach are inclusiveness, transparency, fairness, empathy, equal opportunities, and the force of the better argument (Sager, 2009). This ideal situation is, however, criticized for not recognizing the inherent power dynamics and political nature of planning (Healey, 2007). What many of the approaches have in common is that they emphasize a network-based understanding of planning whereby knowledge, roles, and responsibilities are created in social relations. How to understand what's going on and what should be done about it is thus a result of relationships between individuals, working groups, institutions, and organizations—and the formal and informal norms and spaces for different interpretations that exist in these contexts (Healey, 2007; Schön and Rein, 1994). However, with multiple understandings of what is considered appropriate, uncertainty arises (Healey, 2007; Schön and Rein, 1994). This can be seen in case of Gothenburg where there are multiple understandings for how much influence and responsibility the private developers should have, and what the role and responsibility of the municipality is. Since the 1990s, the private sector has gradually gained influence and Sweden has moved towards 'market-oriented planning,' which means that it is becoming increasingly common for a municipality to formulate goals and plans collaboratively with the private sector (Kalbro and Rosnes, 2013). In the planning literature, several driving forces for this development have been referenced, often under the label 'neoliberalism' (see e.g. Sager, 2009). One suggested driving force is the belief that the private sector holds knowledge and insights on what is needed to create sustainable and attractive cities. Another is that collaboration increases the likelihood that plans will be implemented and realized in a built environment, something that cannot be guaranteed by the municipalities acting in isolation (Kalbro and Rosnes, 2013; Koglin and Pettersson, 2017). Both of these align well with the arguments that explain why private developers have been invited in the Gothenburg case—that is, a stated need for their knowledge about what is sustainable and how to achieve sustainability, as well as increasing the possibilities for the smooth implementation thereof.

The increased expectations of innovation concern not only solutions for the city, but also how this should be achieved. Bladini et al. (2015) emphasize that innovation means adopting ways of 'thinking outside the box,' which necessitates allowing space for failure. This then also challenges the traditional view of the municipality as a bureaucracy, developed over a long period of time to create predictability and to prevent failure and arbitrariness (Bladini et al., 2015). Municipalities are, relatively speaking, free to be innovative at the level of visions and goals for an urban development project. But the closer they come to the implementation thereof, the more they have to be organized into bureaucratic structures, which limits the room for manoeuvre (Bladini et al., 2015).

Trying to find a way through these different ideas puts pressure on the process managers, who must make tough choices about planning ideals that do not always fit well together. In the next section, I describe how conflicts between these ideas create practical challenges for Maria, Daniel, Erik, and Anna.

Navigating between Planning Ideas

In early 2017, it seems as though the process managers are guided by ideas about co-creation and shared responsibilities, as well as the need for, and benefits of, consensus. During this period, the process managers emphasize that they are a group and that this group has made a journey together, which has created trust within the group. They also highlight the agreement on ambition levels and target goals for the city development as a key for further work. The argument put forward is that common ground, reached by consensus, will not only guide the work, but also make collaboration smoother. Another key issue pointed out during this time is the need for joint responsibility and the process managers speak about themselves as facilitators, as bridging different perspectives and inspiring their collaboration partners to step up even more to achieve sustainable development.

Adding to these ideas on trust and consensus is the strong focus on innovation as a premise for achieving sustainable city development. Anna and Daniel have marketed the collaboration process itself as one of their most important innovations. They also argue that several of the target goals are expected to be reached through different forms of innovation. However, as they get closer to the implementation phase and things are not proceeding as desired, or as quickly as might be hoped for, they become doubtful as to whether this is the right, or only way forward. Gradually the process managers' rhetoric shifts to focus more on the need to be able to control the process. Accordingly, they also start to investigate possibilities for taking stronger control, thereby aligning more with the ideas of the municipality in control of planning and the need for systems ensuring predictability. This situation creates ambivalence for how to act and the process managers try to handle this by going in two directions at the same time.

An example of this is how ideas of responsibility are handled. The process managers believe that it is key for them to gradually hand over the responsibility to the private developers. This proves to be problematic, which makes the process managers recurrently give and take back control of the process. They are thus trying to push the process forward by repeatedly putting themselves back in charge, even though they continue to state that the goal is for the private developers to gradually and jointly take over. Thus, handing over responsibility means that in addition to coaching, the process managers are continuously making sure that the private developers take their share of the responsibility for reaching the common target. This means that the process managers act both as inspiring facilitators and as a control function, placing demands on the private developers. This raises questions as to whether and how this kind of double behavior becomes synergistic, or risks weakening the desired effect. Overall, the work initiated is proven to be resource-intensive and creates uncertainty over who decides about what and when, even to the point that the process managers start questioning if this kind of public-private collaboration is the right way forward at all.

Another challenging balance is found between innovation and predictability. Innovation is, as previously mentioned, perceived as a key ideal in the process. This is sometimes expressed by the process managers as the need or ability to find ways forward that are not already known. However, this implies that they want to make space for creativity, preferably not for failing. The balance between creativity and failure is handled by the process managers trying to create predictability and limit the risks for failure. They do this by placing greater demands on the private developers to outline how they plan to proceed in order to meet the need for innovative solutions. This includes requesting detailed information about the individual private developers' organizations and how they plan to bring in new knowledge. This then is a behavior that once again increases control over the private developers and shifts the focus back to the power of the municipality. Nevertheless, the process managers still talk about it as a part of their facilitating role, that is to support and inspire. The oscillation between ideas of innovation, predictability, trust, and control continues to put pressure on the process managers and makes them question their possibilities for influence. Overall, it leads them struggle with being able to feel content with their work.

The difficulties of deciding role distribution between private and public return when it is time to amass the private developers' action plans and from this decide whether they are good enough to meet the sustainability goals. Here is the dilemma: the process managers (together with the municipality) are now the ones that will decide whether the measures suggested by the private developers are good enough, despite the process managers' earlier protestations that they don't possess this expertise, and that they need the group to understand what constitutes a good solution. In this situation, the process managers no longer take the role of facilitators bridging perspectives and knowledge, but rather they assume the role of being the ones with the responsibility of judging what is good enough.

Finally, the ideals of working together to meet agreed goals through the creation of trust and consensus are repeatedly challenged during the process and become more salient the closer they get to implementation phase. During implementation, the private developers begin to worry whether what has been decided in the working group is, actually, in line with what their companies want. There is also, as mentioned, the situation where things previously agreed on no longer seem to be settled. Additionally, the process managers become preoccupied with what they can and cannot do within the framework of their position, and the legal rules within municipal planning. This makes them revert to their more traditional roles, whereby the process managers set the frame and the private developers respond, which was exactly the situation they wanted to move away from. The process managers also struggle with questions of whether it is possible to exclude some of the partners, particularly in a situation in which there is insufficient progression. The urge to reformulate who and which experiences, perspectives and knowledge should be included in the process once again raises the question of the definition and added value of consensus.

Difficulties and Hopes for the Future

The difficulty highlighted in this story is that managing the complexity of planning for sustainable cities also includes managing collaboration processes between the private and public sectors. Today this work means navigating different ideas for what this collaboration should comprise. This is a challenging task as different ideas provide different, sometimes conflicting, guidance for what should be prioritized, how power and responsibilities should be distributed, and which roles and actions are relevant. This, then, is a situation that puts considerable pressure on individual professionals for realizing sustainable city planning through collaboration, but leaves them quite empty-handed when sorting out how they should act in order to meet their goals.

Although these challenges have caused moments of despair, it seems as though the process has also had a positive impact, both in terms of learning and increased opportunities for sustainability. One of the private developers states that they have not previously agreed on such a high ambition level regarding holistic planning. Others express that during this procedure they also have learned a lot about collaborative processes and what makes a sustainable outcome. Relationships in the group continue to grow and there seem to be an overall feeling that they have managed to overcome several of the difficulties.

In particular, Anna, Maria, Daniel, and Erik seem to have gradually developed a more profound basis of experience over the past year, partly by broadening their repertoire of possible ways for dealing with a situation. This seems to have been spurred by the many twists, turns, and moments of introspection, which has given them the experience of dealing with a variety of situations in a variety of ways and provided opportunities for looking at their own practice through different lenses of explanation. This then is argued to be key for being able to foster learning and achieve expertise in a particular area (Watson, 2002). In the long term, this could strengthen the process managers' capacity for making more context-sensitive choices about collaboration. However, whether it has led to organizational learning is not clear.

Hope was restored following several events that had a positive effect on the project. In late 2018, the planning phase of the city district Masthuggskajen was the first project ever to be awarded a Citylab certification for sustainable urban development.[4] Daniel explains that it felt like they had received a 'stamp of approval' that reassured them that they were moving in the right direction. In February 2019, the land and exploration agreement between the members of the consortium was signed, thus marking the end of the planning process. Three months later, the detailed plans for Masthuggskajen were finally given legal force after the courts rejected appeals to halt the development. Politicians, representatives from the consortium, the City of Gothenburg, and other stakeholders gathered for an on-site ceremony to mark the commencement of the construction phase. In 2020, construction was underway, with the first occupants expected to take up residency in 2022. The project is scheduled for completion in 2026. However, it is important not to lose sight of whether and how the sustainability goals will be achieved during the construction phase, and whether it might have been possible to have got this far, or perhaps even further, by adopting less resource-intensive processes. Sustainable city development is a continuous process, and there is still much to do in terms of finding, implementing, and evaluating more concrete solutions that will be built into the physical as well as the organizational environment.

From this chapter, then, we learn that collaboration is an important albeit challenging core aspect for finding and reaching multidimensional solutions for sustainable city development above narrow definitions. Planning is not only about what is achieved, but also about the road there. There is still much to be explored about how this road should be collaboratively organized so that it becomes less challenging for individual professionals and that achievements for sustainability are assured.

Notes

1 All the names that appear in this chapter are pseudonyms.
2 This text is based on the study entitled 'From Vision to Implementation,' which is part of the Vinnova-financed Decode research project. The aim of the study was to explore and support professionals' work to bridge the gap between the planning and implementation phases of city development projects.
3 The overall research method was a collaboration between authorities, a consulting firm and academia. The author acted as project leader. The methods used include document reviews and conversations with practitioners on 15 separate occasions including individual and group interviews, work meetings and workshops from January 2017 to January 2018. The study also includes short interviews with private developers, conducted by Hanna Areslätt, Tyréns AB, in January 2018. The quotations from the professionals were translated into English by the author.
4 Citylab is a recent certification system that was developed by the Sweden Green Building Council and adapted to Swedish conditions.

References

Älvstranden Utveckling, Göteborgs kommun (2017). *Hållbarhetsprogram Masthuggskajen (Sustainability Program for Masthuggskajen)*. Retrieved March 23, 2020, from http://masthuggskajen.se/wp-content/uploads/sites/3/2017/06/H%C3%A5llbarhetsprogram_Masthuggskajen_2017-06-12.pdf.
Bladini, F., Jensen, C., Palm, K., Sandoff, A., & Williamsson, J. (2015). *Planerarens roll i förändring. Boverket & Tillväxtverket Tillväxt kräver planering: En antologi om samverkan i den fysiska planeringen* (The Planner's Role in Change. In *Growth Requires Planning: An Anthology of Collaboration in Physical Planning*). Stockholm: National Board of Housing, Building and Planning & Swedish Agency for Economic and Regional Growth. Retrieved March 23, 2020, from www.boverket.se/globalassets/publikationer/dokument/2015/tillvaxt-kraver-planering-webb.pdf.
City of Gothenburg (2012). RiverCity Gothenburg vision. Retrieved March 23, 2020, from http://alvstaden.goteborg.se/wp-content/uploads/2012/12/rivercity_vision_eng_web.pdf.
Healey, P. (2007). *Urban Complexity and Spatial Strategies: Towards a Relational Planning for Our Times*. New York: Routledge.
IQ Samhällsbyggnad (2017). *Är vi redo för samhällsbyggnad? En idéskrift från omvärlds- och framtidsutskottet. (Are We Ready for Urban Development? A Report from the*

Committee on Competitive Intelligence and the Future). Retrieved March 23, 2020, from www.iqs.se/om-oss/aktuellt/nyheter/2017/170621-var-nya-ideskrift-lanserad/.

Kalbro, T., & Rosnes, A. (2013). Public Planning Monopoly—Or Not? The Right to Initiate Development Plans in Norway and Sweden. In E. Hepperle, R. Dixon-Gough, V. Maliene, R. Mansberger, J. Paulsson, & A. Pödör (Eds.), *Land Management: Potential, Problems and Stumbling Blocks*. Zurich: Vdf Hochschulverlag.

Koglin, T., & Pettersson, F. (2017). Changes, problems, and challenges in Swedish spatial planning: An analysis of power dynamics. *Sustainability*, 9(10), 1836.

Sager, T. (2009). Planners' role: Torn between dialogical ideals and neo-liberal realities. *European Planning Studies*, 17(1), 65–84.

Schön, D.A., & Rein, M. (1994). *Frame Reflection: Toward the Resolution of Intractable Policy Controversies*. New York: Ashgate.

Smas, L., Fredricsson, C., Larsson, V., & Perjo, L. (2015). Ansträngande partnerskap: näringslivet i nordisk stadsplanering (Challenging Partnerships: The Business Sector in Nordic Urban Planning). Nordregio Working Paper 3. Stockholm.

Smedby, N., & Neil, L. (2013). Experiences in urban governance for sustainability: The constructive dialogue in Swedish municipalities. *Journal of Cleaner Production*, 50(1), 148–158.

United Nations, General Assembly (2015). Transforming our world: The 2030 Agenda for Sustainable Development. Resolution adopted by the General Assembly on 25 September. Retrieved March 23, 2020, from www.un.org/ga/search/view_doc.asp?symbol=A/RES/70/1&Lang=E.

Watson, V. (2002). Do we learn from planning practice? The contribution of the practice movement to planning theory. *Journal of Planning Education and Research*, 22(2), 178–187.

Chapter 16

Concluding Commentary
Will Sustainability Be Replaced by Resilience, and If So, Why?

Barbara Czarniawska

For the past 10 years or so, any application for a research grant has had to contain the word 'sustainability.' From its origin in ecology studies, sustainability has come to be translated into practically every domain of social life. We are now exploring sustainable equality alongside sustainable waste management, sustainable relationships, and sustainable cities. And most importantly, economic growth has to be sustainable too.

However, Benson and Craig (2015, p. 781) have suggested that "[t]he time has come to move past the concept of sustainability. As an environmental management goal, sustainability is no longer appropriate, and it cannot be used to meaningfully address the challenges ahead." In line with such reasoning, sustainability has in recent times begun to give way to 'resilience.' In metallurgy, resilience is the ability of a material to absorb energy when it is deformed elastically and to release that energy upon unloading. But resilience is usually used metaphorically, and, like sustainability, resilience translates smoothly from one domain of life to another—perhaps even more easily, because resilience has a great many sources. It pleases even the Actor-Network theoreticians, because it applies to humans and nonhumans alike. During his presentation at the PARSE conference in Gothenburg, in November 2015, Bruno Latour spoke almost exclusively about the studies being done by Stockholm Resilience Center.

The Stockholm Resilience Centre is "an international centre of excellence for resilience and sustainability science," thus indicating the kinship between the two notions. "Since its launch in 2007, SRC has developed into a world-leading science centre for addressing the complex challenges facing humanity." On the centre's webpage, resilience is defined as "the ability to deal with change and continue to develop."[1] But *whose* ability is not specified.

The Stockholm Resilience Centre is a joint initiative between Stockholm University, the Stockholm Environment Institute, and the Beijer International Institute of Ecological Economics at the Royal Swedish Academy of Sciences. The centre is financed by the Foundation for Strategic Environmental Research, MISTRA, previously the major financier of sustainability research, which probably explains the addition of the word 'sustainability,' that was not there in 2013.

But why resilience? Resilience is a desirable trait of systems, because resilience "is a capability to recover" from crises, emergencies, and accidents, wrote organization scholars Karl Weick and Kathleen Sutcliffe in their 2001 bestseller, *Managing the Unexpected: Resilient Performance in an Age of Uncertainty*. The book went into its second edition in 2007. Weick and Sutcliffe referred to the notion of resilience as introduced by Aaron Wildavsky in his 1988 book, *Searching for Safety*. This notion was repeated in the entry 'Risk and safety' that appeared in the Concise Encyclopedia of Economics, co-authored by Aaron Wildavsky's son Adam Wildavsky, in 1993—the year in which his father died. The encyclopedia went into a second edition in 2007. Speak of an idea whose time has come... The Wildavskys concluded their entry as follows:

> A strategy of resilience [in contrast to a strategy of anticipation], requires reliance on experience with adverse consequences once they occur in order to develop a capacity to learn from the harm and bounce back. Resilience, therefore, requires the accumulation of large amounts of generalizable resources—such as organizational capacity, knowledge, wealth, energy, and communication—that can be used to craft solutions to problems that the people involved did not know would occur. Thus, a strategy of resilience requires much less predictive capacity but much more growth, not only in wealth, but also in knowledge.[2]

So, while sustainability required prediction and planning, resilience requires the mobilization of resources, 'just in case.'

The Wildavskys and Weick and Sutcliffe wrote primarily about resilient organizations, but also about resilient performance, thereby alluding to the psychological concept of resilience. In psychology, and I quote,

> [r]esilience is the capacity to withstand stress and catastrophe. Psychologists have long recognized the capabilities of humans to adapt and overcome risk and adversity. Individuals and communities are able to rebuild their lives even after devastating tragedies. Resilience is most commonly understood as a process, and not a trait of an individual.[3]

According to Wikipedia, studies on psychological resilience began in the 1970s, but their number has visibly increased, particularly over the past five years or so. It has even managed to earn a critique,[4] because even if researchers treat it as a process and not a trait, it is still an individual process.

So, why is resilience replacing sustainability, or at least relegating sustainability to second place? Perhaps it is simply a change in research fashion. As Gabriel Tarde (1890) explained almost 130 years ago, people follow fashions, but then become tired, or bored with them, and look around for something new. Yes, but why resilience? And why now?

One explanation, relevant especially in the context of big cities, is the recently produced atmosphere of threat, no matter how much supported by facts. Cities are threatened by incipient terrorists (that is, immigrants), and therefore have to be resilient. Here, Wildavsky's definition fits very well: "resilience … requires reliance on experience with adverse consequences once they occur in order to develop a capacity to learn from the harm and bounce back." Indeed, some cities did experience events with adverse consequences and now claim to have learned from it.

One possible answer is the discovery that sustainability costs money. This observation coincided with, or was even caused by, the economic crisis of 2008–2010—first in the global context of banking and finance, and then in the context of European 'malaise,' as it has recently been called. What we need is a resilient euro, a resilient European Union (once Brexit is over), but also resilient consumers, and resilient computer systems that can recover from zombie attacks and similar misadventures. It seems likely, therefore, that the next shift will not be from economy to ecology, as Bruno Latour (2004) hoped, but from ecology to economy. This may necessitate the economizing of ecological measures and—within the growing movement against Merkel and Macron's austerity programs—the elimination of the adjective 'sustainable' from 'sustainable growth.'

Like the contributors to this book, I believe in sustainability—not the least because in certain languages, for example in French, *durabilité* can be understood both as sustainability and resilience. In this time of the coronavirus pandemic, it is obvious that resilience will become *the* central issue. In future field studies, however, at least with regard to grant applications in English, the safest move is to combine both, as the Stockholm Institute does: promise to study resilience *and* sustainability! As to field studies themselves, my position is firm: we should study actual practices, not just their labels. Only then can we decide whether cities are becoming sustainable, resilient, or even both.

Notes

1 Retrieved April 10, 2019, from www.stockholmresilience.org/research/resilience-dictionary.html.
2 Retrieved April 10, 2019, from www.econlib.org/library/Enc/RiskandSafety.html.
3 Retrieved April 10, 2019, from http://en.wikipedia.org/wiki/Psychological_resilience.
4 Retrieved July 10, 2018, from www.wiley.com/en-us/Resilient+Life%3A+The+Art+of+Living+Dangerously-p-9780745671536.

References

Benson, Melinda Harm, & Craig, Robin Kundis (2015). The end of sustainability. *Society & Natural Resources: An International Journal*, 27 (7): 777–782.
Latour, Bruno (2004). *Politics of Nature. How to Bring the Sciences into Democracy*. Cambridge, MA: Harvard University Press.

Latour, Bruno (2005). *Reassembling the Social*. Oxford: Oxford University Press.
Tarde, Gabriel ([1890] 1962). *The Laws of Imitation*. New York: Henry Holt.
Trivedi, Kishor S., Dong Seong, Kim, & Ghosh, Rajesh (2009). Resilience in computer systems and networks. In *Computer-Aided Design: Digest of Technical Papers*, ICCAD, 2–5 November.
Weick, Karl, & Sutcliffe, Kathleen ([2001] 2007). *Managing the Unexpected: Resilient Performance in an Age of Uncertainty*. San Francisco, CA: Jossey-Bass.
Wildavsky, Aaron (1988). *Searching for Safety*. New York: Routledge.

Index

Page numbers in *italics* refer to figures; those in **bold** indicate tables.

Aalborg Charter, EU 77
Abram, S. and Weszkalnys, G. 117
academic conference panel 133–4
accountability and replicability 187–90
action plans 221–3
adaptive learning 150
Affolderbach, J. and Schulz, C. 81
affordable housing 23, 43, 44, 58–9, 71, 76, 78, 179, 185, 198–9, 200
agenda setting situations 131–6
Agnew, J. 81
agreement of common goals 220–1
Alconbury ruling (2001), England 23
Älvstaden project *see* RiverCity Gothenburg
Älvstranden (property development company) 217–18, 222–3
Amar, G. 89
ambiguous concept and multiple object of sustainable development 1–4
Amin, A. and Thrift, N. 144
APUR, Paris 101, 107–8
Årsta Nature Reserve, Stockholm 42–7, 48–9

Bangalore *see* water management and coproduction (Bangalore, India)
Barends, E. et al. 150; and Rosseau, D. 149, 156
Barthes, R. 91
'Barwood Strategic Land' case, England 30
Basque Declaration, EU 77
Benson, M. H. and Craig, R. K. 231
Bergmark, A. 144
best practices *see* Germany
bicycles 79, 93, 94

biomass: Malmö 167; Paris 111
Bladini, F. et al. 225
'Bloor Homes' case, England 30
Blühdorn, I. 79, 80
Bordeaux Métropole (mobility and intermodality) 86–7, 88; challenges 95–8; interchange stations 88–90; Pont de Pierre 86–7, 98; promises 91–3; studies and experience 93–5
Bordeaux wetland area 115–17; evaluation process 118–20; evaluation and valorization 117–18, 120; grass management 122–3, 124–5, 126–7; workshop and outcomes 120–5
Bostadsbolaget public housing company 148–9, 152, 157–8
'Braintree' decision, England 34, 36
Brown, R. D. and Corry, R. C. 147
'Brown' case, England 28–9
Brundtland Report 26, 27, 76–7
buildings, climate-smart 169–70
Bulkeley, H. 2
bus routes/Bus Rapid Transit (BRT) system, Bordeaux 92, 96, 98

Cambridge *see* land ownership (Cambridge)
Cambridge University Reporter 184–5
Campbell, H. 6
Cardwell, D. 189
cars/traffic reduction 78, 93, 96, 97
centralized decision-making and local government planning 180–1
centralized leadership and emerging-in-practice approaches 135–6

236 Index

challenge-driven research and innovation 136–7, 140
Chalmers School of Technology, Gothenburg 53
citizen engagement and urban commons 206–7
citizen-led collectives 212–13
'City of Edinburgh' planning decision (1997) 25
civil servants 143–4
civil society actors 16–17, 49, 105, 142–3
Climate Contract for Hyllie 160–1, 163, 165–7, 168, 171, 172–3
climate-smart cities *see* smart cities (Malmö)
Code for Sustainable Homes (2015), England 181, 182, 186
collaboration and conflict: dilemmas of 14–17; *see also* public-private collaboration (Gothenburg)
collective learning 70–1
commons *see* water management and coproduction (Bangalore, India)
communication technologies 217–18
Communities and Local Government Select Committee, England 34–5
community building 71–2
competitiveness and best practice 76–9
concretization 52, 197–8
consensus 225–6, 227
Conservative Party/government, UK 175, 182, 189–90; and coalition government (2010–15) 177, 179
construction sites *see* Paris
consultants in planning process, England 178
coproduction: housing development 183; *see also* water management and coproduction (Bangalore, India)
CPCU, Paris 109–11
creative learning 150, 152

'Dartford' case, England 30
Decode project 141
definition and realization, dilemmas of 8–10
Department of Communities and Local Government (DCLG), England 179
Department of Environment, Food and Rural Affairs, England 26, 27
developmental learning 150
dilemma-driven approach 138–9

directors' group, RiverCity Gothenburg 53, 54, 55–7
disagreement in urban planning 135
disconnect: local and national policy 179–80
discretion of local government, loss of 180–1
documents and formulations 56–7

'Earl Shilton' case, England 29
ecology and economy 233
Eddington Development, Cambridge 184–7, 189–90
egalitarianism through coproduction 214–15
electricity: networks *see* smart cities (Malmö); *see also* heating systems
Ellström, P.-E. 150, 153
emerging-in-practice approach 135–6
emission reduction 77, 96; *see also* Paris (construction sites of low carbon transition)
engagement and frustration, dilemmas of 17–19
English planning law 21–2, 36; courts and Supreme Court decisions 28–33; legal system 22–6; national framework (NPPF) (2012) 27–34, 36; national framework (NPPF) (2019) 34–5, 36; planning balance 24–6, 36; planning decisions 23–4; sustainable development, definitions and strategies 26–7; *see also* land ownership (Cambridge)
Eon, Malmö 160, 161, 165, 166, 167, 168, 169, 170, 171, 172
EU: Aalborg Charter 77; Basque Declaration 77; Lund Declaration 137; *see also* programming (EU)
European Conference on Sustainable Cities & Towns 77
European Research Area (ERA) 129
European Strategy for Sustainable Development 26
evaluation and valorization *see* Bordeaux wetland area
evidence-based approach (Gothenburg) 147–8; new approach to old problem 148–9; organizations and stakeholders 152–3; practitioners 153–4; scientific literature 154–6; solving urban difficulties 149–52; summary and discussion 156–8

Financial Times 185, 186, 188–9
Freiburg, Germany 75–6, 80, 82, 175–6, 187
friction universals, concept of 3–4
Frihamnen and Jubilee Park 58–61, 64, 198–9, 200
frustration *see* engagement and frustration, dilemmas of

'Gallagher Estates' case, England 29
Gare de Bordeaux-Saint-Jean 89, 90, 91
geothermal energy, Paris 111
Germany (best practices) 75–6, 83; Freiburg 75–6, 80, 82, 175–6, 187; new Green competitiveness 76–9; participation: postpolitics and planning 82–3; sustainability transition and growth trajectories 79–80; territorial trap/spatial container 80–1
gilet jaunes ('yellow vests') movement 95
Gironde department, Bordeaux Métropole 94, 95, 96–7
goal conflicts: housing vs nature reserves 39–41, 44–7, 48–9
Gore, A. 130
Gothenburg 50–3; *see also* evidence-based approach; public-private collaboration; RiverCity Gothenburg
governance: English planning law 176, 177; frustrations of existing 211–12; gaps: Sydney (strategy 2030) 71–2
grass management, Bordeaux wetland area 122–3, 124–5, 126–7
Greater Cambridge Housing Development Agency (HDA) 182, 183
Green Party, Stockholm 40, 41, 49
Gunder, M. and Hillier, J. 1

Hale, T. 185, 186, 189
Hambleton, R. 82
Hammarkullen, Gothenburg 148–9, 154, 156, 158
Haughton, G. et al. 188
Healey, P. 224–5
heating systems: Hyllie, Malmö 167, 170, 171–2; Paris 107–8, 109–11
Helgesson, C. and Muniesa, F. 118
high-level policy conference setting 132, *133*
Höijer, B. et al. 4–5, 6
Hoppe, R. 151
housing: affordable 23, 43, 44, 58–9, 71, 76, 78, 179, 185, 198–9, 200; and grass management 122–3, 124–5, 126–7;

public 148–9, 177; segregation and polarization 195–7; vs nature reserves 39–41, 44–7, 48–9; *see also specific developments*
Hyllie *see* smart cities (Malmö)

India *see* water management and coproduction (Bangalore, India)
information systems and intermodal transport network 94
innovation: and predictability 226–7; priorities and 55–6; research and 129, 136–7, 140
interest groups/communities 45, 53–4, 213
Intergovernmental Panel on Climate Change (IPCC) 80, 176
international perspective 54

Jacobs, J. 69
'Jelson' decision, England 34
Joint Programming Initiative (JPI) 129–30, 137, 139, 144
Jullien, F. 73

Kalbro, T. and Rosnes, A. 224, 225
Kaufman, V. and Paulhiac, F. 92
'Kere Habba' festival, Bangalore 201–2
knowledge: dilemmas of 12–14; forms of 151
Kornberger, M. 118, 120

land consumption: North-Rhine-Westphalia 78–9
land ownership (Cambridge) 175–6; bargain for sustainable development 182–4; disconnect 179–80; Eddington Development 184–7, 189–90; interviewees **191**; local government and national policy (NPPF) 179–84; loss of discretion 180–1; role of 176–9; summary: accountability and replicability 187–90
land politics *see* Stockholm (politics of land use)
Latour, B. 143, 231, 233
learning 70–1, 150–1
Left Party, Stockholm 40
Local Agenda 21 51–2, 77, 102
local authorities/government, England 177; and national policy (NPPF) 179–84
Lund Declaration, EU 137

Malmö *see* smart cities (Malmö)
Malmö Environmental Programme (MEP) 165–6
'Malvern Hills' case, England 29
Masthuggskajen, Gothenburg 219–20, 228–9
Metzger, J. 82–3
Ministry of the Environment, Sweden 51–2
Ministry of Housing, Communities and Local Government, England 22–3, 27–8, 31, 35
mobility *see* Bordeaux (mobility and intermodality); *specific forms of transport*
Mol, A. 2–3
Monbiot, G. et al. 177, 190
Moore, C. 67
multinational technology companies 162–3
multiple object, concept of 2–3
multiple planning models 224–5
Münster, Westphalia 75, 76, 79

naming and framing problems 150, 151, 156
National Planning Policy Framework (NPPF) *see under* English planning law; land ownership (Cambridge)
nature reserves *see* Stockholm (politics of land use)
networks: of cities/peers 70–1; and organizations 183–4
Neurath, O. 136

organizations and networks 183–4
ownership *see* land ownership (Cambridge)

Paris (construction sites of low carbon transition) 101–2; internal organization of public authority action 102–6; production of urban energy plans 107–8; reconfiguration of technical infrastructure 109–12; summary and conclusions 112–13
participation: civil 55; and drafting process 53–8; postpolitics and planning 82–3; workshops 53–4, 120–5, 141–3
path stability/dependency 79–80, 150
'Paul Newman New Homes' case, England 35

PCET (*Plans Climat Energie Territorial*) and Territorial Project, Paris 102–6
place-building initiative and team, Frihamnen 59–61
planning *see* English planning law; *specific cities, developments and approaches*
Planning and Compulsory Purchase Act (2004) England 23
Planning Inspectorate, England 23
Plato 73
policy-makers' meeting room 132
Pont de Pierre, Bordeaux Métropole 86–7, 98
practice-centered approach: ambiguous concept and multiple object 1–4; conceptualizing dilemmas 4–6; overview of dilemmas 8–19; view 6–7
predictability and innovation 226–7
priorities and innovation 55–6
private consultants 178
private developers 176–7, 182–3, 189, 199, 217–18, 222–3, 227
private landowners 176–7, 189
'problems' and 'solutions' 5–6
process managers 222–3, 225–7
programming (EU) 129–30; academic conference panel 133–4; agenda setting situations 131–6; dilemmas 130–1, 136–9; high-level policy conference setting 132, *133*; Joint Programming Initiative (JPI) 129–30, 137, 139, 144; new hope 139–40; new protocol 143–4; policy-makers' meeting room 132; reflections on settings 134–6; SRIA 129–31, 137, 138, 144; swarm intelligence 144–5; transdisciplinary working, requirements for 140–4; workshop 141–3
prototypes/prototyping 59, 61, 64
public administration and civil servants 143–4
public creation 71–2
public housing 148–9, 177
public transport *see* Bordeaux Métropole (mobility and intermodality); *specific forms*
public-private collaboration (Gothenburg) 217–18; action plans 221–3; agreement of common goals 220–1; multiple planning models 224–5; nature of difficulties 223–7; navigating between planning ideas 225–6; realization of vision 219–20; RiverCity 198–9;

summary: difficulties and hopes for future 227–8
public-private partnership (PPP) models 206, 211, 213

rail networks: Bordeaux Métropole 89, 89–90, 90, 91, 97–8; Malmö-Copenhagen 165; Sydney 68
Rancière, J. 135
realization of vision 61–5, 219–20; concretization 52, 197–8; definition and 8–10
Red-Green-Pink coalition government (2014–18), Stockholm 39–40, 41, 44–5
reflection-in-practice 6
renewable energy 166–8
replicability 189–90
research and innovation 129, 136–7, 140
resilience and sustainability 231–4
Rio Earth Summit 76–7
Rittle, H. and Webber, M. 4, 12–13, 14, 116, 148
RiverCity Gothenburg 52–3; civil participation 55; concretization of social and urban design challenges 197–8; documents and formulations 56–7; Frihamnen and Jubilee Park 58–61, 64, 198–9, 200; interest groups and workshops 53–4; international perspective 54; new organizing solutions 57–8; participants and drafting process 53–8; priorities and innovative working 55–6; public-private collaboration 198–9; segregation and polarization in housing market 195–7; vision 61–5, 194–5
role distribution: public-private collaboration 227

Salomon, D. 82
Schön, D. 6, 148, 150, 151
'Scrivens' case, England 29–30
shared responsibilities 225–6
Simmel, G. 69, 72
'situated ethical judgement' 6
smart cities (Malmö) 160–1, 171–3; buildings 169–70; renewable energy 166–8; sustainable and 162–6
Smart Grids for Hyllie 169–70, 171–2
SNFC, Bordeaux Métropole 91, 92, 98
Social Democrat party, Stockholm 40
social housing and mixed tenure 196–7
social problems 148–9

socioeconomic/ethnic segregation and inequalities 195–7
space and time, dilemmas of 10–12
spatial container, green city as 80–1
'St Modwen' decision, England 34
stakeholders 139–40, 152–3, 199–200
Stockholm (politics of land use) 39; Årsta Nature Reserve 42–7, 48–9; goals conflicts: housing vs nature reserves 39–41, 44–7, 48–9
Stockholm Resilience Centre 231
Strategic Research and Innovation Agenda (SRIA), EU 129–31, 137, 138, 144
Suffolk Coastal District, England 31–2
sustainability and resilience 231–4
sustainability transition and growth trajectories 79–80
Sustainable Development Goal (SDG) 11 136
swarm intelligence 144–5
Sweden see evidence-based approach (Gothenburg); Gothenburg; public-private collaboration (Gothenburg); RiverCity Gothenburg; smart cities (Malmö); Stockholm (politics of land use)
Sydney (strategy 2030) 67–8; collective discovery and learning 70–1; community building and public creation 71–2; impact beyond implementation 68–72; new sensibilities 68–9; solutions 72–4

technical infrastructure, reconfiguration of 109–12
technology 80; communication 217–18; multinational companies 162–3; trigeneration of 71; see also smart cities (Malmö)
territorial trap 80–1
time and space, dilemmas of 10–12
Town and Country Planning Act, England (1947) 180; (1990) 23
'Trafford' case, England 29
trams and tram network, Bordeaux 87, 91, 92, 93, 95–6, 97–8
transdisciplinary working 140–4
translation concept 52
transport see Bordeaux Métropole (mobility and intermodality); specific forms
trigeneration of technology 71
Tsing, A. L. 3

UN: -Habitat principles for sustainable neighborhood planning 154, *155*, 156; Brundtland Report 26, 27, 76–7; Local Agenda 21 51–2, 77, 102; Summit on Sustainable Development 26; Sustainable Development Goal (SDG) 11 136
universals in sustainable development 3–4
urban commons 207
Urban Transformations Journal 142

VA Syd, Malmö 160, 165, 166
valorization and evaluation *see* Bordeaux wetland area
valuation, concept of 118
Vatin, F. 118, 120

Wachsmuth, D. et al. 80–1
water management and coproduction (Bangalore, India) 201–2, 206–7; cultural contexts 209–10; frustrations of existing governance 211–12; geophysical contexts 208–9; historical context 207–8; history 203–5; motivating factors 210–13; nostalgia 210–11; power dynamics 213–14; practical motivations 211; state and public-private partnerships (PPPs) 205–6; summary: egalitarianism 214–15
Weick, K. and Sutcliffe, K. 232
'West Berkshire' (2016) planning decision, England 23
West Harbour development, Malmö 163–5
wetlands *see* Bordeaux wetland area
Whitehead, M. 117
wicked problems and structured problems 151–2, 156
Wildavsky, A. 232, 233
Willaston Cheshire residential development case, England 32–3
'William Davis' case, England 29, 30
wind turbines 160–1, 166–8, 171
workshops 53–4, 120–5, 141–3
Wrangsten, C. and Bylund, J. 138–9
'Wychavon' case, England 29

'Young RiverCity' group, Gothenburg 55

Zhou, N. et al. 77